PURGATORIO

Dante Alighieri

Translated and with Notes by
Henry Wadsworth Longfellow

DOVER PUBLICATIONS, INC.
MINEOLA, NEW YORK

DOVER THRIFT EDITIONS

GENERAL EDITOR: SUSAN L. RATTINER
EDITOR OF THIS VOLUME: JIM MILLER

Copyright

Copyright © 2017 by Dover Publications, Inc.
All rights reserved.

Bibliographical Note

This Dover edition, first published in 2017, is an unabridged republication of *Purgatorio*, translated and with notes by Henry Wadsworth Longfellow, originally published in 1867 by George Routledge & Sons, London, as the second part of *The Divine Comedy of Dante Alighieri*.

International Standard Book Number

ISBN-13: 978-0-486-81533-6
ISBN-10: 0-486-81533-1

Manufactured in the United States by LSC Communications
81533101   2017
www.doverpublications.com

Note

DANTE ALIGHIERI (1265–1321), born in Florence, would have a life-long affinity with his beloved city, even after being exiled in his later years. At the time of his birth, Italy was divided between those who supported the papacy, and those who were loyal to the German rulers of the Holy Roman Empire. Shortly after his birth, the Guelfs, with the help of French and papal troops, were successful in driving the pro-imperial Ghibellines from the city of Florence. This victory ushered in a period of Florentine prosperity, as well as its heightened stature among other Italian cities, and attracted a host of intellectuals there with whom Dante came to associate.

As a disciple of master rhetorician Brunetto Latini, Dante was influenced by his mentor's approach to philosophy and politics, and was also schooled in the burgeoning poetical movement in Italy. Dante became instrumental in the advancement of Stilnuovo ("New Style") poetry, by which he and friends Guido Cavalcanti and Cino de Pistoia used verse to analyze the psychology of love. Inspired by Latini's desire to employ the vernacular in literary works, Dante also pioneered the practice of using the laymen's Italian in literature, rather than the more technical Latin. At that time, there was no single Italian language; rather, people spoke local dialects that were all derived from Latin. Predictably, Dante chose to write many of his works in his native Florentine dialect.

Dante soon entered into local politics, joining a medical guild by way of his reputation as a philosopher. In 1300, he was elected *priore,* an office that granted him the power and burden of political involvement in turbulent Florence. At this time, the Florentine Guelfs were experiencing division within its party, and split into two factions—the Blacks and the Whites. Dante was a member of the Whites, who objected to the imperialistic ambitions of Pope Boniface VIII, and eventually lost control of the city. Detained at the Vatican, where he had gone as an emissary to speak to the pope, Dante was tried in absentia for crimes fabricated by the Blacks. Sentenced to death by burning should he ever return, Dante never again set foot in Florence. Instead, he roamed from city to city in Italy, where he was welcomed by scholars and nobles alike. He continued in his interest in politics, recording observations and writing a number of discourses on the volatile events of his time. He died in the city of Ravenna in 1321.

Dante began work on *The Divine Comedy* around 1308, and completed it shortly before his death. Originally titled *Commedia* (Comedy), the work adopted its lofty epithet after Dante was named "Divine Poet" by scholar Giovanni Boccaccio a few decades after his death. An epic poem that was his masterpiece, *The Divine Comedy* traces Dante's imagined journey through the three levels of the Roman Catholic afterlife—Hell, Purgatory, and Heaven. The first canto of *The Inferno* serves as an introduction to the entire poem, followed by the standard thirty-three cantos that serve as the structure for the two other canticles. At once an allegory of man's spiritual pilgrimage through life, as well as a thinly veiled political commentary on the circumstances of Dante's own exile, *The Divine Comedy* is a brilliant, multi-layered work that transcends time and culture in its ability to captivate readers and scholars alike.

It was in Italy, during a mandatory tour of Europe to qualify as a professor of modern languages, that Henry Wadsworth Longfellow (1807–1882) first encountered Dante's writings. Spending his evenings poring over the "gloomy pages," Longfellow later converted his many notes into lectures on Dante at Bowdoin College and Harvard University. Thus began Longfellow's lifelong interest in the poet, and, in 1843, he committed himself to the translation of *The Divine Comedy*—an endeavor that would span several decades, due to long respites from the project. Of the three canticles, he completed *The Inferno* last, marking the occasion in a diary entry on April 16, 1863. After several more years spent revising and annotating the translation, Longfellow finally published his work in 1867.

Contents

PURGATORIO

I enter, and I see thee in the gloom
    Of the long aisles, O poet saturnine!
    And strive to make my steps keep pace with thine.
    The air is filled with some unknown perfume;
The congregation of the dead make room
    For thee to pass; the votive tapers shine;
    Like rooks that haunt Ravenna's groves of pine
    The hovering echoes fly from tomb to tomb.
From the confessionals I hear arise
    Rehearsals of forgotten tragedies,
    And lamentations from the crypts below;
And then a voice celestial that begins
    With the pathetic words, "Although your sins
    As scarlet be," and ends with "as the snow."

PURGATORIO

Canto I

To run o'er better waters hoists its sail
    The little vessel of my genius now,
    That leaves behind itself a sea so cruel;
And of that second kingdom will I sing
    Wherein the human spirit doth purge itself,
    And to ascend to heaven becometh worthy.
But let dead Poesy here rise again,
    O holy Muses, since that I am yours,
    And here Calliope somewhat ascend,
My song accompanying with that sound,   10
    Of which the miserable magpies felt
    The blow so great, that they despaired of pardon.
Sweet colour of the oriental sapphire,
    That was upgathered in the cloudless aspect
    Of the pure air, as far as the first circle,
Unto mine eyes did recommence delight
    Soon as I issued forth from the dead air,
    Which had with sadness filled mine eyes and breast.
The beauteous planet, that to love incites,
    Was making all the orient to laugh,   20
    Veiling the Fishes that were in her escort.
To the right hand I turned, and fixed my mind
    Upon the other pole, and saw four stars
    Ne'er seen before save by the primal people.
Rejoicing in their flamelets seemed the heaven.
    O thou septentrional and widowed site,
    Because thou art deprived of seeing these!
When from regarding them I had withdrawn,
    Turning a little to the other pole,
    There where the Wain had disappeared already,   30

I saw beside me an old man alone,
  Worthy of so much reverence in his look,
  That more owes not to father any son.
A long beard and with white hair intermingled
  He wore, in semblance like unto the tresses,
  Of which a double list fell on his breast.
The rays of the four consecrated stars
  Did so adorn his countenance with light,
  That him I saw as were the sun before him.
"Who are you? ye who, counter the blind river,   40
  Have fled away from the eternal prison?"
  Moving those venerable plumes, he said:
"Who guided you? or who has been your lamp
  In issuing forth out of the night profound,
  That ever black makes the infernal valley?
The laws of the abyss, are they thus broken?
  Or is there changed in heaven some council new,
  That being damned ye come unto my crags?"
Then did my Leader lay his grasp upon me,
  And with his words, and with his hands and signs,   50
  Reverent he made in me my knees and brow;
Then answered him: "I came not of myself;
  A Lady from Heaven descended, at whose prayers
  I aided this one with my company.
But since it is thy will more be unfolded
  Of our condition, how it truly is,
  Mine cannot be that this should be denied thee.
This one has never his last evening seen,
  But by his folly was so near to it
  That very little time was there to turn.   60
As I have said, I unto him was sent
  To rescue him, and other way was none
  Than this to which I have myself betaken.
I've shown him all the people of perdition,
  And now those spirits I intend to show
  Who purge themselves beneath thy guardianship.
How I have brought him would be long to tell thee.
  Virtue descendeth from on high that aids me
  To lead him to behold thee and to hear thee.
Now may it please thee to vouchsafe his coming;   70

He seeketh Liberty, which is so dear,
    As knoweth he who life for her refuses.
Thou know'st it; since, for her, to thee not bitter
    Was death in Utica, where thou didst leave
    The vesture, that will shine so, the great day.
By us the eternal edicts are not broken;
    Since this one lives, and Minos binds not me;
    But of that circle I, where are the chaste
Eyes of thy Marcia, who in looks still prays thee,
    O holy breast, to hold her as thine own;   80
    For her love, then, incline thyself to us.
Permit us through thy sevenfold realm to go;
    I will take back this grace from thee to her,
    If to be mentioned there below thou deignest."
"Marcia so pleasing was unto mine eyes
    While I was on the other side," then said he,
    "That every grace she wished of me I granted;
Now that she dwells beyond the evil river,
    She can no longer move me, by that law
    Which, when I issued forth from there, was made.   90
But if a Lady of Heaven do move and rule thee,
    As thou dost say, no flattery is needful;
    Let it suffice thee that for her thou ask me.
Go, then, and see thou gird this one about
    With a smooth rush, and that thou wash his face,
    So that thou cleanse away all stain therefrom,
For 'twere not fitting that the eye o'ercast
    By any mist should go before the first
    Angel, who is of those of Paradise.
This little island round about its base   100
    Below there, yonder, where the billow beats it,
    Doth rushes bear upon its washy ooze;
No other plant that putteth forth the leaf,
    Or that doth indurate, can there have life,
    Because it yieldeth not unto the shocks.
Thereafter be not this way your return;
    The sun, which now is rising, will direct you
    To take the mount by easier ascent."
With this he vanished; and I raised me up
    Without a word, and wholly drew myself   110

Unto my Guide, and turned mine eyes to him.
And he began: "Son, follow thou my steps;
    Let us turn back, for on this side declines
    The plain unto its lower boundaries."
The dawn was vanquishing the matin hour
    Which fled before it, so that from afar
    I recognised the trembling of the sea.
Along the solitary plain we went
    As one who unto the lost road returns,
    And till he finds it seems to go in vain.   120
As soon as we were come to where the dew
    Fights with the sun, and, being in a part
    Where shadow falls, little evaporates,
Both of his hands upon the grass outspread
    In gentle manner did my Master place;
    Whence I, who of his action was aware,
Extended unto him my tearful cheeks;
    There did he make in me uncovered wholly
    That hue which Hell had covered up in me.
Then came we down upon the desert shore   130
    Which never yet saw navigate its waters
    Any that afterward had known return.
There he begirt me as the other pleased;
    O marvellous! for even as he culled
    The humble plant, such it sprang up again
Suddenly there where he uprooted it.

Canto II

Already had the sun the horizon reached
    Whose circle of meridian covers o'er
    Jerusalem with its most lofty point,
And night that opposite to him revolves
    Was issuing forth from Ganges with the Scales
    That fall from out her hand when she exceedeth;
So that the white and the vermilion cheeks
    Of beautiful Aurora, where I was,
    By too great age were changing into orange.
We still were on the border of the sea,   10
    Like people who are thinking of their road,

Who go in heart, and with the body stay;
And lo! as when, upon the approach of morning,
    Through the gross vapours Mars grows fiery red
    Down in the West upon the ocean floor,
Appeared to me—may I again behold it!—
    A light along the sea so swiftly coming,
    Its motion by no flight of wing is equalled;
From which when I a little had withdrawn
    Mine eyes, that I might question my Conductor,   20
    Again I saw it brighter grown and larger.
Then on each side of it appeared to me
    I knew not what of white, and underneath it
    Little by little there came forth another.
My Master yet had uttered not a word
    While the first whiteness into wings unfolded;
    But when he clearly recognised the pilot,
He cried: "Make haste, make haste to bow the knee!
    Behold the Angel of God! fold thou thy hands!
    Henceforward shalt thou see such officers!   30
See how he scorneth human arguments,
    So that nor oar he wants, nor other sail
    Than his own wings, between so distant shores.
See how he holds them pointed up to heaven,
    Fanning the air with the eternal pinions,
    That do not moult themselves like mortal hair!"
Then as still nearer and more near us came
    The Bird Divine, more radiant he appeared,
    So that near by the eye could not endure him,
But down I cast it; and he came to shore   40
    With a small vessel, very swift and light,
    So that the water swallowed naught thereof.
Upon the stern stood the Celestial Pilot;
    Beatitude seemed written in his face,
    And more than a hundred spirits sat within.
"*In exitu Israel de Ægypto!*"
    They chanted all together in one voice,
    With whatso in that psalm is after written.
Then made he sign of holy rood upon them,
    Whereat all cast themselves upon the shore,   50
    And he departed swiftly as he came.
The throng which still remained there unfamiliar

Seemed with the place, all round about them gazing,
  As one who in new matters makes essay.
On every side was darting forth the day
  The sun, who had with his resplendent shafts
  From the mid-heaven chased forth the Capricorn,
When the new people lifted up their faces
  Towards us, saying to us: "If ye know,
  Show us the way to go unto the mountain." 60
And answer made Virgilius: "Ye believe
  Perchance that we have knowledge of this place,
  But we are strangers even as yourselves.
Just now we came, a little while before you,
  Another way, which was so rough and steep,
  That mounting will henceforth seem sport to us."
The souls who had, from seeing me draw breath,
  Become aware that I was still alive,
  Pallid in their astonishment became;
And as to messenger who bears the olive 70
  The people throng to listen to the news,
  And no one shows himself afraid of crowding,
So at the sight of me stood motionless
  Those fortunate spirits, all of them, as if
  Oblivious to go and make them fair.
One from among them saw I coming forward,
  As to embrace me, with such great affection,
  That it incited me to do the like.
O empty shadows, save in aspect only!
  Three times behind it did I clasp my hands, 80
  As oft returned with them to my own breast!
I think with wonder I depicted me;
  Whereat the shadow smiled and backward drew;
  And I, pursuing it, pressed farther forward.
Gently it said that I should stay my steps;
  Then knew I who it was, and I entreated
  That it would stop awhile to speak with me.
It made reply to me: "Even as I loved thee
  In mortal body, so I love thee free;
  Therefore I stop; but wherefore goest thou?" 90
"My own Casella! to return once more
  There where I am, I make this journey," said I;
  "But how from thee has so much time be taken?"

And he to me: "No outrage has been done me,
   If he who takes both when and whom he pleases
   Has many times denied to me this passage,
For of a righteous will his own is made.
   He, sooth to say, for three months past has taken
   Whoever wished to enter with all peace;
Whence I, who now had turned unto that shore   100
   Where salt the waters of the Tiber grow,
   Benignantly by him have been received.
Unto that outlet now his wing is pointed,
   Because for evermore assemble there
   Those who tow'rds Acheron do not descend."
And I: "If some new law take not from thee
   Memory or practice of the song of love,
   Which used to quiet in me all my longings,
Thee may it please to comfort therewithal
   Somewhat this soul of mine, that with its body   110
   Hitherward coming is so much distressed."
"Love, that within my mind discourses with me,"
   Forthwith began he so melodiously,
   The melody within me still is sounding.
My Master, and myself, and all that people
   Which with him were, appeared as satisfied
   As if naught else might touch the mind of any.
We all of us were moveless and attentive
   Unto his notes; and lo! the grave old man,
   Exclaiming: "What is this, ye laggard spirits?   120
What negligence, what standing still is this?
   Run to the mountain to strip off the slough,
   That lets not God be manifest to you."
Even as when, collecting grain or tares,
   The doves, together at their pasture met,
   Quiet, nor showing their accustomed pride,
If aught appear of which they are afraid,
   Upon a sudden leave their food alone,
   Because they are assailed by greater care;
So that fresh company did I behold   130
   The song relinquish, and go tow'rds the hill,
   As one who goes, and knows not whitherward;
Nor was our own departure less in haste.

Canto III

Inasmuch as the instantaneous flight
    Had scattered them asunder o'er the plain,
    Turned to the mountain whither reason spurs us,
I pressed me close unto my faithful comrade,
    And how without him had I kept my course?
    Who would have led me up along the mountain?
He seemed to me within himself remorseful;
    O noble conscience, and without a stain,
    How sharp a sting is trivial fault to thee!
After his feet had laid aside the haste   10
    Which mars the dignity of every act,
    My mind, that hitherto had been restrained,
Let loose its faculties as if delighted,
    And I my sight directed to the hill
    That highest tow'rds the heaven uplifts itself.
The sun, that in our rear was flaming red,
    Was broken in front of me into the figure
    Which had in me the stoppage of its rays;
Unto one side I turned me, with the fear
    Of being left alone, when I beheld   20
    Only in front of me the ground obscured.
"Why dost thou still mistrust?" my Comforter
    Began to say to me turned wholly round;
    "Dost thou not think me with thee, and that I guide thee?
'Tis evening there already where is buried
    The body within which I cast a shadow;
    'Tis from Brundusium ta'en, and Naples has it.
Now if in front of me no shadow fall,
    Marvel not at it more than at the heavens,
    Because one ray impedeth not another.   30
To suffer torments, both of cold and heat,
    Bodies like this that Power provides, which wills
    That how it works be not unveiled to us.
Insane is he who hopeth that our reason
    Can traverse the illimitable way,
    Which the one Substance in three Persons follows!
Mortals, remain contented at the *Quia*;
    For if ye had been able to see all,
    No need there were for Mary to give birth;

And ye have seen desiring without fruit,   40
  Those whose desire would have been quieted,
  Which evermore is given them for a grief.
I speak of Aristotle and of Plato,
  And many others";—and here bowed his head,
  And more he said not, and remained disturbed.
We came meanwhile unto the mountain's foot;
  There so precipitate we found the rock,
  That nimble legs would there have been in vain.
'Twixt Lerici and Turbìa, the most desert,
  The most secluded pathway is a stair   50
  Easy and open, if compared with that.
"Who knoweth now upon which hand the hill
  Slopes down," my Master said, his footsteps staying,
  "So that who goeth without wings may mount?"
And while he held his eyes upon the ground
  Examining the nature of the path,
  And I was looking up around the rock,
On the left hand appeared to me a throng
  Of souls, that moved their feet in our direction,
  And did not seem to move, they came so slowly.   60
"Lift up thine eyes," I to the Master said;
  "Behold, on this side, who will give us counsel,
  If thou of thine own self can have it not."
Then he looked at me, and with frank expression
  Replied: "Let us go there, for they come slowly,
  And thou be steadfast in thy hope, sweet son."
Still was that people as far off from us,
  After a thousand steps of ours I say,
  As a good thrower with his hand would reach,
When they all crowded unto the hard masses   70
  Of the high bank, and motionless stood and close,
  As he stands still to look who goes in doubt.
"O happy dead! O spirits elect already!"
  Virgilius made beginning, "by that peace
  Which I believe is waiting for you all,
Tell us upon what side the mountain slopes,
  So that the going up be possible,
  For to lose time irks him most who most knows."
As sheep come issuing forth from out the fold
  By ones and twos and threes, and the others stand   80

Timidly, holding down their eyes and nostrils,
And what the foremost does the others do,
  Huddling themselves against her, if she stop,
  Simple and quiet and the wherefore know not;
So moving to approach us thereupon
  I saw the leader of that fortunate flock,
  Modest in face and dignified in gait.
As soon as those in the advance saw broken
  The light upon the ground at my right side,
  So that from me the shadow reached the rock,   90
They stopped, and backward drew themselves somewhat;
  And all the others, who came after them,
  Not knowing why nor wherefore, did the same.
"Without your asking, I confess to you
  This is a human body which you see,
  Whereby the sunshine on the ground is cleft.
Marvel ye not thereat, but be persuaded
  That not without a power which comes from Heaven
  Doth he endeavour to surmount this wall."
The Master thus; and said those worthy people: 100
  "Return ye then, and enter in before us,"
  Making a signal with the back o' the hand.
And one of them began: "Whoe'er thou art,
  Thus going turn thine eyes, consider well
  If e'er thou saw me in the other world."
I turned me tow'rds him, and looked at him closely;
  Blond was he, beautiful, and of noble aspect,
  But one of his eyebrows had a blow divided.
When with humility I had disclaimed
  E'er having seen him, "Now behold!" he said,   110
  And showed me high upon his breast a wound.
Then said he with a smile: "I am Manfredi,
  The grandson of the Empress Costanza;
  Therefore, when thou returnest, I beseech thee
Go to my daughter beautiful, the mother
  Of Sicily's honour and of Aragon's,
  And the truth tell her, if aught else be told.
After I had my body lacerated
  By these two mortal stabs, I gave myself
  Weeping to Him, who willingly doth pardon.   120
Horrible my iniquities had been;

But Infinite Goodness hath such ample arms,
    That it receives whatever turns to it.
Had but Cosenza's pastor, who in chase
    Of me was sent by Clement at that time,
    In God read understandingly this page,
The bones of my dead body still would be
    At the bridge-head, near unto Benevento,
    Under the safeguard of the heavy cairn.
Now the rain bathes and moveth them the wind,   130
    Beyond the realm, almost beside the Verde,
    Where he transported them with tapers quenched.
By malison of theirs is not so lost
    Eternal Love, that it cannot return,
    So long as hope has anything of green.
True is it, who in contumacy dies
    Of Holy Church, though penitent at last,
    Must wait upon the outside this bank
Thirty times told the time that he has been
    In his presumption, unless such decree   140
    Shorter by means of righteous prayers become.
See now if thou hast power to make me happy,
    By making known unto my good Costanza
    How thou hast seen me, and this ban beside,
For those on earth can much advance us here."

Canto IV

Whenever by delight or else by pain,
    That seizes any faculty of ours,
    Wholly to that the soul collects itself,
It seemeth that no other power it heeds;
    And this against that error is which thinks
    One soul above another kindles in us.
And hence, whenever aught is heard or seen
    Which keeps the soul intently bent upon it,
    Time passes on, and we perceive it not,
Because one faculty is that which listens,   10
    And other that which the soul keeps entire;
    This is as if in bonds, and that is free.
Of this I had experience positive

In hearing and in gazing at that spirit;
  For fifty full degrees uprisen was
The sun, and I had not perceived it, when
  We came to where those souls with one accord
  Cried out unto us: "Here is what you ask."
A greater opening ofttimes hedges up
  With but a little forkful of his thorns   20
  The villager, what time the grape imbrowns,
Than was the passage-way through which ascended
  Only my Leader and myself behind him,
  After that company departed from us.
One climbs Sanleo and descends in Noli,
  And mounts the summit of Bismantova,
  With feet alone; but here one needs must fly;
With the swift pinions and the plumes I say
  Of great desire, conducted after him
  Who gave me hope, and made a light for me.   30
We mounted upward through the rifted rock,
  And on each side the border pressed upon us,
  And feet and hands the ground beneath required.
When we were come upon the upper rim
  Of the high bank, out on the open slope,
  "My Master," said I, "what way shall we take?"
And he to me: "No step of thine descend;
  Still up the mount behind me win thy way,
  Till some sage escort shall appear to us."
The summit was so high it vanquished sight,   40
  And the hillside precipitous far more
  Than line from middle quadrant to the centre.
Spent with fatigue was I, when I began:
  "O my sweet Father! turn thee and behold
  How I remain alone, unless thou stay!"
"O son," he said, "up yonder drag thyself,"
  Pointing me to a terrace somewhat higher,
  Which on that side encircles all the hill.
These words of his so spurred me on, that I
  Strained every nerve, behind him scrambling up,   50
  Until the circle was beneath my feet.
Thereon ourselves we seated both of us
  Turned to the East, from which we had ascended,
  For all men are delighted to look back.

To the low shores mine eyes I first directed,
　　Then to the sun uplifted them, and wondered
　　That on the left hand we were smitten by it.
The Poet well perceived that I was wholly
　　Bewildered at the chariot of the light,
　　Where 'twixt us and the Aquilon it entered.   60
Whereon he said to me: "If Castor and Pollux
　　Were in the company of yonder mirror,
　　That up and down conducteth with its light,
Thou wouldst behold the zodiac's jagged wheel
　　Revolving still more near unto the Bears,
　　Unless it swerved aside from its old track.
How that may be wouldst thou have power to think,
　　Collected in thyself, imagine Zion
　　Together with this mount on earth to stand,
So that they both one sole horizon have,   70
　　And hemispheres diverse; whereby the road
　　Which Phaeton, alas! knew not to drive,
Thou'lt see how of necessity must pass
　　This on one side, when that upon the other,
　　If thine intelligence right clearly heed."
"Truly, my Master," said I, "never yet
　　Saw I so clearly as I now discern,
　　There where my wit appeared incompetent,
That the mid-circle of supernal motion,
　　Which in some art is the Equator called,   80
　　And aye remains between the Sun and Winter,
For reason which thou sayest, departeth hence
　　Tow'rds the Septentrion, what time the Hebrews
　　Beheld it tow'rds the region of the heat.
But, if it pleaseth thee, I fain would learn
　　How far we have to go; for the hill rises
　　Higher than eyes of mine have power to rise."
And he to me: "This mount is such, that ever
　　At the beginning down below 'tis tiresome,
　　And aye the more one climbs, the less it hurts.   90
Therefore, when it shall seem so pleasant to thee,
　　That going up shall be to thee as easy
　　As going down the current in a boat,
Then at this pathway's ending thou wilt be;
　　There to repose thy panting breath expect;

No more I answer; and this I know for true."
And as he finished uttering these words,
   A voice close by us sounded: "Peradventure
   Thou wilt have need of sitting down ere that."
At sound thereof each one of us turned round,   100
   And saw upon the left hand a great rock,
   Which neither I nor he before had noticed.
Thither we drew; and there were persons there
   Who in the shadow stood behind the rock,
   As one through indolence is wont to stand.
And one of them, who seemed to me fatigued,
   Was sitting down, and both his knees embraced,
   Holding his face low down between them bowed.
"O my sweet Lord," I said, "do turn thine eye
   On him who shows himself more negligent   110
   Then even Sloth herself his sister were."
Then he turned round to us, and he gave heed,
   Just lifting up his eyes above his thigh,
   And said: "Now go thou up, for thou art valiant."
Then knew I who he was; and the distress,
   That still a little did my breathing quicken,
   My going to him hindered not; and after
I came to him he hardly raised his head,
   Saying: "Hast thou seen clearly how the sun
   O'er thy left shoulder drives his chariot?"   120
His sluggish attitude and his curt words
   A little unto laughter moved my lips;
   Then I began: "Belacqua, I grieve not
For thee henceforth; but tell me, wherefore seated
   In this place art thou? Waitest thou an escort?
   Or has thy usual habit seized upon thee?"
And he: "O brother, what's the use of climbing?
   Since to my torment would not let me go
   The Angel of God, who sitteth at the gate.
First heaven must needs so long revolve me round   130
   Outside thereof, as in my life it did,
   Since the good sighs I to the end postponed,
Unless, e'er that, some prayer may bring me aid
   Which rises from a heart that lives in grace;
   What profit others that in heaven are heard not?"
Meanwhile the Poet was before me mounting,

And saying: "Come now; see the sun has touched
   Meridian, and from the shore the night
Covers already with her foot Morocco."

Canto V

I had already from those shades departed,
   And followed in the footsteps of my Guide,
   When from behind, pointing his finger at me,
One shouted: "See, it seems as if shone not
   The sunshine on the left of him below,
   And like one living seems he to conduct him."
Mine eyes I turned at utterance of these words,
   And saw them watching with astonishment
   But me, but me, and the light which was broken!
"Why doth thy mind so occupy itself,"   10
   The Master said, "that thou thy pace dost slacken?
   What matters it to thee what here is whispered?
Come after me, and let the people talk;
   Stand like a steadfast tower, that never wags
   Its top for all the blowing of the winds;
For evermore the man in whom is springing
   Thought upon thought, removes from him the mark,
   Because the force of one the other weakens."
What could I say in answer but "I come"?
   I said it somewhat with that colour tinged   20
   Which makes a man of pardon sometimes worthy.
Meanwhile along the mountain-side across
   Came people in advance of us a little,
   Singing the Miserere verse by verse.
When they became aware I gave no place
   For passage of the sunshine through my body,
   They changed their song into a long, hoarse "Oh!"
And two of them, in form of messengers,
   Ran forth to meet us, and demanded of us,
   "Of your condition make us cognisant."   30
And said my Master: "Ye can go your way
   And carry back again to those who sent you,
   That this one's body is of very flesh.
If they stood still because they saw his shadow,

As I suppose, enough is answered them;
    Him let them honour, it may profit them."
Vapours enkindled saw I ne'er so swiftly
    At early nightfall cleave the air serene,
    Nor, at the set of sun, the clouds of August,
But upward they returned in briefer time,   40
    And, on arriving, with the others wheeled
    Tow'rds us, like troops that run without a rein.
"This folk that presses unto us is great,
    And cometh to implore thee," said the Poet;
    "So still go onward, and in going listen."
"O soul that goest to beatitude
    With the same members wherewith thou wast born,"
    Shouting they came, "a little stay thy steps,
Look, if thou e'er hast any of us seen,
    So that o'er yonder thou bear news of him;   50
    Ah, why dost thou go on? Ah, why not stay?
Long since we all were slain by violence,
    And sinners even to the latest hour;
    Then did a light from heaven admonish us,
So that, both penitent and pardoning, forth
    From life we issued reconciled to God,
    Who with desire to see Him stirs our hearts."
And I: "Although I gaze into your faces,
    No one I recognize; but if may please you
    Aught I have power to do, ye well-born spirits,   60
Speak ye, and I will do it, by that peace
    Which, following the feet of such a Guide,
    From world to world makes itself sought by me."
And one began: "Each one has confidence
    In thy good offices without an oath,
    Unless the I cannot cut off the I will;
Whence I, who speak alone before the others,
    Pray thee, if ever thou dost see the land
    That 'twixt Romagna lies and that of Charles,
Thou be so courteous to me of thy prayers   70
    In Fano, that they pray for me devoutly,
    That I may purge away my grave offences.
From thence was I; but the deep wounds, through which
    Issued the blood wherein I had my seat,
    Were dealt me in bosom of the Antenori,

There where I thought to be the most secure;
   'Twas he of Este had it done, who held me
   In hatred far beyond what justice willed.
But if towards the Mira I had fled,
   When I was overtaken at Oriaco,   80
   I still should be o'er yonder where men breathe.
I ran to the lagoon, and reeds and mire
   Did so entangle me I fell, and saw there
   A lake made from my veins upon the ground."
Then said another: "Ah, be that desire
   Fulfilled that draws thee to the lofty mountain,
   As thou with pious pity aidest mine.
I was of Montefeltro, and am Buonconte;
   Giovanna, nor none other cares for me;
   Hence among these I go with downcast front."   90
And I to him: "What violence or what chance
   Led thee astray so far from Campaldino,
   That never has thy sepulture been known?"
"Oh," he replied, "at Casentino's foot
   A river crosses named Archiano, born
   Above the Hermitage in Apennine.
There where the name thereof becometh void
   Did I arrive, pierced through and through the throat,
   Fleeing on foot, and bloodying the plain;
There my sight lost I, and my utterance   100
   Ceased in the name of Mary, and thereat
   I fell, and tenantless my flesh remained.
Truth will I speak, repeat it to the living;
   God's Angel took me up, and he of hell
   Shouted: 'O thou from heaven, why dost thou rob me?
Thou bearest away the eternal part of him,
   For one poor little tear, that takes him from me;
   But with the rest I'll deal in other fashion!'
Well knowest thou how in the air is gathered
   That humid vapour which to water turns,   110
   Soon as it rises where the cold doth grasp it.
He joined that evil will, which aye seeks evil,
   To intellect, and moved the mist and wind
   By means of power, which his own nature gave;
Thereafter, when the day was spent, the valley
   From Pratomagno to the great yoke covered

With fog, and made the heaven above intent,
So that the pregnant air to water changed;
    Down fell the rain, and to the gullies came
    Whate'er of it earth tolerated not;   120
And as it mingled with the mighty torrents,
    Towards the royal river with such speed
    It headlong rushed, that nothing held it back.
My frozen body near unto its outlet
    The robust Archian found, and into Arno
    Thrust it, and loosened from my breast the cross
I made of me, when agony o'ercame me;
    It rolled me on the banks and on the bottom;
    Then with its booty covered and begirt me."
"Ah, when thou hast returned unto the world,   130
    And rested thee from thy long journeying,"
    After the second followed the third spirit,
"Do thou remember me who am the Pia;
    Siena made me, unmade me Maremma;
    He knoweth it, who had encircled first,
Espousing me, my finger with his gem."

Canto VI

Whene'er is broken up the game of Zara,
    He who has lost remains behind despondent,
    The throws repeating, and in sadness learns;
The people with the other all depart;
    One goes in front, and one behind doth pluck him,
    And at his side one brings himself to mind;
He pauses not, and this and that one hears;
    They crowd no more to whom his hand he stretches,
    And from the throng he thus defends himself.
Even such was I in that dense multitude,   10
    Turning to them this way and that my face,
    And, promising, I freed myself therefrom.
There was the Aretine, who from the arms
    Untamed of Ghin di Tacco had his death,
    And he who fleeing from pursuit was drowned.
There was imploring with his hands outstretched
    Frederick Novello, and that one of Pisa

Who made the good Marzucco seem so strong.
I saw Count Orso; and the soul divided
   By hatred and by envy from its body,   20
   As it declared, and not for crime committed,
Pierre de la Brosse I say; and here provide
   While still on earth the Lady of Brabant,
   So that for this she be of no worse flock!
As soon as I was free from all those shades
   Who only prayed that some one else may pray,
   So as to hasten their becoming holy,
Began I: "It appears that thou deniest,
   O light of mine, expressly in some text,
   That orison can bend decree of Heaven;   30
And ne'ertheless these people pray for this.
   Might then their expectation bootless be?
   Or is to me thy saying not quite clear?"
And he to me: "My writing is explicit,
   And not fallacious is the hope of these,
   If with sane intellect 'tis well regarded;
For top of judgment doth not vail itself,
   Because the fire of love fulfils at once
   What he must satisfy who here installs him.
And there, where I affirmed that proposition,   40
   Defect was not amended by a prayer,
   Because the prayer from God was separate.
Verily, in so deep a questioning
   Do not decide, unless she tell it thee,
   Who light 'twixt truth and intellect shall be.
I know not if thou understand; I speak
   Of Beatrice; her shalt thou see above,
   Smiling and happy, on this mountain's top."
And I: "Good Leader, let us make more haste,
   For I no longer tire me as before;   50
   And see, e'en now the hill a shadow casts."
"We will go forward with this day," he answered,
   "As far as now is possible for us;
   But otherwise the fact is than thou thinkest.
Ere thou art up there, thou shalt see return
   Him, who now hides himself behind the hill,
   So that thou dost not interrupt his rays.
But yonder there behold! a soul that stationed

All, all alone is looking hitherward;
   It will point out to us the quickest way."   60
We came up unto it; O Lombard soul,
   How lofty and disdainful thou didst bear thee,
   And grand and slow in moving of thine eyes!
Nothing whatever did it say to us,
   But let us go our way, eying us only
   After the manner of a couchant lion;
Still near to it Virgilius drew, entreating
   That it would point us out the best ascent;
   And it replied not unto his demand,
But of our native land and of our life   70
   It questioned us; and the sweet Guide began:
   "Mantua,"—and the shade, all in itself recluse,
Rose tow'rds him from the place where first it was,
   Saying: "O Mantuan, I am Sordello
   Of thine own land!" and one embraced the other.
Ah! servile Italy, grief's hostelry!
   A ship without a pilot in great tempest!
   No Lady thou of Provinces, but brothel!
That noble soul was so impatient, only
   At the sweet sound of his own native land,   80
   To make its citizen glad welcome there;
And now within thee are not without war
   Thy living ones, and one doth gnaw the other
   Of those whom one wall and one fosse shut in!
Search, wretched one, all round about the shores
   Thy seaboard, and then look within thy bosom,
   If any part of thee enjoyeth peace!
What boots it, that for thee Justinian
   The bridle mend, if empty be the saddle?
   Withouten this the shame would be the less.   90
Ah! people, thou that oughtest to be devout,
   And to let Cæsar sit upon the saddle,
   If well thou hearest what God teacheth thee,
Behold how fell this wild beast has become,
   Being no longer by the spur corrected,
   Since thou hast laid thy hand upon the bridle.
O German Albert! who abandonest
   Her that has grown recalcitrant and savage,
   And oughtest to bestride her saddle-bow,

May a just judgment from the stars down fall   100
  Upon thy blood, and be it new and open,
  That thy successor may have fear thereof;
Because thy father and thyself have suffered,
  By greed of those transalpine lands distrained,
  The garden of the empire to be waste.
Come and behold Montecchi and Cappelletti,
  Monaldi and Fillippeschi, careless man!
  Those sad already, and these doubt-depressed!
Come, cruel one! come and behold the oppression
  Of thy nobility, and cure their wounds,   110
  And thou shalt see how safe is Santafiore!
Come and behold thy Rome, that is lamenting,
  Widowed, alone, and day and night exclaims,
  "My Cæsar, why hast thou forsaken me?"
Come and behold how loving are the people;
  And if for us no pity moveth thee,
  Come and be made ashamed of thy renown!
And if it lawful be, O Jove Supreme!
  Who upon earth for us wast crucified,
  Are thy just eyes averted otherwhere?   120
Or preparation is 't, that, in the abyss
  Of thine own counsel, for some good thou makest
  From our perception utterly cut off?
For all the towns of Italy are full
  Of tyrants, and becometh a Marcellus
  Each peasant churl who plays the partisan!
My Florence! well mayst thou contented be
  With this digression, which concerns thee not,
  Thanks to thy people who such forethought take!
Many at heart have justice, but shoot slowly,   130
  That unadvised they come not to the bow,
  But on their very lips thy people have it!
Many refuse to bear the common burden;
  But thy solicitous people answereth
  Without being asked, and crieth: "I submit."
Now be thou joyful, for thou hast good reason;
  Thou affluent, thou in peace, thou full of wisdom!
  If I speak true, the event conceals it not.
Athens and Lacedæmon, they who made
  The ancient laws, and were so civilized,   140

Made towards living well a little sign
Compared with thee, who makest such fine-spun
   Provisions, that to middle of November
   Reaches not what thou in October spinnest.
How oft, within the time of thy remembrance,
   Laws, money, offices, and usages
   Hast thou remodelled, and renewed thy members?
And if thou mind thee well, and see the light,
   Thou shalt behold thyself like a sick woman,
   Who cannot find repose upon her down,   150
But by her tossing wardeth off her pain.

Canto VII

After the gracious and glad salutations
   Had three and four times been reiterated,
   Sordello backward drew and said, "Who are you?"
"Or ever to this mountain were directed
   The souls deserving to ascend to God,
   My bones were buried by Octavian.
I am Virgilius; and for no crime else
   Did I lose heaven, than for not having faith;"
   In this wise then my Leader made reply.
As one who suddenly before him sees   10
   Something whereat he marvels, who believes
   And yet does not, saying, "It is! it is not!"
So he appeared; and then bowed down his brow,
   And with humility returned towards him,
   And, where inferiors embrace, embraced him.
"O glory of the Latians, thou," he said,
   "Through whom our language showed what it could do,
   O pride eternal of the place I came from,
What merit or what grace to me reveals thee?
   If I to hear thy words be worthy, tell me   20
   If thou dost come from Hell, and from what cloister."
"Through all the circles of the doleful realm,"
   Responded he, "have I come hitherward;
   Heaven's power impelled me, and with that I come.
I by not doing, not by doing, lost
   The sight of that high sun which thou desirest,

And which too late by me was recognized.
A place there is below not sad with torments,
    But darkness only, where the lamentations
    Have not the sound of wailing, but are sighs.   30
There dwell I with the little innocents
    Snatched by the teeth of Death, or ever they
    Were from our human sinfulness exempt.
There dwell I among those who the three saintly
    Virtues did not put on, and without vice
    The others knew and followed all of them.
But if thou know and can, some indication
    Give us by which we may the sooner come
    Where Purgatory has its right beginning."
He answered: "No fixed place has been assigned us;   40
    'Tis lawful for me to go up and round;
    So far as I can go, as guide I join thee.
But see already how the day declines,
    And to go up by night we are not able;
    Therefore 'tis well to think of some fair sojourn.
Souls are there on the right hand here withdrawn;
    If thou permit me I will lead thee to them,
    And thou shalt know them not without delight."
"How is this?" was the answer; "should one wish
    To mount by night would he prevented be   50
    By others? or mayhap would not have power?"
And on the ground the good Sordello drew
    His finger, saying, "See, this line alone
    Thou couldst not pass after the sun is gone;
Not that aught else would hindrance give, however,
    To going up, save the nocturnal darkness;
    This with the want of power the will perplexes.
We might indeed therewith return below,
    And, wandering, walk the hill-side round about,
    While the horizon holds the day imprisoned."   60
Thereon my Lord, as if in wonder, said:
    "Do thou conduct us thither, where thou sayest
    That we can take delight in tarrying."
Little had we withdrawn us from that place,
    When I perceived the mount was hollowed out
    In fashion as the valleys here are hollowed.
"Thitherward," said that shade, "will we repair,

Where of itself the hill-side makes a lap,
    And there for the new day will we await."
'Twixt hill and plain there was a winding path   70
    Which led us to the margin of that dell,
    Where dies the border more than half away
Gold and fine silver, and scarlet and pearl-white,
    The Indian wood resplendent and serene,
    Fresh emerald the moment it is broken,
By herbage and by flowers within that hollow
    Planted, each one in colour would be vanquished,
    As by its greater vanquished is the less.
Nor in that place had nature painted only,
    But of the sweetness of a thousand odours   80
    Made there a mingled fragrance and unknown.
"*Salve Regina*," on the green and flowers
    There seated, singing, spirits I beheld,
    Which were not visible outside the valley.
"Before the scanty sun now seeks his nest,"
    Began the Mantuan who had led us thither,
    "Among them do not wish me to conduct you.
Better from off this ledge the acts and faces
    Of all of them will you discriminate,
    Than in the plain below received among them.   90
He who sits highest, and the semblance bears
    Of having what he should have done neglected,
    And to the others' song moves not his lips,
Rudolph the Emperor was, who had the power
    To heal the wounds that Italy have slain,
    So that through others slowly she revives.
The other, who in look doth comfort him,
    Governed the region where the water springs,
    The Moldau bears the Elbe, and Elbe the sea.
His name was Ottocar; and in swaddling-clothes   100
    Far better he than bearded Winceslaus
    His son, who feeds in luxury and ease.
And the small-nosed, who close in council seems
    With him that has an aspect so benign,
    Died fleeing and disflowering the lily;
Look there, how he is beating at his breast!
    Behold the other one, who for his cheek
    Sighing has made of his own palm a bed;

Father and father-in-law of France's Pest
   Are they, and know his vicious life and lewd,   110
   And hence proceeds the grief that so doth pierce them.
He who appears so stalwart, and chimes in,
   Singing, with that one of the manly nose,
   The cord of every valour wore begirt;
And if as King had after him remained
   The stripling who in rear of him is sitting,
   Well had the valour passed from vase to vase,
Which cannot of the other heirs be said.
   Frederick and Jacomo possess the realms,
   But none the better heritage possesses.   120
Not oftentimes upriseth through the branches
   The probity of man; and this He wills
   Who gives it, so that we may ask of Him.
Eke to the large-nosed reach my words, no less
   Than to the other, Pier, who with him sings;
   Whence Provence and Apulia grieve already
The plant is as inferior to its seed,
   As more than Beatrice and Margaret
   Costanza boasteth of her husband still.
Behold the monarch of the simple life,   130
   Harry of England, sitting there alone;
   He in his branches has a better issue.
He who the lowest on the ground among them
   Sits looking upward, is the Marquis William,
   For whose sake Alessandria and her war
Make Monferrat and Canavese weep."

Canto VIII

'Twas now the hour that turneth back desire
   In those who sail the sea, and melts the heart,
   The day they've said to their sweet friends farewell,
And the new pilgrim penetrates with love,
   If he doth hear from far away a bell
   That seemeth to deplore the dying day,
When I began to make of no avail
   My hearing, and to watch one of the souls
   Uprisen, that begged attention with its hand.

It joined and lifted upward both its palms,
  Fixing its eyes upon the orient,
    As if it said to God, "Naught else I care for."   10
"*Te lucis ante*" so devoutly issued
  Forth from its mouth, and with such dulcet notes,
    It made me issue forth from my own mind.
And then the others, sweetly and devoutly,
  Accompanied it through all the hymn entire,
    Having their eyes on the supernal wheels.
Here, Reader, fix thine eyes well on the truth,
  For now indeed so subtile is the veil,   20
    Surely to penetrate within is easy.
I saw that army of the gentle-born
  Thereafterward in silence upward gaze,
    As if in expectation, pale and humble;
And from on high come forth and down descend,
  I saw two Angels with two flaming swords,
    Truncated and deprived of their points.
Green as the little leaflets just now born
  Their garments were, which, by their verdant pinions
    Beaten and blown abroad, they trailed behind.   30
One just above us came to take his station,
  And one descended to the opposite bank,
    So that the people were contained between them.
Clearly in them discerned I the blond head;
  But in their faces was the eye bewildered,
    As faculty confounded by excess.
"From Mary's bosom both of them have come,"
  Sordello said, "as guardians of the valley
    Against the serpent, that will come anon."
Whereupon I, who knew not by what road,   40
  Turned round about, and closely drew myself,
    Utterly frozen, to the faithful shoulders.
And once again Sordello: "Now descend we
  'Mid the grand shades, and we will speak to them;
    Right pleasant will it be for them to see you."
Only three steps I think that I descended,
  And was below, and saw one who was looking
    Only at me, as if he fain would know me.
Already now the air was growing dark,
  But not so that between his eyes and mine   50

It did not show what it before locked up.
Tow'rds me he moved, and I tow'rds him did move;
   Noble Judge Nino! how it me delighted,
   When I beheld thee not among the damned!
No greeting fair was left unsaid between us;
   Then asked he: "How long is it since thou camest
   O'er the far waters to the mountain's foot?"
"Oh!" said I to him, "through the dismal places
   I came this morn; and am in the first life,
   Albeit the other, going thus, I gain."   60
And on the instant my reply was heard,
   He and Sordello both shrank back from me,
   Like people who are suddenly bewildered.
One to Virgilius, and the other turned
   To one who sat there, crying, "Up, Currado!
   Come and behold what God in grace has willed!"
Then, turned to me: "By that especial grace
   Thou owest unto Him, who so conceals
   His own first wherefore, that it has no ford,
When thou shalt be beyond the waters wide,   70
   Tell my Giovanna that she pray for me,
   Where answer to the innocent is made.
I do not think her mother loves me more,
   Since she has laid aside her wimple white,
   Which she, unhappy, needs must wish again.
Through her full easily is comprehended
   How long in woman lasts the fire of love,
   If eye or touch do not relight it often.
So fair a hatchment will not make for her
   The Viper marshalling the Milanese   80
   A-field, as would have made Gallura's Cock."
In this wise spake he, with the stamp impressed
   Upon his aspect of that righteous zeal
   Which measurably burneth in the heart.
My greedy eyes still wandered up to heaven,
   Still to that point where slowest are the stars,
   Even as a wheel the nearest to its axle.
And my Conductor: "Son, what dost thou gaze at
   Up there?" And I to him: "At those three torches
   With which this hither pole is all on fire."   90
And he to me: "The four resplendent stars

Thou sawest this morning are down yonder low,
    And these have mounted up to where those were."
As he was speaking, to himself Sordello
    Drew him, and said, "Lo there our Adversary!"
    And pointed with his finger to look thither.
Upon the side on which the little valley
    No barrier hath, a serpent was; perchance
    The same which gave to Eve the bitter food.
'Twixt grass and flowers came on the evil streak,   100
    Turning at times its head about, and licking
    Its back like to a beast that smoothes itself.
I did not see, and therefore cannot say
    How the celestial falcons 'gan to move,
    But well I saw that they were both in motion.
Hearing the air cleft by their verdant wings,
    The serpent fled, and round the Angels wheeled,
    Up to their stations flying back alike.
The shade that to the Judge had near approached
    When he had called, throughout that whole assault   110
    Had not a moment loosed its gaze on me.
"So may the light that leadeth thee on high
    Find in thine own free-will as much of wax
    As needful is up to the highest azure,"
Began it, "if some true intelligence
    Of Valdimagra or its neighbourhood
    Thou knowest, tell it me, who once was great there.
Currado Malaspina was I called;
    I'm not the elder, but from him descended;
    To mine I bore the love which here refineth."   120
"O," said I unto him, "through your domains
    I never passed, but where is there a dwelling
    Throughout all Europe, where they are not known?
That fame, which doeth honour to your house,
    Proclaims its Signors and proclaims its land,
    So that he knows of them who ne'er was there.
And, as I hope for heaven, I swear to you
    Your honoured family in naught abates
    The glory of the purse and of the sword.
It is so privileged by use and nature,   130
    That though a guilty head misguide the world,
    Sole it goes right, and scorns the evil way."

And he: "Now go; for the sun shall not lie
   Seven times upon the pillow which the Ram
   With all his four feet covers and bestrides,
Before that such a courteous opinion
   Shall in the middle of thy head be nailed
   With greater nails than of another's speech,
Unless the course of justice standeth still."

Canto IX

The concubine of old Tithonus now
   Gleamed white upon the eastern balcony,
   Forth from the arms of her sweet paramour;
With gems her forehead all relucent was,
   Set in the shape of that cold animal
   Which with its tail doth smite amain the nations,
And of the steps, with which she mounts, the Night
   Had taken two in that place where we were,
   And now the third was bending down its wings;
When I, who something had of Adam in me,   10
   Vanquished by sleep, upon the grass reclined,
   There were all five of us already sat.
Just at the hour when her sad lay begins
   The little swallow, near unto the morning,
   Perchance in memory of her former woes,
And when the mind of man, a wanderer
   More from the flesh, and less by thought imprisoned,
   Almost prophetic in its visions is,
In dreams it seemed to me I saw suspended
   An eagle in the sky, with plumes of gold,   20
   With wings wide open, and intent to stoop,
And this, it seemed to me, was where had been
   By Ganymede his kith and kin abandoned,
   When to the high consistory he was rapt.
I thought within myself, perchance he strikes
   From habit only here, and from elsewhere
   Disdains to bear up any in his feet.
Then wheeling somewhat more, it seemed to me,
   Terrible as the lightning he descended,
   And snatched me upward even to the fire.   30

Therein it seemed that he and I were burning,
   And the imagined fire did scorch me so,
   That of necessity my sleep was broken.
Not otherwise Achilles started up,
   Around him turning his awakened eyes,
   And knowing not the place in which he was,
What time from Chiron stealthily his mother
   Carried him sleeping in her arms to Scyros,
   Wherefrom the Greeks withdrew him afterwards,
Than I upstarted, when from off my face   40
   Sleep fled away; and pallid I became,
   As doth the man who freezes with affright.
Only my Comforter was at my side,
   And now the sun was more than two hours high,
   And turned towards the sea-shore was my face.
"Be not intimidated," said my Lord,
   "Be reassured, for all is well with us;
   Do not restrain, but put forth all thy strength.
Thou hast at length arrived at Purgatory;
   See there the cliff that closes it around;   50
   See there the entrance, where it seems disjoined.
Whilom at dawn, which doth precede the day,
   When inwardly thy spirit was asleep
   Upon the flowers that deck the land below,
There came a Lady and said: 'I am Lucìa;
   Let me take this one up, who is asleep;
   So will I make his journey easier for him.'
Sordello and the other noble shapes
   Remained; she took thee, and, as day grew bright,
   Upward she came, and I upon her footsteps.   60
She laid thee here; and first her beauteous eyes
   That open entrance pointed out to me;
   Then she and sleep together went away."
In guise of one whose doubts are reassured,
   And who to confidence his fear doth change,
   After the truth has been discovered to him,
So did I change; and when without disquiet
   My Leader saw me, up along the cliff
   He moved, and I behind him, tow'rd the height
Reader, thou seest well how I exalt   70
   My theme, and therefore if with greater art

I fortify it, marvel not thereat.
Nearer approached we, and were in such place,
    That there, where first appeared to me a rift
    Like to a crevice that disparts a wall,
I saw a portal, and three stairs beneath,
    Diverse in colour, to go up to it,
    And a gate-keeper, who yet spake no word.
And as I opened more and more mine eyes,
    I saw him seated on the highest stair,   80
    Such in the face that I endured it not.
And in his hand he had a naked sword,
    Which so reflected back the sunbeams tow'rds us,
    That oft in vain I lifted up mine eyes.
"Tell it from where you are, what is't you wish?"
    Began he to exclaim; "where is the escort?
    Take heed your coming hither harm you not!"
"A Lady of Heaven, with these things conversant,"
    My Master answered him, "but even now
    Said to us, 'Thither go; there is the portal.'"   90
"And may she speed your footsteps in all good,"
    Again began the courteous janitor;
    "Come forward then unto these stairs of ours."
Thither did we approach; and the first stair
    Was marble white, so polished and so smooth,
    I mirrored myself therein as I appear.
The second, tint of deeper hue than perse,
    Was of a calcined and uneven stone,
    Cracked all asunder lengthwise and across.
The third, that uppermost rests massively,   100
    Porphyry seemed to me, as flaming red
    As blood that from a vein is spirting forth.
Both of his feet was holding upon this
    The Angel of God, upon the threshold seated,
    Which seemed to me a stone of diamond.
Along the three stairs upward with good will
    Did my Conductor draw me, saying: "Ask
    Humbly that he the fastening may undo."
Devoutly at the holy feet I cast me,
    For mercy's sake besought that he would open,   110
    But first upon my breast three times I smote.
Seven P's upon my forehead he described

With the sword's point, and, "Take heed that thou wash
These wounds, when thou shalt be within," he said.
Ashes, or earth that dry is excavated,
Of the same colour were with his attire,
And from beneath it he drew forth two keys.
One was of gold, and the other was of silver;
First with the white, and after with the yellow,
Plied he the door, so that I was content.   120
"Whenever faileth either of these keys
So that it turn not rightly in the lock,"
He said to us, "this entrance doth not open.
More precious one is, but the other needs
More art and intellect ere it unlock,
For it is that which doth the knot unloose.
From Peter I have them; and he bade me err
Rather in opening than in keeping shut,
If people but fall down before my feet."
Then pushed the portals of the sacred door,   130
Exclaiming: "Enter; but I give you warning
That forth returns whoever looks behind."
And when upon their hinges were turned round
The swivels of that consecrated gate,
Which are of metal, massive and sonorous,
Roared not so loud, nor so discordant seemed
Tarpeia, when was ta'en from it the good
Metellus, wherefore meagre it remained.
At the first thunder-peal I turned attentive,
And "*Te Deum laudamus*" seemed to hear   140
In voices mingled with sweet melody.
Exactly such an image rendered me
That which I heard, as we are wont to catch,
When people singing with the organ stand;
For now we hear, and now hear not, the words.

Canto X

When we had crossed the threshold of the door
Which the perverted love of souls disuses,
Because it makes the crooked way seem straight,
Re-echoing I heard it closed again;

And if I had turned back mine eyes upon it,
   What for my failing had been fit excuse?
We mounted upward through a rifted rock,
   Which undulated to this side and that,
   Even as a wave receding and advancing.
"Here it behoves us use a little art,"   10
   Began my Leader, "to adapt ourselves
   Now here, now there, to the receding side."
And this our footsteps so infrequent made,
   That sooner had the moon's decreasing disk
   Regained its bed to sink again to rest,
Than we were forth from out that needle's eye;
   But when we free and in the open were,
   There where the mountain backward piles itself,
I wearied out, and both of us uncertain
   About our way, we stopped upon a plain   20
   More desolate than roads across the deserts.
From where its margin borders on the void,
   To foot of the high bank that ever rises,
   A human body three times told would measure;
And far as eye of mine could wing its flight,
   Now on the left, and on the right flank now,
   The same this cornice did appear to me.
Thereon our feet had not been moved as yet,
   When I perceived the embankment round about,
   Which all right of ascent had interdicted,   30
To be of marble white, and so adorned
   With sculptures, that not only Polycletus,
   But Nature's self, had there been put to shame.
The Angel, who came down to earth with tidings
   Of peace, that had been wept for many a year,
   And opened Heaven from its long interdict,
In front of us appeared so truthfully
   There sculptured in a gracious attitude,
   He did not seem an image that is silent.
One would have sworn that he was saying, "*Ave*";   40
   For she was there in effigy portrayed
   Who turned the key to ope the exalted love,
And in her mien this language had impressed,
   "*Ecce ancilla Dei*," as distinctly
   As any figure stamps itself in wax.

"Keep not thy mind upon one place alone,"
  The gentle Master said, who had me standing
  Upon that side where people have their hearts;
Whereat I moved mine eyes, and I beheld
  In rear of Mary, and upon that side   50
  Where he was standing who conducted me,
Another story on the rock imposed;
  Wherefore I passed Virgilius and drew near,
  So that before mine eyes it might be set.
There sculptured in the self-same marble were
  The cart and oxen, drawing the holy ark,
  Wherefore one dreads an office not appointed.
People appeared in front, and all of them
  In seven choirs divided, of two senses
  Made one say "No," the other, "Yes, they sing."   60
Likewise unto the smoke of the frankincense,
  Which there was imaged forth, the eyes and nose
  Were in the yes and no discordant made.
Preceded there the vessel benedight,
  Dancing with girded loins, the humble Psalmist,
  And more and less than King was he in this.
Opposite, represented at the window
  Of a great palace, Michal looked upon him,
  Even as a woman scornful and afflicted.
I moved my feet from where I had been standing,   70
  To examine near at hand another story,
  Which after Michal glimmered white upon me.
There the high glory of the Roman Prince
  Was chronicled, whose great beneficence
  Moved Gregory to his great victory;
'Tis of the Emperor Trajan I am speaking;
  And a poor widow at his bridle stood,
  In attitude of weeping and of grief.
Around about him seemed it thronged and full
  Of cavaliers, and the eagles in the gold   80
  Above them visibly in the wind were moving.
The wretched woman in the midst of these
  Seemed to be saying: "Give me vengeance, Lord,
  For my dead son, for whom my heart is breaking."
And he to answer her: "Now wait until
  I shall return." And she: "My Lord," like one

In whom grief is impatient, "shouldst thou not
Return?" And he: "Who shall be where I am
    Will give it thee." And she: "Good deed of others
    What boots it thee, if thou neglect thine own?"   90
Whence he: "Now comfort thee, for it behoves me
    That I discharge my duty ere I move;
    Justice so wills, and pity doth retain me."
He who on no new thing has ever looked
    Was the creator of this visible language,
    Novel to us, for here it is not found.
While I delighted me in contemplating
    The images of such humility,
    And dear to look on for their Maker's sake,
"Behold, upon this side, but rare they make   100
    Their steps," the Poet murmured, "many people;
    These will direct us to the lofty stairs."
Mine eyes, that in beholding were intent
    To see new things, of which they curious are,
    In turning round towards him were not slow.
But still I wish not, Reader, thou shouldst swerve
    From thy good purposes, because thou hearest
    How God ordaineth that the debt be paid;
Attend not to the fashion of the torment,
    Think of what follows; think that at the worst   110
    It cannot reach beyond the mighty sentence.
"Master," began I, "that which I behold
    Moving towards us seems to me not persons,
    And what I know not, so in sight I waver."
And he to me: "The grievous quality
    Of this their torment bows them so to earth,
    That my own eyes at first contended with it;
But look there fixedly, and disentangle
    By sight what cometh underneath those stones;
    Already canst thou see how each is stricken."   120
O ye proud Christians! wretched, weary ones!
    Who, in the vision of the mind infirm,
    Confidence have in your backsliding steps,
Do ye not comprehend that we are worms,
    Born to bring forth the angelic butterfly
    That flieth unto judgment without screen?
Why floats aloft your spirit high in air?

Like are ye unto insects undeveloped,
Even as the worm in whom formation fails!
As to sustain a ceiling or a roof,   130
    In place of corbel, oftentimes a figure
    Is seen to join its knees unto its breast,
Which makes of the unreal real anguish
    Arise in him who sees it; fashioned thus
    Beheld I those, when I had ta'en good heed.
True is it, they were more or less bent down,
    According as they more or less were laden;
    And he who had most patience in his looks
Weeping did seem to say, "I can no more!"

Canto XI

"Our Father, thou who dwellest in the heavens,
    Not circumscribed, but from the greater love
    Thou bearest to the first effects on high,
Praised be thy name and thine omnipotence
    By every creature, as befitting is
    To render thanks to thy sweet effluence.
Come unto us the peace of thy dominion,
    For unto it we cannot of ourselves,
    If it come not, with all our intellect.
Even as thine own Angels of their will   10
    Make sacrifice to thee, Hosanna singing,
    So may all men make sacrifice of theirs.
Give unto us this day our daily manna,
    Withouten which in this rough wilderness
    Backward goes he who toils most to advance.
And even as we the trespass we have suffered
    Pardon in one another, pardon thou
    Benignly, and regard not our desert.
Our virtue, which is easily o'ercome,
    Put not to proof with the old Adversary,   20
    But thou from him who spurs it so, deliver.
This last petition verily, dear Lord,
    Not for ourselves is made, who need it not,
    But for their sake who have remained behind us."
Thus for themselves and us good furtherance
    Those shades imploring, went beneath a weight

Like unto that of which we sometimes dream,
Unequally in anguish round and round
   And weary all, upon that foremost cornice,
   Purging away the smoke-stains of the world.   30
If there good words are always said for us,
   What may not here be said and done for them,
   By those who have a good root to their will?
Well may we help them wash away the marks
   That hence they carried, so that clean and light
   They may ascend unto the starry wheels!
"Ah! so may pity and justice you disburden
   Soon, that ye may have power to move the wing,
   That shall uplift you after your desire,
Show us on which hand tow'rd the stairs the way   40
   Is shortest, and if more than one the passes,
   Point us out that which least abruptly falls;
For he who cometh with me, through the burden
   Of Adam's flesh wherewith he is invested,
   Against his will is chary of his climbing."
The words of theirs which they returned to those
   That he whom I was following had spoken,
   It was not manifest from whom they came,
But it was said: "To the right hand come with us
   Along the bank, and ye shall find a pass   50
   Possible for living person to ascend.
And were I not impeded by the stone,
   Which this proud neck of mine doth subjugate,
   Whence I am forced to hold my visage down,
Him, who still lives and does not name himself,
   Would I regard, to see if I may know him
   And make him piteous unto this burden.
A Latian was I, and born of a great Tuscan;
   Guglielmo Aldobrandeschi was my father;
   I know not if his name were ever with you.   60
The ancient blood and deeds of gallantry
   Of my progenitors so arrogant made me
   That, thinking not upon the common mother,
All men I held in scorn to such extent
   I died therefor, as know the Sienese,
   And every child in Campagnatico.
I am Omberto; and not to me alone
   Has pride done harm, but all my kith and kin

Has with it dragged into adversity.
And here must I this burden bear for it   70
  Till God be satisfied, since I did not
  Among the living, here among the dead."
Listening I downward bent my countenance;
  And one of them, not this one who was speaking,
  Twisted himself beneath the weight that cramps him,
And looked at me, and knew me, and called out,
  Keeping his eyes laboriously fixed
  On me, who all bowed down was going with them.
"O," asked I him, "art thou not Oderisi,
  Agobbio's honour, and honour of that art   80
  Which is in Paris called illuminating?"
"Brother," said he, "more laughing are the leaves
  Touched by the brush of Franco Bolognese;
  All his the honour now, and mine in part.
In sooth I had not been so courteous
  While I was living, for the great desire
  Of excellence, on which my heart was bent.
Here of such pride is paid the forfeiture;
  And yet I should not be here, were it not
  That, having power to sin, I turned to God.   90
O thou vain glory of the human powers,
  How little green upon thy summit lingers,
  If't be not followed by an age of grossness!
In painting Cimabue thought that he
  Should hold the field, now Giotto has the cry,
  So that the other's fame is growing dim.
So has one Guido from the other taken
  The glory of our tongue, and he perchance
  Is born, who from the nest shall chase them both.
Naught is this mundane rumour but a breath   100
  Of wind, that comes now this way and now that,
  And changes name, because it changes side.
What fame shalt thou have more, if old peel off
  From thee thy flesh, than if thou hadst been dead
  Before thou left the *pappo* and the *dindi,*
Ere pass a thousand years? which is a shorter
  Space to the eterne, than twinkling of an eye
  Unto the circle that in heaven wheels slowest.
With him, who takes so little of the road

In front of me, all Tuscany resounded;   110
    And now he scarce is lisped of in Siena,
Where he was lord, what time was overthrown
    The Florentine delirium, that superb
    Was at that day as now 'tis prostitute.
Your reputation is the colour of grass
    Which comes and goes, and that discolours it
    By which it issues green from out the earth."
And I: "Thy true speech fills my heart with good
    Humility, and great tumour thou assuagest;
    But who is he, of whom just now thou spakest?"   120
"That," he replied, "is Provenzan Salvani,
    And he is here because he had presumed
    To bring Siena all into his hands.
He has gone thus, and goeth without rest
    E'er since he died; such money renders back
    In payment he who is on earth too daring."
And I: "If every spirit who awaits
    The verge of life before that he repent,
    Remains below there and ascends not hither,
(Unless good orison shall him bestead,)   130
    Until as much time as he lived be passed,
    How was the coming granted him in largess?"
"When he in greatest splendour lived," said he,
    "Freely upon the Campo of Siena,
    All shame being laid aside, he placed himself;
And there to draw his friend from the duress
    Which in the prison-house of Charles he suffered,
    He brought himself to tremble in each vein.
I say no more, and know that I speak darkly;
    Yet little time shall pass before thy neighbours   140
    Will so demean themselves that thou canst gloss it.
This action has released him from those confines."

Canto XII

Abreast, like oxen going in a yoke,
    I with that heavy-laden soul went on,
    As long as the sweet pedagogue permitted;
But when he said, "Leave him, and onward pass,

For here 'tis good that with the sail and oars,
  As much as may be, each push on his barque;"
Upright, as walking wills it, I redressed
  My person, notwithstanding that my thoughts
  Remained within me downcast and abashed.
I had moved on, and followed willingly   10
  The footsteps of my Master, and we both
  Already showed how light of foot we were,
When unto me he said: "Cast down thine eyes;
  'Twere well for thee, to alleviate the way,
  To look upon the bed beneath thy feet."
As, that some memory may exist of them,
  Above the buried dead their tombs in earth
  Bear sculptured on them what they were before;
Whence often there we weep for them afresh,
  From pricking of remembrance, which alone   20
  To the compassionate doth set its spur;
So saw I there, but of a better semblance
  In point of artifice, with figures covered
  Whate'er as pathway from the mount projects.
I saw that one who was created noble
  More than all other creatures, down from heaven
  Flaming with lightnings fall upon one side.
I saw Briareus smitten by the dart
  Celestial, lying on the other side,
  Heavy upon the earth by mortal frost.   30
I saw Thymbræus, Pallas saw, and Mars,
  Still clad in armour round about their father,
  Gaze at the scattered members of the giants.
I saw, at foot of his great labour, Nimrod,
  As if bewildered, looking at the people
  Who had been proud with him in Sennaar.
O Niobe! with what afflicted eyes
  Thee I beheld upon the pathway traced,
  Between thy seven and seven children slain!
O Saul! how fallen upon thy proper sword   40
  Didst thou appear there lifeless in Gilboa,
  That felt thereafter neither rain nor dew!
O mad Arachne! so I thee beheld
  E'en then half spider, sad upon the shreds
  Of fabric wrought in evil hour for thee!

O Rehoboam! no more seems to threaten
   Thine image there; but full of consternation
   A chariot bears it off, when none pursues!
Displayed moreo'er the adamantine pavement
   How unto his own mother made Alcmæon   50
   Costly appear the luckless ornament;
Displayed how his own sons did throw themselves
   Upon Sennacherib within the temple,
   And how, he being dead, they left him there;
Displayed the ruin and the cruel carnage
   That Tomyris wrought, when she to Cyrus said,
   "Blood didst thou thirst for, and with blood I glut thee!"
Displayed how routed fled the Assyrians
   After that Holofernes had been slain,
   And likewise the remainder of that slaughter.   60
I saw there Troy in ashes and in caverns;
   O Ilion! thee, how abject and debased,
   Displayed the image that is there discerned!
Whoe'er of pencil master was or stile,
   That could portray the shades and traits which there
   Would cause each subtile genius to admire?
Dead seemed the dead, the living seemed alive;
   Better than I saw not who saw the truth,
   All that I trod upon while bowed I went.
Now wax ye proud, and on with looks uplifted,   70
   Ye sons of Eve, and bow not down your faces
   So that ye may behold your evil ways!
More of the mount by us was now encompassed,
   And far more spent the circuit of the sun,
   Than had the mind preoccupied imagined,
When he, who ever watchful in advance
   Was going on, began: "Lift up thy head,
   'Tis no more time to go thus meditating.
Lo there an Angel who is making haste
   To come towards us; lo, returning is   80
   From service of the day the sixth handmaiden.
With reverence thine acts and looks adorn,
   So that he may delight to speed us upward;
   Think that this day will never dawn again."
I was familiar with his admonition
   Ever to lose no time; so on this theme

He could not unto me speak covertly.
Towards us came the being beautiful
   Vested in white, and in his countenance
   Such as appears the tremulous morning star.   90
His arms he opened, and opened then his wings;
   "Come," said he, "near at hand here are the steps,
   And easy from henceforth is the ascent."
At this announcement few are they who come!
   O human creatures, born to soar aloft,
   Why fall ye thus before a little wind?
He led us on to where the rock was cleft;
   There smote upon my forehead with his wings,
   Then a safe passage promised unto me.
As on the right hand, to ascend the mount   100
   Where seated is the church that lordeth it
   O'er the well-guided, above Rubaconte,
The bold abruptness of the ascent is broken
   By stairways that were made there in the age
   When still were safe the ledger and the stave,
E'en thus attempered is the bank which falls
   Sheer downward from the second circle there;
   But on this side and that the high rock grazes.
As we were turning thitherward our persons,
   "*Beati pauperes spiritu,*" voices   110
   Sang in such wise that speech could tell it not.
Ah me! how different are these entrances
   From the Infernal! for with anthems here
   One enters, and below with wild laments.
We now were mounting up the sacred stairs,
   And it appeared to me by far more easy
   Than on the plain it had appeared before.
Whence I: "My Master, say, what heavy thing
   Has been uplifted from me, so that hardly
   Aught of fatigue is felt by me in walking?"   120
He answered: "When the P's which have remained
   Still on thy face almost obliterate
   Shall wholly, as the first is, be erased,
Thy feet will be so vanquished by good will,
   That not alone they shall not feel fatigue,
   But urging up will be to them delight."
Then did I even as they do who are going

With something on the head to them unknown,
   Unless the signs of others make them doubt,
Wherefore the hand to ascertain is helpful,   130
   And seeks and finds, and doth fulfil the office
   Which cannot be accomplished by the sight;
And with the fingers of the right hand spread
   I found but six the letters, that had carved
   Upon my temples he who bore the keys;
Upon beholding which my Leader smiled.

Canto XIII

We were upon the summit of the stairs,
   Where for the second time is cut away
   The mountain, which ascending shriveth all.
There in like manner doth a cornice bind
   The hill all round about, as does the first,
   Save that its arc more suddenly is curved.
Shade is there none, nor sculpture that appears;
   So seems the bank, and so the road seems smooth,
   With but the livid colour of the stone.
"If to inquire we wait for people here,"   10
   The Poet said, "I fear that peradventure
   Too much delay will our election have."
Then steadfast on the sun his eyes he fixed,
   Made his right side the centre of his motion,
   And turned the left part of himself about.
"O thou sweet light! with trust in whom I enter
   Upon this novel journey, do thou lead us,"
   Said he, "as one within here should be led.
Thou warmest the world, thou shinest over it;
   If other reason prompt not otherwise,   20
   Thy rays should evermore our leaders be!"
As much as here is counted for a mile,
   So much already there had we advanced
   In little time, by dint of ready will;
And tow'rds us there were heard to fly, albeit
   They were not visible, spirits uttering
   Unto Love's table courteous invitations,
The first voice that passed onward in its flight,

"*Vinum non habent*," said in accents loud,
    And went reiterating it behind us.   30
And ere it wholly grew inaudible
    Because of distance, passed another, crying,
    "I am Orestes!" and it also stayed not.
"O," said I, "Father, these, what voices are they?"
    And even as I asked, behold the third,
    Saying: "Love those from whom ye have had evil!"
And the good Master said: "This circle scourges
    The sin of envy, and on that account
    Are drawn from love the lashes of the scourge.
The bridle of another sound shall be;   .   40
    I think that thou wilt hear it, as I judge,
    Before thou comest to the Pass of Pardon.
But fix thine eyes athwart the air right steadfast,
    And people thou wilt see before us sitting,
    And each one close against the cliff is seated."
Then wider than at first mine eyes I opened;
    I looked before me, and saw shades with mantles
    Not from the colour of the stone diverse.
And when we were a little farther onward,
    I heard a cry of, "Mary, pray for us!"   50
    A cry of, "Michael, Peter, and all Saints!"
I do not think there walketh still on earth
    A man so hard, that he would not be pierced
    With pity at what afterward I saw.
For when I had approached so near to them
    That manifest to me their acts became,
    Drained was I at the eyes by heavy grief.
Covered with sackcloth vile they seemed to me,
    And one sustained the other with his shoulder,
    And all of them were by the bank sustained.   60
Thus do the blind, in want of livelihood,
    Stand at the doors of churches asking alms,
    And one upon another leans his head,
So that in others pity soon may rise,
    Not only at the accent of their words,
    But at their aspect, which no less implores.
And as unto the blind the sun comes not,
    So to the shades, of whom just now I spake,
    Heaven's light will not be bounteous of itself;

For all their lids an iron wire transpierces,   70
    And sews them up, as to a sparhawk wild
    Is done, because it will not quiet stay.
To me it seemed, in passing, to do outrage,
    Seeing the others without being seen;
    Wherefore I turned me to my counsel sage.
Well knew he what the mute one wished to say,
    And therefore waited not for my demand,
    But said: "Speak, and be brief, and to the point."
I had Virgilius upon that side
    Of the embankment from which one may fall,   80
    Since by no border 'tis engarlanded;
Upon the other side of me I had
    The shades devout, who through the horrible seam
    Pressed out the tears so that they bathed their cheeks.
To them I turned me, and, "O people, certain,"
    Began I, "of beholding the high light,
    Which your desire has solely in its care,
So may grace speedily dissolve the scum
    Upon your consciences, that limpidly
    Through them descend the river of the mind,   90
Tell me, for dear 'twill be to me and gracious,
    If any soul among you here is Latian,
    And 'twill perchance be good for him I learn it."
"O brother mine, each one is citizen
    Of one true city; but thy meaning is,
    Who may have lived in Italy a pilgrim."
By way of answer this I seemed to hear
    A little farther on than where I stood,
    Whereat I made myself still nearer heard.
Among the rest I saw a shade that waited   100
    In aspect, and should any one ask how,
    Its chin it lifted upward like a blind man.
"Spirit," I said, "who stoopest to ascend,
    If thou art he who did reply to me,
    Make thyself known to me by place or name."
"Sienese was I," it replied, "and with
    The others here recleanse my guilty life,
    Weeping to Him to lend himself to us.
Sapient I was not, although I Sapia
    Was called, and I was at another's harm   110

More happy far than at my own good fortune.
And that thou mayst not think that I deceive thee,
    Hear if I was as foolish as I tell thee.
    The arc already of my years descending,
My fellow-citizens near unto Colle
    Were joined in battle with their adversaries,
    And I was praying God for what he willed.
Routed were they, and turned into the bitter
    Passes of flight; and I, the chase beholding,
    A joy received unequalled by all others;   120
So that I lifted upward my bold face
    Crying to God, 'Henceforth I fear thee not,'
    As did the blackbird at the little sunshine.
Peace I desired with God at the extreme
    Of my existence, and as yet would not
    My debt have been by penitence discharged,
Had it not been that in remembrance held me
    Pier Pettignano in his holy prayers,
    Who out of charity was grieved for me.
But who art thou, that into our conditions   130
    Questioning goest, and hast thine eyes unbound
    As I believe, and breathing dost discourse?"
"Mine eyes," I said, "will yet be here ta'en from me,
    But for short space; for small is the offence
    Committed by their being turned with envy.
Far greater is the fear, wherein suspended
    My soul is, of the torment underneath,
    For even now the load down there weighs on me."
And she to me: "Who led thee, then, among us
    Up here, if to return below thou thinkest?"   140
    And I: "He who is with me, and speaks not;
And living am I; therefore ask of me,
    Spirit elect, if thou wouldst have me move
    O'er yonder yet my mortal feet for thee."
"O, this is such a novel thing to hear,"
    She answered, "that great sign it is God loves thee;
    Therefore with prayer of thine sometimes assist me.
And I implore, by what thou most desirest,
    If e'er thou treadest the soil of Tuscany,
    Well with my kindred reinstate my fame.   150
Them wilt thou see among that people vain

Who hope in Talamone, and will lose there
   More hope than in discovering the Diana;
But there still more the admirals will lose."

Canto XIV

"Who is this one that goes about our mountain,
   Or ever Death has given him power of flight,
   And opes his eyes and shuts them at his will?"
"I know not who, but know he's not alone;
   Ask him thyself, for thou art nearer to him,
   And gently, so that he may speak, accost him."
Thus did two spirits, leaning tow'rds each other,
   Discourse about me there on the right hand;
   Then held supine their faces to address me.
And said the one: "O soul, that, fastened still   10
   Within the body, tow'rds the heaven art going,
   For charity console us, and declare
Whence comest and who art thou; for thou mak'st us
   As much to marvel at this grace of thine
   As must a thing that never yet has been."
And I: "Through midst of Tuscany there wanders
   A streamlet that is born in Falterona,
   And not a hundred miles of course suffice it;
From thereupon do I this body bring.
   To tell you who I am were speech in vain,   20
   Because my name as yet makes no great noise."
"If well thy meaning I can penetrate
   With intellect of mine," then answered me
   He who first spake, "thou speakest of the Arno."
And said the other to him: "Why concealed
   This one the appellation of that river,
   Even as a man doth of things horrible?"
And thus the shade that questioned was of this
   Himself acquitted: "I know not; but truly
   'Tis fit the name of such a valley perish;   30
For from its fountain head (where is so pregnant
   The Alpine mountain whence is cleft Peloro
   That in few places it that mark surpasses)
To where it yields itself in restoration

Of what the heaven doth of the sea dry up,
    Whence have the rivers that which goes with them,
Virtue is like an enemy avoided
    By all, as is a serpent, through misfortune
    Of place, or through bad habit that impels them;
On which account have so transformed their nature   40
    The dwellers in that miserable valley,
    It seems that Circe had them in her pasture.
'Mid ugly swine, of acorns worthier
    Than other food for human use created,
    It first directeth its impoverished way.
Curs findeth it thereafter, coming downward,
    More snarling than their puissance demands,
    And turns from them disdainfully its muzzle.
It goes on falling, and the more it grows,
    The more it finds the dogs becoming wolves,   50
    This maledict and misadventurous ditch.
Descended then through many a hollow gulf,
    It finds the foxes so replete with fraud,
    They fear no cunning that may master them.
Nor will I cease because another hears me;
    And well 'twill be for him, if still he mind him
    Of what a truthful spirit to me unravels.
Thy grandson I behold, who doth become
    A hunter of those wolves upon the bank
    Of the wild stream, and terrifies them all.   60
He sells their flesh, it being yet alive;
    Thereafter slaughters them like ancient beeves
    Many of life, himself of praise, deprives.
Blood-stained he issues from the dismal forest;
    He leaves it such, a thousand years from now
    In its primeval state 'tis not re-wooded."
As at the announcement of impending ills
    The face of him who listens is disturbed,
    From whate'er side the peril seize upon him;
So I beheld that other soul, which stood   70
    Turned round to listen, grow disturbed and sad,
    When it had gathered to itself the word.
The speech of one and aspect of the other
    Had me desirous made to know their names,
    And question mixed with prayers I made thereof,
Whereat the spirit which first spake to me

Began again: "Thou wishest I should bring me
  To do for thee what thou'lt not do for me;
But since God willeth that in thee shine forth
  Such grace of his, I'll not be chary with thee;   80
  Know, then, that I Guido del Duca am.
My blood was so with envy set on fire,
  That if I had beheld a man make merry,
  Thou wouldst have seen me sprinkled o'er with pallor.
From my own sowing such the straw I reap!
  O human race! why dost thou set thy heart
  Where interdict of partnership must be?
This is Renier; this is the boast and honour
  Of the house of Calboli, where no one since
  Has made himself the heir of his desert.   90
And not alone his blood is made devoid,
  'Twixt Po and mount, and sea-shore and the Reno,
  Of good required for truth and for diversion;
For all within these boundaries is full
  Of venomous roots, so that too tardily
  By cultivation now would they diminish.
Where is good Lizio, and Arrigo Manardi,
  Pier Traversaro, and Guido di Carpigna,
  O Romagnuoli into bastards turned?
When in Bologna will a Fabbro rise?   100
  When in Faenza a Bernardin di Fosco,
  The noble scion of ignoble seed?
Be not astonished, Tuscan, if I weep,
  When I remember, with Guido da Prata,
  Ugolin d'Azzo, who was living with us,
Frederick Tignoso and his company,
  The house of Traversara, and th' Anastagi,
  And one race and the other is extinct;
The dames and cavaliers, the toils and ease
  That filled our souls with love and courtesy,   110
  There where the hearts have so malicious grown!
O Brettinoro! why dost thou not flee,
  Seeing that all thy family is gone,
  And many people, not to be corrupted?
Bagnacaval does well in not begetting
  And ill does Castrocaro, and Conio worse,
  In taking trouble to beget such Counts.
Will do well the Pagani, when their Devil

Shall have departed; but not therefore pure
    Will testimony of them e'er remain.   120
O Ugolin de' Fantoli, secure
    Thy name is, since no longer is awaited
    One who, degenerating, can obscure it!
But go now, Tuscan, for it now delights me
    To weep far better than it does to speak,
    So much has our discourse my mind distressed."
We were aware that those beloved souls
    Heard us depart; therefore, by keeping silent,
    They made us of our pathway confident.
When we became alone by going onward,   130
    Thunder, when it doth cleave the air, appeared
    A voice, that counter to us came, exclaiming:
"Shall slay me whosoever findeth me!"
    And fled as the reverberation dies
    If suddenly the cloud asunder bursts.
As soon as hearing had a truce from this,
    Behold another, with so great a crash,
    That it resembled thunderings following fast:
"I am Aglaurus, who became a stone!"
    And then, to press myself close to the Poet,   140
    I backward, and not forward, took a step.
Already on all sides the air was quiet;
    And said he to me: "That was the hard curb
    That ought to hold a man within his bounds;
But you take in the bait so that the hook
    Of the old Adversary draws you to him,
    And hence availeth little curb or call.
The heavens are calling you, and wheel around you,
    Displaying to you their eternal beauties,
    And still your eye is looking on the ground;   150
Whence He, who all discerns, chastises you."

Canto XV

As much as 'twixt the close of the third hour
    And dawn of day appeareth of that sphere
    Which aye in fashion of a child is playing,
So much it now appeared, towards the night,

Was of his course remaining to the sun;
   There it was evening, and 'twas midnight here;
And the rays smote the middle of our faces,
   Because by us the mount was so encircled,
   That straight towards the west we now were going;
When I perceived my forehead overpowered   10
   Beneath the splendour far more than at first,
   And stupor were to me the things unknown,
Whereat towards the summit of my brow
   I raised my hands, and made myself the visor
   Which the excessive glare diminishes.
As when from off the water, or a mirror,
   The sunbeam leaps unto the opposite side,
   Ascending upward in the selfsame measure
That it descends, and deviates as far
   From falling of a stone in line direct,   20
   (As demonstrate experiment and art,)
So it appeared to me that by a light
   Refracted there before me I was smitten;
   On which account my sight was swift to flee.
"What is that, Father sweet, from which I cannot
   So fully screen my sight that it avail me,"
   Said I, "and seems towards us to be moving?"
"Marvel thou not, if dazzle thee as yet
   The family of heaven," he answered me;
   "An angel 'tis, who comes to invite us upward.   30
Soon will it be, that to behold these things
   Shall not be grievous, but delightful to thee
   As much as nature fashioned thee to feel."
When we had reached the Angel benedight,
   With joyful voice he said: "Here enter in
   To stairway far less steep than are the others."
We mounting were, already thence departed.
   And "*Beati misericordes*" was
   Behind us sung, "Rejoice, thou that o'ercomest!"
My Master and myself, we two alone   40
   Were going upward, and I thought, in going,
   Some profit to acquire from words of his;
And I to him directed me, thus asking:
   "What did the spirit of Romagna mean,
   Mentioning interdict and partnership?"

Whence he to me: "Of his own greatest failing
   He knows the harm; and therefore wonder not
   If he reprove us, that we less may rue it.
Because are thither pointed your desires
   Where by companionship each share is lessened,   50
   Envy doth ply the bellows to your sighs.
But if the love of the supernal sphere
   Should upwardly direct your aspiration,
   There would not be that fear within your breast;
For there, as much the more as one says *Our*,
   So much the more of good each one possesses,
   And more of charity in that cloister burns."
"I am more hungering to be satisfied,"
   I said, "than if I had before been silent,
   And more of doubt within my mind I gather.   60
How can it be, that boon distributed
   The more possessors can more wealthy make
   Therein, than if by few it be possessed?"
And he to me: "Because thou fixest still
   Thy mind entirely upon earthly things,
   Thou pluckest darkness from the very light.
That goodness infinite and ineffable
   Which is above there, runneth unto love,
   As to a lucid body comes the sunbeam.
So much it gives itself as it finds ardour,   70
   So that as far as charity extends,
   O'er it increases the eternal valour.
And the more people thitherward aspire,
   More are there to love well, and more they love there,
   And, as a mirror, one reflects the other.
And if my reasoning appease thee not,
   Thou shalt see Beatrice; and she will fully
   Take from thee this and every other longing.
Endeavour, then, that soon may be extinct,
   As are the two already, the five wounds   80
   That close themselves again by being painful."
Even as I wished to say, "Thou dost appease me,"
   I saw that I had reached another circle,
   So that my eager eyes made me keep silence.
There it appeared to me that in a vision
   Ecstatic on a sudden I was rapt,

And in a temple many persons saw;
And at the door a woman, with the sweet
  Behaviour of a mother, saying: "Son,
  Why in this manner hast thou dealt with us?   90
Lo, sorrowing, thy father and myself
  Were seeking for thee;"—and as here she ceased,
  That which appeared at first had disappeared.
Then I beheld another with those waters
  Adown her cheeks which grief distils whenever
  From great disdain of others it is born,
And saying: "If of that city thou art lord,
  For whose name was such strife among the gods,
  And whence doth every science scintillate,
Avenge thyself on those audacious arms   100
  That clasped our daughter, O Pisistratus;"
  And the lord seemed to me benign and mild
To answer her with aspect temperate:
  "What shall we do to those who wish us ill,
  If he who loves us be by us condemned?"
Then saw I people hot in fire of wrath,
  With stones a young man slaying, clamorously
  Still crying to each other, "Kill him! kill him!"
And him I saw bow down, because of death
  That weighed already on him, to the earth,   110
  But of his eyes made ever gates to heaven,
Imploring the high Lord, in so great strife,
  That he would pardon those his persecutors,
  With such an aspect as unlocks compassion.
Soon as my soul had outwardly returned
  To things external to it which are true,
  Did I my not false errors recognize.
My Leader, who could see me bear myself
  Like to a man that rouses him from sleep,
  Exclaimed: "What ails thee, that thou canst not stand?   120
But hast been coming more than half a league
  Veiling thine eyes, and with thy legs entangled,
  In guise of one whom wine or sleep subdues?"
"O my sweet Father, if thou listen to me,
  I'll tell thee," said I, "what appeared to me,
  When thus from me my legs were ta'en away."
And he: "If thou shouldst have a hundred masks

Upon thy face, from me would not be shut
 Thy cogitations, howsoever small.
What thou hast seen was that thou mayst not fail   130
 To ope thy heart unto the waters of peace,
 Which from the eternal fountain are diffused.
I did not ask, 'What ails thee?' as he does
 Who only looketh with the eyes that see not
 When of the soul bereft the body lies,
But asked it to give vigour to thy feet;
 Thus must we needs urge on the sluggards, slow
 To use their wakefulness when it returns."
We passed along, athwart the twilight peering
 Forward as far as ever eye could stretch   140
 Against the sunbeams serotine and lucent;
And lo! by slow degrees a smoke approached
 In our direction, sombre as the night,
 Nor was there place to hide one's self therefrom.
This of our eyes and the pure air bereft us.

Canto XVI

Darkness of hell, and of a night deprived
 Of every planet under a poor sky,
 As much as may be tenebrous with cloud,
Ne'er made unto my sight so thick a veil,
 As did that smoke which there enveloped us,
 Nor to the feeling of so rough a texture;
For not an eye it suffered to stay open;
 Whereat mine escort, faithful and sagacious,
 Drew near to me and offered me his shoulder.
E'en as a blind man goes behind his guide,   10
 Lest he should wander, or should strike against
 Aught that may harm or peradventure kill him,
So went I through the bitter and foul air,
 Listening unto my Leader, who said only,
 "Look that from me thou be not separated."
Voices I heard, and every one appeared
 To supplicate for peace and misericord
 The Lamb of God who takes away our sins.
Still "*Agnus Dei*" their exordium was;

One word there was in all, and metre one,   20
  So that all harmony appeared among them.
"Master," I said, "are spirits those I hear?"
  And he to me: "Thou apprehendest truly,
  And they the knot of anger go unloosing."
"Now who art thou, that cleavest through our smoke,
  And art discoursing of us even as though
  Thou didst by calends still divide the time?"
After this manner by a voice was spoken;
  Whereon my Master said: "Do thou reply,
  And ask if on this side the way go upward."   30
And I: "O creature that dost cleanse thyself
  To return beautiful to Him who made thee,
  Thou shalt hear marvels if thou follow me."
"Thee will I follow far as is allowed me,"
  He answered; "and if smoke prevent our seeing,
  Hearing shall keep us joined instead thereof."
Thereon began I: "With that swathing band
  Which death unwindeth am I going upward,
  And hither came I through the infernal anguish.
And if God in his grace has me infolded,   40
  So that he wills that I behold his court
  By method wholly out of modern usage,
Conceal not from me who ere death thou wast,
  But tell it me, and tell me if I go
  Right for the pass, and be thy words our escort."
"Lombard was I, and I was Marco called;
  The world I knew, and loved that excellence,
  At which has each one now unbent his bow.
For mounting upward, thou art going right."
  Thus he made answer, and subjoined: "I pray thee   50
  To pray for me when thou shalt be above."
And I to him: "My faith I pledge to thee
  To do what thou dost ask me; but am bursting
  Inly with doubt, unless I rid me of it.
First it was simple, and is now made double
  By thy opinion, which makes certain to me,
  Here and elsewhere, that which I couple with it.
The world forsooth is utterly deserted
  By every virtue, as thou tellest me,
  And with iniquity is big and covered;   60

But I beseech thee point me out the cause,
    That I may see it, and to others show it;
    For one in the heavens, and here below one puts it."
A sigh profound, that grief forced into Ai!
    He first sent forth, and then began he: "Brother,
    The world is blind, and sooth thou comest from it!
Ye who are living every cause refer
    Still upward to the heavens, as if all things
    They of necessity moved with themselves.
If this were so, in you would be destroyed   70
    Free will, nor any justice would there be
    In having joy for good, or grief for evil.
The heavens your movements do initiate,
    I say not all; but granting that I say it,
    Light has been given you for good and evil,
And free volition; which, if some fatigue
    In the first battles with the heavens it suffers,
    Afterwards conquers all, if well 'tis nurtured.
To greater force and to a better nature,
    Though free, ye subject are, and that creates   80
    The mind in you the heavens have not in charge.
Hence, if the present world doth go astray,
    In you the cause is, be it sought in you;
    And I therein will now be thy true spy.
Forth from the hand of Him, who fondles it
    Before it is, like to a little girl
    Weeping and laughing in her childish sport,
Issues the simple soul, that nothing knows,
    Save that, proceeding from a joyous Maker,
    Gladly it turns to that which gives it pleasure.   90
Of trivial good at first it tastes the savour;
    Is cheated by it, and runs after it,
    If guide or rein turn not aside its love.
Hence it behoved laws for a rein to place,
    Behoved a king to have, who at the least
    Of the true city should discern the tower.
The laws exist, but who sets hand to them?
    No one; because the shepherd who precedes
    Can ruminate, but cleaveth not the hoof;
Wherefore the people that perceives its guide   100
    Strike only at the good for which it hankers,

Feeds upon that, and farther seeketh not.
Clearly canst thou perceive that evil guidance
 The cause is that has made the world depraved,
 And not that nature is corrupt in you.
Rome, that reformed the world, accustomed was
 Two suns to have, which one road and the other,
 Of God and of the world, made manifest.
One has the other quenched, and to the crosier
 The sword is joined, and ill beseemeth it   110
 That by main force one with the other go,
Because, being joined, one feareth not the other;
 If thou believe not, think upon the grain,
 For by its seed each herb is recognized.
In the land laved by Po and Adige,
 Valour and courtesy used to be found,
 Before that Frederick had his controversy;
Now in security can pass that way
 Whoever will abstain, through sense of shame,
 From speaking with the good, or drawing near them.   120
True, three old men are left, in whom upbraids
 The ancient age the new, and late they deem it
 That God restore them to the better life:
Currado da Palazzo, and good Gherardo,
 And Guido da Castel, who better named is,
 In fashion of the French, the simple Lombard:
Say thou henceforward that the Church of Rome,
 Confounding in itself two governments,
 Falls in the mire, and soils itself and burden."
"O Marco mine," I said, "thou reasonest well;   130
 And now discern I why the sons of Levi
 Have been excluded from the heritage.
But what Gherardo is it, who, as sample
 Of a lost race, thou sayest has remained
 In reprobation of the barbarous age?"
"Either thy speech deceives me, or it tempts me,"
 He answered me; "for speaking Tuscan to me,
 It seems of good Gherardo naught thou knowest.
By other surname do I know him not,
 Unless I take it from his daughter Gaia.   140
 May God be with you, for I come no farther.
Behold the dawn, that through the smoke rays out,

Already whitening; and I must depart—
    Yonder the Angel is—ere he appear."
Thus did he speak, and would no farther hear me.

Canto XVII

Remember, Reader, if e'er in the Alps
    A mist o'ertook thee, through which thou couldst see
    Not otherwise than through its membrane mole,
How, when the vapours humid and condensed
    Begin to dissipate themselves, the sphere
    Of the sun feebly enters in among them,
And thy imagination will be swift
    In coming to perceive how I re-saw
    The sun at first, that was already setting.
Thus, to the faithful footsteps of my Master   10
    Mating mine own, I issued from that cloud
    To rays already dead on the low shores.
O thou, Imagination, that dost steal us
    So from without sometimes, that man perceives not,
    Although around may sound a thousand trumpets,
Who moveth thee, if sense impel thee not?
    Moves thee a light, which in the heaven takes form,
    By self, or by a will that downward guides it.
Of her impiety, who changed her form
    Into the bird that most delights in singing,   20
    In my imagining appeared the trace;
And hereupon my mind was so withdrawn
    Within itself, that from without there came
    Nothing that then might be received by it.
Then reigned within my lofty fantasy
    One crucified, disdainful and ferocious
    In countenance, and even thus was dying.
Around him were the great Ahasuerus,
    Esther his wife, and the just Mordecai,
    Who was in word and action so entire.   30
And even as this image burst asunder
    Of its own self, in fashion of a bubble
    In which the water it was made of fails,
There rose up in my vision a young maiden

Bitterly weeping, and she said: "O queen,
Why hast thou wished in anger to be naught?
Thou'st slain thyself, Lavinia not to lose;
Now hast thou lost me; I am she who mourns,
Mother, at thine ere at another's ruin."
As sleep is broken, when upon a sudden   40
New light strikes in upon the eyelids closed,
And broken quivers ere it dieth wholly,
So this imagining of mine fell down
As soon as the effulgence smote my face,
Greater by far than what is in our wont.
I turned me round to see where I might be,
When said a voice, "Here is the passage up;"
Which from all other purposes removed me,
And made my wish so full of eagerness
To look and see who was it that was speaking,   50
It never rests till meeting face to face;
But as before the sun, which quells the sight,
And in its own excess its figure veils,
Even so my power was insufficient here.
"This is a spirit divine, who in the way
Of going up directs us without asking,
And who with his own light himself conceals.
He does with us as man doth with himself;
For he who sees the need, and waits the asking,
Malignly leans already tow'rds denial.   60
Accord we now our feet to such inviting,
Let us make haste to mount ere it grow dark;
For then we could not till the day return."
Thus my Conductor said; and I and he
Together turned our footsteps to a stairway;
And I, as soon as the first step I reached,
Near me perceived a motion as of wings,
And fanning in the face, and saying, "*Beati
Pacifici,* who are without ill anger."
Already over us were so uplifted   70
The latest sunbeams, which the night pursues,
That upon many sides the stars appeared.
"O manhood mine, why dost thou vanish so?"
I said within myself; for I perceived
The vigour of my legs was put in truce.

We at the point were where no more ascends
   The stairway upward, and were motionless,
   Even as a ship, which at the shore arrives;
And I gave heed a little, if I might hear
   Aught whatsoever in the circle new;   80
   Then to my Master turned me round and said:
"Say, my sweet Father, what delinquency
   Is purged here in the circle where we are?
   Although our feet may pause, pause not thy speech."
And he to me: "The love of good, remiss
   In what it should have done, is here restored;
   Here plied again the ill-belated oar;
But still more openly to understand,
   Turn unto me thy mind, and thou shalt gather
   Some profitable fruit from our delay.   90
Neither Creator nor a creature ever,
   Son," he began, "was destitute of love
   Natural or spiritual; and thou knowest it.
The natural was ever without error;
   But err the other may by evil object,
   Or by too much, or by too little vigour.
While in the first it well directed is,
   And in the second moderates itself,
   It cannot be the cause of sinful pleasure;
But when to ill it turns, and, with more care   100
   Or lesser than it ought, runs after good,
   'Gainst the Creator works his own creation.
Hence thou mayst comprehend that love must be
   The seed within yourselves of every virtue,
   And every act that merits punishment.
Now inasmuch as never from the welfare
   Of its own subject can love turn its sight,
   From their own hatred all things are secure;
And since we cannot think of any being
   Standing alone, nor from the First divided,   110
   Of hating Him is all desire cut off.
Hence if, discriminating, I judge well,
   The evil that one loves is of one's neighbour,
   And this is born in three modes in your clay.
There are, who, by abasement of their neighbour,
   Hope to excel, and therefore only long

That from his greatness he may be cast down;
There are, who power, grace, honour, and renown
   Fear they may lose because another rises,
   Thence are so sad that the reverse they love;   120
And there are those whom injury seems to chafe,
   So that it makes them greedy for revenge,
   And such must needs shape out another's harm.
This threefold love is wept for down below;
   Now of the other will I have thee hear,
   That runneth after good with measure faulty.
Each one confusedly a good conceives
   Wherein the mind may rest, and longeth for it;
   Therefore to overtake it each one strives.
If languid love to look on this attract you,   130
   Or in attaining unto it, this cornice,
   After just penitence, torments you for it.
There's other good that does not make man happy;
   'Tis not felicity, 'tis not the good
   Essence, of every good the fruit and root.
The love that yields itself too much to this
   Above us is lamented in three circles;
   But how tripartite it may be described,
I say not, that thou seek it for thyself."

Canto XVIII

An end had put unto his reasoning
   The lofty Teacher, and attent was looking
   Into my face, if I appeared content;
And I, whom a new thirst still goaded on,
   Without was mute, and said within: "Perchance
   The too much questioning I make annoys him."
But that true Father, who had comprehended
   The timid wish, that opened not itself,
   By speaking gave me hardihood to speak.
Whence I: "My sight is, Master, vivified   10
   So in thy light, that clearly I discern
   Whate'er thy speech importeth or describes.
Therefore I thee entreat, sweet Father dear,
   To teach me love, to which thou dost refer

Every good action and its contrary."
"Direct," he said, "towards me the keen eyes
   Of intellect, and clear will be to thee
   The error of the blind, who would be leaders.
The soul, which is created apt to love,
   Is mobile unto everything that pleases,   20
   Soon as by pleasure she is waked to action.
Your apprehension from some real thing
   An image draws, and in yourselves displays it
   So that it makes the soul turn unto it.
And if, when turned, towards it she incline,
   Love is that inclination; it is nature,
   Which is by pleasure bound in you anew
Then even as the fire doth upward move
   By its own form, which to ascend is born,
   Where longest in its matter it endures,   30
So comes the captive soul into desire,
   Which is a motion spiritual, and ne'er rests
   Until she doth enjoy the thing beloved.
Now may apparent be to thee how hidden
   The truth is from those people, who aver
   All love is in itself a laudable thing;
Because its matter may perchance appear
   Aye to be good; but yet not each impression
   Is good, albeit good may be the wax."
"Thy words, and my sequacious intellect,"   40
   I answered him, "have love revealed to me;
   But that has made me more impregned with doubt;
For if love from without be offered us,
   And with another foot the soul go not,
   If right or wrong she go, 'tis not her merit."
And he to me: "What reason seeth here,
   Myself can tell thee; beyond that await
   For Beatrice, since 'tis a work of faith.
Every substantial form, that segregate
   From matter is, and with it is united,   50
   Specific power has in itself collected,
Which without act is not perceptible,
   Nor shows itself except by its effect,
   As life does in a plant by the green leaves.
But still, whence cometh the intelligence

Of the first notions, man is ignorant,
  And the affection for the first allurements,
Which are in you as instinct in the bee
  To make its honey; and this first desire
  Merit of praise or blame containeth not.   60
Now, that to this all others may be gathered,
  Innate within you is the power that counsels,
  And it should keep the threshold of assent.
This is the principle, from which is taken
  Occasion of desert in you, according
  As good and guilty loves it takes and winnows.
Those who, in reasoning, to the bottom went,
  Were of this innate liberty aware,
  Therefore bequeathed they Ethics to the world.
Supposing, then, that from necessity   70
  Springs every love that is within you kindled,
  Within yourselves the power is to restrain it.
The noble virtue Beatrice understands
  By the free will; and therefore see that thou
  Bear it in mind, if she should speak of it."
The moon, belated almost unto midnight,
  Now made the stars appear to us more rare,
  Formed like a bucket, that is all ablaze,
And counter to the heavens ran through those paths
  Which the sun sets aflame, when he of Rome   80
  Sees it 'twixt Sardes and Corsicans go down;
And that patrician shade, for whom is named
  Pietola more than any Mantuan town,
  Had laid aside the burden of my lading;
Whence I, who reason manifest and plain
  In answer to my questions had received,
  Stood like a man in drowsy reverie.
But taken from me was this drowsiness
  Suddenly by a people, that behind
  Our backs already had come round to us.   90
And as, of old, Ismenus and Asopus
  Beside them saw at night the rush and throng,
  If but the Thebans were in need of Bacchus,
So they along that circle curve their step,
  From what I saw of those approaching us,
  Who by good-will and righteous love are ridden.

Full soon they were upon us, because running
    Moved onward all that mighty multitude,
    And two in the advance cried out, lamenting,
"Mary in haste unto the mountain ran,   100
    And Cæsar, that he might subdue Ilerda,
    Thrust at Marseilles, and then ran into Spain."
"Quick! quick! so that the time may not be lost
    By little love!" forthwith the others cried,
    "For ardour in well-doing freshens grace!"
"O folk, in whom an eager fervour now
    Supplies perhaps delay and negligence,
    Put by you in well-doing, through lukewarmness,
This one who lives, and truly I lie not,
    Would fain go up, if but the sun relight us;   110
    So tell us where the passage nearest is."
These were the words of him who was my Guide;
    And some one of those spirits said: "Come on
    Behind us, and the opening shalt thou find;
So full of longing are we to move onward,
    That stay we cannot; therefore pardon us,
    If thou for churlishness our justice take.
I was San Zeno's Abbot at Verona,
    Under the empire of good Barbarossa,
    Of whom still sorrowing Milan holds discourse;   120
And he has one foot in the grave already,
    Who shall erelong lament that monastery,
    And sorry be of having there had power,
Because his son, in his whole body sick,
    And worse in mind, and who was evil-born,
    He put into the place of its true pastor."
If more he said, or silent was, I know not,
    He had already passed so far beyond us;
    But this I heard, and to retain it pleased me.
And he who was in every need my succour   130
    Said: "Turn thee hitherward; see two of them
    Come fastening upon slothfulness their teeth."
In rear of all they shouted: "Sooner were
    The people dead to whom the sea was opened,
    Than their inheritors the Jordan saw;
And those who the fatigue did not endure
    Unto the issue, with Anchises' son,

Themselves to life withouten glory offered."
Then when from us so separated were
   Those shades, that they no longer could be seen,   140
   Within me a new thought did entrance find,
Whence others many and diverse were born;
   And so I lapsed from one into another,
   That in a reverie mine eyes I closed,
And meditation into dream transmuted.

Canto XIX

It was the hour when the diurnal heat
   No more can warm the coldness of the moon,
   Vanquished by earth, or peradventure Saturn,
When geomancers their Fortuna Major
   See in the orient before the dawn
   Rise by a path that long remains not dim,
There came to me in dreams a stammering woman,
   Squint in her eyes, and in her feet distorted,
   With hands dissevered, and of sallow hue.
I looked at her; and as the sun restores   10
   The frigid members, which the night benumbs,
   Even thus my gaze did render voluble
Her tongue, and made her all erect thereafter
   In little while, and the lost countenance
   As love desires it so in her did colour.
When in this wise she had her speech unloosed,
   She 'gan to sing so, that with difficulty
   Could I have turned my thoughts away from her.
"I am," she sang, "I am the Siren sweet
   Who mariners amid the main unman   20
   So full am I of pleasantness to hear.
I drew Ulysses from his wandering way
   Unto my song, and he who dwells with me
   Seldom departs, so wholly I content him."
Her mouth was not yet closed again, before
   Appeared a Lady saintly and alert
   Close at my side to put her to confusion.
"Virgilius, O Virgilius! who is this?"
   Sternly she said; and he was drawing near

With eyes still fixed upon that modest one.   30
She seized the other and in front laid open,
    Rending her garments, and her belly showed me;
    This waked me with the stench that issued from it.
I turned mine eyes, and good Virgilius said:
    "At least thrice have I called thee; rise and come;
    Find we the opening by which thou mayst enter."
I rose; and full already of high day
    Were all the circles of the Sacred Mountain,
    And with the new sun at our back we went.
Following behind him, I my forehead bore   40
    Like unto one who has it laden with thought,
    Who makes himself the half arch of a bridge,
When I heard say, "Come, here the passage is,"
    Spoken in a manner gentle and benign,
    Such as we hear not in this mortal region.
With open wings, which of a swan appeared,
    Upward he turned us who thus spake to us,
    Between the two walls of the solid granite.
He moved his pinions afterwards and fanned us,
    Affirming those *qui lugent* to be blessed,   50
    For they shall have their souls with comfort filled.
"What aileth thee, that aye to earth thou gazest?"
    To me my Guide began to say, we both
    Somewhat beyond the Angel having mounted.
And I: "With such misgiving makes me go
    A vision new, which bends me to itself,
    So that I cannot from the thought withdraw me."
"Didst thou behold," he said, "that old enchantress,
    Who sole above us henceforth is lamented?
    Didst thou behold how man is freed from her?   60
Suffice it thee, and smite earth with thy heels,
    Thine eyes lift upward to the lure, that whirls
    The Eternal King with revolutions vast."
Even as the hawk, that first his feet surveys,
    Then turns him to the call and stretches forward,
    Through the desire of food that draws him thither,
Such I became, and such, as far as cleaves
    The rock to give a way to him who mounts,
    Went on to where the circling doth begin.
On the fifth circle when I had come forth,   70

People I saw upon it who were weeping,
   Stretched prone upon the ground, all downward turned.
"*Adhæsit pavimento anima mea,*"
   I heard them say with sighings so profound,
   That hardly could the words be understood.
"O ye elect of God, whose sufferings
   Justice and Hope both render less severe,
   Direct ye us towards the high ascents."
"If ye are come secure from this prostration,
   And wish to find the way most speedily,   80
   Let your right hands be evermore outside."
Thus did the Poet ask, and thus was answered
   By them somewhat in front of us; whence I
   In what was spoken divined the rest concealed,
And unto my Lord's eyes mine eyes I turned;
   Whence he assented with a cheerful sign
   To what the sight of my desire implored.
When of myself I could dispose at will,
   Above that creature did I draw myself,
   Whose words before had caused me to take note,   90
Saying: "O Spirit, in whom weeping ripens
   That without which to God we cannot turn,
   Suspend awhile for me thy greater care.
Who wast thou, and why are your backs turned upwards,
   Tell me, and if thou wouldst that I procure thee
   Anything there whence living I departed."
And he to me: "Wherefore our backs the heaven
   Turns to itself, know shalt thou; but beforehand
   Scias quod ego fui successor Petri.
Between Siestri and Chiaveri descends   100
   A river beautiful, and of its name
   The title of my blood its summit makes.
A month and little more essayed I how
   Weighs the great cloak on him from mire who keeps it;
   For all the other burdens seem a feather.
Tardy, ah woe is me! was my conversion;
   But when the Roman Shepherd I was made,
   Then I discovered life to be a lie.
I saw that there the heart was not at rest,
   Nor farther in that life could one ascend;   110
   Whereby the love of this was kindled in me.

Until that time a wretched soul and parted
    From God was I, and wholly avaricious;
    Now, as thou seest, I here am punished for it.
What avarice does is here made manifest
    In the purgation of these souls converted,
    And no more bitter pain the Mountain has.
Even as our eye did not uplift itself
    Aloft, being fastened upon earthly things,
    So justice here has merged it in the earth.   120
As avarice had extinguished our affection
    For every good, whereby was action lost,
    So justice here doth hold us in restraint,
Bound and imprisoned by the feet and hands;
    And so long as it pleases the just Lord
    Shall we remain immovable and prostrate."
I on my knees had fallen, and wished to speak;
    But even as I began, and he was 'ware,
    Only by listening, of my reverence,
"What cause," he said, "has downward bent thee thus?"   130
    And I to him: "For your own dignity,
    Standing, my conscience stung me with remorse."
"Straighten thy legs, and upward raise thee, brother,"
    He answered: "Err not, fellow-servant am I
    With thee and with the others to one power.
If e'er that holy, evangelic sound,
    Which sayeth *neque nubent,* thou hast heard,
    Well canst thou see why in this wise I speak.
Now go; no longer will I have thee linger,
    Because thy stay doth incommode my weeping,   140
    With which I ripen that which thou hast said.
On earth I have a grandchild named Alagia,
    Good in herself, unless indeed our house
    Malevolent may make her by example,
And she alone remains to me on earth."

Canto XX

Ill strives the will against a better will;
    Therefore, to pleasure him, against my pleasure
    I drew the sponge not saturate from the water.
Onward I moved, and onward moved my Leader,

Through vacant places, skirting still the rock,
   As on a wall close to the battlements;
For they that through their eyes pour drop by drop
   The malady which all the world pervades,
   On the other side too near the verge approach.
Accursed mayst thou be, thou old she-wolf,   10
   That more than all the other beasts hast prey,
   Because of hunger infinitely hollow!
O heaven, in whose gyrations some appear
   To think conditions here below are changed,
   When will he come through whom she shall depart?
Onward we went with footsteps slow and scarce,
   And I attentive to the shades I heard
   Piteously weeping and bemoaning them;
And I by peradventure heard "Sweet Mary!"
   Uttered in front of us amid the weeping   20
   Even as a woman does who is in child-birth;
And in continuance: "How poor thou wast
   Is manifested by that hostelry
   Where thou didst lay thy sacred burden down."
Thereafterward I heard: "O good Fabricius,
   Virtue with poverty didst thou prefer
   To the possession of great wealth with vice."
So pleasurable were these words to me
   That I drew farther onward to have knowledge
   Touching that spirit whence they seemed to come.   30
He furthermore was speaking of the largess
   Which Nicholas unto the maidens gave,
   In order to conduct their youth to honour.
"O soul that dost so excellently speak,
   Tell me who wast thou," said I, "and why only
   Thou dost renew these praises well deserved?
Not without recompense shall be thy word,
   If I return to finish the short journey
   Of that life which is flying to its end."
And he: "I'll tell thee, not for any comfort   40
   I may expect from earth, but that so much
   Grace shines in thee or ever thou art dead.
I was the root of that malignant plant
   Which overshadows all the Christian world,
   So that good fruit is seldom gathered from it;
But if Douay and Ghent, and Lille and Bruges

Had power, soon vengeance would be taken on it;
    And this I pray of Him who judges all.
Hugh Capet was I called upon the earth;
    From me were born the Louises and Philips,   50
    By whom in later days has France been governed.
I was the son of a Parisian butcher,
    What time the ancient kings had perished all,
    Excepting one, contrite in cloth of gray.
I found me grasping in my hands the rein
    Of the realm's government, and so great power
    Of new acquest, and so with friends abounding,
That to the widowed diadem promoted
    The head of mine own offspring was, from whom
    The consecrated bones of these began.   60
So long as the great dowry of Provence
    Out of my blood took not the sense of shame,
    'Twas little worth, but still it did no harm.
Then it began with falsehood and with force
    Its rapine; and thereafter, for amends,
    Took Ponthieu, Normandy, and Gascony.
Charles came to Italy, and for amends
    A victim made of Conradin, and then
    Thrust Thomas back to heaven, for amends.
A time I see, not very distant now,   70
    Which draweth forth another Charles from France,
    The better to make known both him and his.
Unarmed he goes, and only with the lance
    That Judas jousted with; and that he thrusts
    So that he makes the paunch of Florence burst.
He thence not land, but sin and infamy,
    Shall gain, so much more grievous to himself
    As the more light such damage he accounts.
The other, now gone forth, ta'en in his ship,
    See I his daughter sell, and chaffer for her   80
    As corsairs do with other female slaves.
What more, O Avarice, canst thou do to us,
    Since thou my blood so to thyself hast drawn,
    It careth not for its own proper flesh?
That less may seem the future ill and past,
    I see the flower-de-luce Alagna enter,
    And Christ in his own Vicar captive made.

I see him yet another time derided;
    I see renewed the vinegar and gall,
    And between living thieves I see him slain.   90
I see the modern Pilate so relentless,
    This does not sate him, but without decretal
    He to the temple bears his sordid sails!
When, O my Lord! shall I be joyful made
    By looking on the vengeance which, concealed,
    Makes sweet thine anger in thy secrecy?
What I was saying of that only bride
    Of the Holy Ghost, and which occasioned thee
    To turn towards me for some commentary,
So long has been ordained to all our prayers   100
    As the day lasts; but when the night comes on,
    Contrary sound we take instead thereof.
At that time we repeat Pygmalion,
    Of whom a traitor, thief, and parricide
    Made his insatiable desire of gold;
And the misery of avaricious Midas,
    That followed his inordinate demand,
    At which forevermore one needs but laugh.
The foolish Achan each one then records,
    And how he stole the spoils; so that the wrath   110
    Of Joshua still appears to sting him here.
Then we accuse Sapphira with her husband,
    We laud the hoof-beats Heliodorus had,
    And the whole mount in infamy encircles
Polymnestor who murdered Polydorus.
    Here finally is cried: 'O Crassus, tell us,
    For thou dost know, what is the taste of gold?'
Sometimes we speak, one loud, another low,
    According to desire of speech, that spurs us
    To greater now and now to lesser pace.   120
But in the good that here by day is talked of,
    Erewhile alone I was not; yet near by
    No other person lifted up his voice."
From him already we departed were,
    And made endeavour to o'ercome the road
    As much as was permitted to our power,
When I perceived, like something that is falling,
    The mountain tremble, whence a chill seized on me,

As seizes him who to his death is going.
Certes so violently shook not Delos,   130
   Before Latona made her nest therein
   To give birth to the two eyes of the heaven.
Then upon all sides there began a cry,
   Such that the Master drew himself towards me,
   Saying, "Fear not, while I am guiding thee."
"*Gloria in excelsis Deo,*" all
   Were saying, from what near I comprehended,
   Where it was possible to hear the cry.
We paused immovable and in suspense,
   Even as the shepherds who first heard that song,   140
   Until the trembling ceased, and it was finished.
Then we resumed again our holy path,
   Watching the shades that lay upon the ground,
   Already turned to their accustomed plaint.
No ignorance ever with so great a strife
   Had rendered me importunate to know,
   If erreth not in this my memory,
As meditating then I seemed to have;
   Nor out of haste to question did I dare,
   Nor of myself I there could aught perceive;   150
So I went onward timorous and thoughtful.

Canto XXI

The natural thirst, that ne'er is satisfied
   Excepting with the water for whose grace
   The woman of Samaria besought,
Put me in travail, and haste goaded me
   Along the encumbered path behind my Leader
   And I was pitying that righteous vengeance;
And lo! in the same manner as Luke writeth
   That Christ appeared to two upon the way
   From the sepulchral cave already risen,
A shade appeared to us, and came behind us,   10
   Down gazing on the prostrate multitude,
   Nor were we ware of it, until it spake,
Saying, "My brothers, may God give you peace!"
   We turned us suddenly, and Virgilius rendered

To him the countersign thereto conforming.
Thereon began he: "In the blessed council,
    Thee may the court veracious place in peace,
    That me doth banish in eternal exile!"
"How," said he, and the while we went with speed,
    "If ye are shades whom God deigns not on high,   20
    Who up his stairs so far has guided you?"
And said my Teacher: "If thou note the marks
    Which this one bears, and which the Angel traces
    Well shalt thou see he with the good must reign,
But because she who spinneth day and night
    For him had not yet drawn the distaff off,
    Which Clotho lays for each one and compacts,
His soul, which is thy sister and my own,
    In coming upwards could not come alone,
    By reason that it sees not in our fashion.   30
Whence I was drawn from out the ample throat
    Of Hell to be his guide, and I shall guide him
    As far on as my school has power to lead.
But tell us, if thou knowest, why such a shudder
    Erewhile the mountain gave, and why together
    All seemed to cry, as far as its moist feet?"
In asking he so hit the very eye
    Of my desire, that merely with the hope
    My thirst became the less unsatisfied.
"Naught is there," he began, "that without order   40
    May the religion of the mountain feel,
    Nor aught that may be foreign to its custom.
Free is it here from every permutation;
    What from itself heaven in itself receiveth
    Can be of this the cause, and naught beside;
Because that neither rain, nor hail, nor snow,
    Nor dew, nor hoar-frost any higher falls
    Than the short, little stairway of three steps.
Dense clouds do not appear, nor rarefied,
    Nor coruscation, nor the daughter of Thaumas,   50
    That often upon earth her region shifts;
No arid vapour any farther rises
    Than to the top of the three steps I spake of,
    Whereon the Vicar of Peter has his feet.
Lower down perchance it trembles less or more,

But, for the wind that in the earth is hidden
I know not how, up here it never trembled.
It trembles here, whenever any soul
    Feels itself pure, so that it soars, or moves
    To mount aloft, and such a cry attends it.   60
Of purity the will alone gives proof,
    Which, being wholly free to change its convent,
    Takes by surprise the soul, and helps it fly.
First it wills well; but the desire permits not,
    Which divine justice with the self-same will
    There was to sin, upon the torment sets.
And I, who have been lying in this pain
    Five hundred years and more, but just now felt
    A free volition for a better seat.
Therefore thou heardst the earthquake, and the pious   70
    Spirits along the mountain rendering praise
    Unto the Lord, that soon he speed them upwards."
So said he to him; and since we enjoy
    As much in drinking as the thirst is great,
    I could not say how much it did me good.
And the wise Leader: "Now I see the net
    That snares you here, and how ye are set free,
    Why the earth quakes, and wherefore ye rejoice.
Now who thou wast be pleased that I may know;
    And why so many centuries thou hast here   80
    Been lying, let me gather from thy words."
"In days when the good Titus, with the aid
    Of the supremest King, avenged the wounds
    Whence issued forth the blood by Judas sold,
Under the name that most endures and honours,
    Was I on earth," that spirit made reply,
    "Greatly renowned, but not with faith as yet.
My vocal spirit was so sweet, that Rome
    Me, a Thoulousian, drew unto herself,
    Where I deserved to deck my brows with myrtle.   90
Statius the people name me still on earth;
    I sang of Thebes, and then of great Achilles;
    But on the way fell with my second burden.
The seeds unto my ardour were the sparks
    Of that celestial flame which heated me,
    Whereby more than a thousand have been fired;

Of the Æneid speak I, which to me
   A mother was, and was my nurse in song;
   Without this weighed I not a drachma's weight.
And to have lived upon the earth what time   100
   Virgilius lived, I would accept one sun
   More than I must ere issuing from my ban."
These words towards me made Virgilius turn
   With looks that in their silence said, "Be silent!"
   But yet the power that wills cannot do all things;
For tears and laughter are such pursuivants
   Unto the passion from which each springs forth,
   In the most truthful least the will they follow.
I only smiled, as one who gives the wink;
   Whereat the shade was silent, and it gazed   110
   Into mine eyes, where most expression dwells;
And, "As thou well mayst consummate a labour
   So great," it said, "why did thy face just now
   Display to me the lightning of a smile?"
Now am I caught on this side and on that;
   One keeps me silent, one to speak conjures me,
   Wherefore I sigh, and I am understood.
"Speak," said my Master, "and be not afraid
   Of speaking, but speak out, and say to him
   What he demands with such solicitude."   120
Whence I: "Thou peradventure marvellest,
   O antique spirit, at the smile I gave;
   But I will have more wonder seize upon thee.
This one, who guides on high these eyes of mine,
   Is that Virgilius, from whom thou didst learn
   To sing aloud of men and of the Gods.
If other cause thou to my smile imputedst,
   Abandon it as false, and trust it was
   Those words which thou hast spoken concerning him."
Already he was stooping to embrace   130
   My Teacher's feet; but he said to him: "Brother,
   Do not; for shade thou art, and shade beholdest."
And he uprising: "Now canst thou the sum
   Of love which warms me to thee comprehend,
   When this our vanity I disremember,
Treating a shadow as substantial thing."

Canto XXII

Already was the Angel left behind us,
    The Angel who to the sixth round had turned us,
    Having erased one mark from off my face;
And those who have in justice their desire
    Had said to us, "*Beati*," in their voices,
    With "*sitio*," and without more ended it.
And I, more light than through the other passes,
    Went onward so, that without any labour
    I followed upward the swift-footed spirits;
When thus Virgilius began: "The love   10
    Kindled by virtue aye another kindles,
    Provided outwardly its flame appear.
Hence from the hour that Juvenal descended
    Among us into the infernal Limbo,
    Who made apparent to me thy affection,
My kindliness towards thee was as great
    As ever bound one to an unseen person,
    So that these stairs will now seem short to me.
But tell me, and forgive me as a friend,
    If too great confidence let loose the rein,   20
    And as a friend now hold discourse with me;
How was it possible within thy breast
    For avarice to find place, 'mid so much wisdom
    As thou wast filled with by thy diligence?"
These words excited Statius at first
    Somewhat to laughter; afterward he answered:
    "Each word of thine is love's dear sign to me.
Verily oftentimes do things appear
    Which give fallacious matter to our doubts,
    Instead of the true causes which are hidden!   30
Thy question shows me thy belief to be
    That I was niggard in the other life,
    It may be from the circle where I was;
Therefore know thou, that avarice was removed
    Too far from me; and this extravagance
    Thousands of lunar periods have punished.
And were it not that I my thoughts uplifted,
    When I the passage heard where thou exclaimest,
    As if indignant, unto human nature,

'To what impellest thou not, O cursed hunger   40
   Of gold, the appetite of mortal men?'
   Revolving I should feel the dismal joustings.
Then I perceived the hands could spread too wide
   Their wings in spending, and repented me
   As well of that as of my other sins;
How many with shorn hair shall rise again
   Because of ignorance, which from this sin
   Cuts off repentance living and in death!
And know that the transgression which rebuts
   By direct opposition any sin   50
   Together with it here its verdure dries.
Therefore if I have been among that folk
   Which mourns its avarice, to purify me,
   For its opposite has this befallen me."
"Now when thou sangest the relentless weapons
   Of the twofold affliction of Jocasta,"
   The singer of the Songs Bucolic said,
"From that which Clio there with thee preludes,
   It does not seem that yet had made thee faithful
   That faith without which no good works suffice.   60
If this be so, what candles or what sun
   Scattered thy darkness so that thou didst trim
   Thy sails behind the Fisherman thereafter?"
And he to him: "Thou first directedst me
   Towards Parnassus, in its grots to drink,
   And first concerning God didst me enlighten.
Thou didst as he who walketh in the night,
   Who bears his light behind, which helps him not,
   But wary makes the persons after him,
When thou didst say: 'The age renews itself,   70
   Justice returns, and man's primeval time,
   And a new progeny descends from heaven.'
Through thee I Poet was, through thee a Christian;
   But that thou better see what I design,
   To colour it will I extend my hand.
Already was the world in every part
   Pregnant with the true creed, disseminated
   By messengers of the eternal kingdom;
And thy assertion, spoken of above,
   With the new preachers was in unison;   80

Whence I to visit them the custom took.
Then they became so holy in my sight,
    That, when Domitian persecuted them,
    Not without tears of mine were their laments;
And all the while that I on earth remained,
    Them I befriended, and their upright customs
    Made me disparage all the other sects.
And ere I led the Greeks unto the rivers
    Of Thebes, in poetry, I was baptized,
    But out of fear was covertly a Christian,   90
For a long time professing paganism;
    And this lukewarmness caused me the fourth circle
    To circuit round more than four centuries.
Thou, therefore, who hast raised the covering
    That hid from me whatever good I speak of,
    While in ascending we have time to spare,
Tell me, in what place is our friend Terentius,
    Cæcilius, Plautus, Varro, if thou knowest;
    Tell me if they are damned, and in what alley."
"These, Persius and myself, and others many,"   100
    Replied my Leader, "with that Grecian are
    Whom more than all the rest the Muses suckled,
In the first circle of the prison blind;
    Ofttimes we of the mountain hold discourse
    Which has our nurses ever with itself.
Euripides is with us, Antiphon,
    Simonides, Agatho, and many other
    Greeks who of old their brows with laurel decked.
There some of thine own people may be seen,
    Antigone, Deiphile and Argìa,   110
    And there Ismene mournful as of old.
There she is seen who pointed out Langìa;
    There is Tiresias' daughter, and there Thetis,
    And there Deidamia with her sisters."
Silent already were the poets both,
    Attent once more in looking round about,
    From the ascent and from the walls released;
And four handmaidens of the day already
    Were left behind, and at the pole the fifth
    Was pointing upward still its burning horn,   120
What time my Guide: "I think that tow'rds the edge

Our dexter shoulders it behoves us turn,
  Circling the mount as we are wont to do."
Thus in that region custom was our ensign;
  And we resumed our way with less suspicion
  For the assenting of that worthy soul
They in advance went on, and I alone
  Behind them, and I listened to their speech,
  Which gave me lessons in the art of song.
But soon their sweet discourses interrupted   130
  A tree which midway in the road we found,
  With apples sweet and grateful to the smell.
And even as a fir-tree tapers upward
  From bough to bough, so downwardly did that;
  I think in order that no one might climb it.
On that side where our pathway was enclosed
  Fell from the lofty rock a limpid water,
  And spread itself abroad upon the leaves.
The Poets twain unto the tree drew near,
  And from among the foliage a voice   140
  Cried: "Of this food ye shall have scarcity."
Then said: "More thoughtful Mary was of making
  The marriage feast complete and honourable,
  Than of her mouth which now for you responds;
And for their drink the ancient Roman women
  With water were content; and Daniel
  Disparaged food, and understanding won.
The primal age was beautiful as gold;
  Acorns it made with hunger savorous,
  And nectar every rivulet with thirst.   150
Honey and locusts were the aliments
  That fed the Baptist in the wilderness;
  Whence he is glorious, and so magnified
As by the Evangel is revealed to you."

Canto XXIII

The while among the verdant leaves mine eyes
  I riveted, as he is wont to do
  Who wastes his life pursuing little birds,
My more than Father said unto me: "Son,

Come now; because the time that is ordained us
   More usefully should be apportioned out."
I turned my face and no less soon my steps
   Unto the Sages, who were speaking so
   They made the going of no cost to me;
And lo! were heard a song and a lament,   10
   "*Labia mea, Domine,*" in fashion
   Such that delight and dolence it brought forth.
"O my sweet Father, what is this I hear?"
   Began I; and he answered: "Shades that go
   Perhaps the knot unloosing of their debt."
In the same way that thoughtful pilgrims do,
   Who, unknown people on the road o'ertaking,
   Turn themselves round to them, and do not stop,
Even thus, behind us with a swifter motion
   Coming and passing onward, gazed upon us   20
   A crowd of spirits silent and devout.
Each in his eyes was dark and cavernous,
   Pallid in face, and so emaciate
   That from the bones the skin did shape itself.
I do not think that so to merest rind
   Could Erisichthon have been withered up
   By famine, when most fear he had of it.
Thinking within myself I said: "Behold,
   This is the folk who lost Jerusalem,
   When Mary made a prey of her own son."   30
Their sockets were like rings without the gems;
   Whoever in the face of men reads *omo*
   Might well in these have recognised the *m*.
Who would believe the odour of an apple,
   Begetting longing, could consume them so,
   And that of water, without knowing how?
I still was wondering what so famished them,
   For the occasion not yet manifest
   Of their emaciation and sad squalor;
And lo! from out the hollow of his head   40
   His eyes a shade turned on me, and looked keenly;
   Then cried aloud: "What grace to me is this?"
Never should I have known him by his look;
   But in his voice was evident to me
   That which his aspect had suppressed within it.

This spark within me wholly re-enkindled
  My recognition of his altered face,
  And I recalled the features of Forese.
"Ah, do not look at this dry leprosy,"
  Entreated he, "which doth my skin discolour,   50
  Nor at default of flesh that I may have;
But tell me truth of thee, and who are those
  Two souls, that yonder make for thee an escort;
  Do not delay in speaking unto me."
"That face of thine, which dead I once bewept,
  Gives me for weeping now no lesser grief,"
  I answered him, "beholding it so changed!
But tell me, for God's sake, what thus denudes you?
  Make me not speak while I am marvelling,
  For ill speaks he who's full of other longings."   60
And he to me: "From the eternal council
  Falls power into the water and the tree
  Behind us left, whereby I grow so thin.
All of this people who lamenting sing,
  For following beyond measure appetite
  In hunger and thirst are here re-sanctified.
Desire to eat and drink enkindles in us
  The scent that issues from the apple-tree,
  And from the spray that sprinkles o'er the verdure;
And not a single time alone, this ground   70
  Encircling, is renewed our pain,—
  I say our pain, and ought to say our solace,—
For the same wish doth lead us to the tree
  Which led the Christ rejoicing to say *Eli,*
  When with his veins he liberated us."
And I to him: "Forese, from that day
  When for a better life thou changedst worlds,
  Up to this time five years have not rolled round.
If sooner were the power exhausted in thee
  Of sinning more, than thee the hour surprised   80
  Of that good sorrow which to God reweds us,
How hast thou come up hitherward already?
  I thought to find thee down there underneath,
  Where time for time doth restitution make."
And he to me: "Thus speedily has led me
  To drink of the sweet wormwood of these torments,

My Nella with her overflowing tears;
She with her prayers devout and with her sighs
    Has drawn me from the coast where one awaits,
    And from the other circles set me free.   90
So much more dear and pleasing is to God
    My little widow, whom so much I loved,
    As in good works she is the more alone;
For the Barbagia of Sardinia
    By far more modest in its women is
    Than the Barbagia I have left her in.
O brother sweet, what wilt thou have me say?
    A future time is in my sight already,
    To which this hour will not be very old,
When from the pulpit shall be interdicted   100
    To the unblushing womankind of Florence
    To go about displaying breast and paps.
What savages were e'er, what Saracens,
    Who stood in need, to make them covered go,
    Of spiritual or other discipline?
But if the shameless women were assured
    Of what swift Heaven prepares for them, already
    Wide open would they have their mouths to howl;
For if my foresight here deceive me not,
    They shall be sad ere he has bearded cheeks   110
    Who now is hushed to sleep with lullaby.
O brother, now no longer hide thee from me;
    See that not only I, but all these people
    Are gazing there, where thou dost veil the sun."
Whence I to him: "If thou bring back to mind
    What thou with me hast been and I with thee,
    The present memory will be grievous still.
Out of that life he turned me back who goes
    In front of me, two days agone when round
    The sister of him yonder showed herself,"   120
And to the sun I pointed. "Through the deep
    Night of the truly dead has this one led me,
    With this true flesh, that follows after him.
Thence his encouragements have led me up,
    Ascending and still circling round the mount
    That you doth straighten, whom the world made crooked.
He says that he will bear me company,

Till I shall be where Beatrice will be;
　　There it behoves me to remain without him.
This is Virgilius, who thus says to me,"   130
　　And him I pointed at; "the other is
　　That shade for whom just now shook every slope
Your realm, that from itself discharges him."

Canto XXIV

Nor speech the going, nor the going that
　　Slackened; but talking we went bravely on,
　　Even as a vessel urged by a good wind.
And shadows, that appeared things doubly dead,
　　From out the sepulchres of their eyes betrayed
　　Wonder at me, aware that I was living.
And I, continuing my colloquy,
　　Said: "Peradventure he goes up more slowly
　　Than he would do, for other people's sake.
But tell me, if thou knowest, where is Piccarda;   10
　　Tell me if any one of note I see
　　Among this folk that gazes at me so."
"My sister, who, 'twixt beautiful and good,
　　I know not which was more, triumphs rejoicing
　　Already in her crown on high Olympus."
So said he first, and then: "'Tis not forbidden
　　To name each other here, so milked away
　　Is our resemblance by our dieting.
This," pointing with his finger, "is Buonagiunta,
　　Buonagiunta, of Lucca; and that face   20
　　Beyond him there, more peaked than the others,
Has held the holy Church within his arms;
　　From Tours was he, and purges by his fasting
　　Bolsena's eels and the Vernaccia wine."
He named me many others one by one;
　　And all contented seemed at being named,
　　So that for this I saw not one dark look.
I saw for hunger bite the empty air
　　Ubaldin dalla Pila, and Boniface,
　　Who with his crook had pastured many people.   30
I saw Messer Marchese, who had leisure

Once at Forlì for drinking with less dryness,
    And he was one who ne'er felt satisfied.
But as he does who scans, and then doth prize
    One more than others, did I him of Lucca,
    Who seemed to take most cognizance of me.
He murmured, and I know not what Gentucca
    From that place heard I, where he felt the wound
    Of justice, that doth macerate them so.
"O soul," I said, "that seemest so desirous   40
    To speak with me, do so that I may hear thee,
    And with thy speech appease thyself and me."
"A maid is born, and wears not yet the veil,"
    Began he, "who to thee shall pleasant make
    My city, howsoever men may blame it.
Thou shalt go on thy way with this prevision;
    If by my murmuring thou hast been deceived,
    True things hereafter will declare it to thee.
But say if him I here behold, who forth
    Evoked the new-invented rhymes, beginning,   50
    Ladies, that have intelligence of love?"
And I to him: "One am I, who, whenever
    Love doth inspire me, note, and in that measure
    Which he within me dictates, singing go."
"O brother, now I see," he said, "the knot
    Which me, the Notary, and Guittone held
    Short of the sweet new style that now I hear.
I do perceive full clearly how your pens
    Go closely following after him who dictates,
    Which with our own forsooth came not to pass;   60
And he who sets himself to go beyond,
    No difference sees from one style to another;"
    And as if satisfied, he held his peace.
Even as the birds, that winter tow'rds the Nile,
    Sometimes into a phalanx form themselves,
    Then fly in greater haste, and go in file;
In such wise all the people who were there,
    Turning their faces, hurried on their steps,
    Both by their leanness and their wishes light.
And as a man, who weary is with trotting,   70
    Lets his companions onward go, and walks,
    Until he vents the panting of his chest;

So did Forese let the holy flock
   Pass by, and came with me behind it, saying,
   "When will it be that I again shall see thee?"
"How long," I answered, "I may live, I know not;
   Yet my return will not so speedy be,
   But I shall sooner in desire arrive;
Because the place where I was set to live
   From day to day of good is more depleted,   80
   And unto dismal ruin seems ordained."
"Now go," he said, "for him most guilty of it
   At a beast's tail behold I dragged along
   Towards the valley where is no repentance.
Faster at every step the beast is going,
   Increasing evermore until it smites him,
   And leaves the body vilely mutilated.
Not long those wheels shall turn," and he uplifted
   His eyes to heaven, "ere shall be clear to thee
   That which my speech no farther can declare.   90
Now stay behind; because the time so precious
   Is in this kingdom, that I lose too much
   By coming onward thus abreast with thee."
As sometimes issues forth upon a gallop
   A cavalier from out a troop that ride,
   And seeks the honour of the first encounter,
So he with greater strides departed from us;
   And on the road remained I with those two,
   Who were such mighty marshals of the world.
And when before us he had gone so far   100
   Mine eyes became to him such pursuivants
   As was my understanding to his words,
Appeared to me with laden and living boughs
   Another apple-tree, and not far distant,
   From having but just then turned thitherward.
People I saw beneath it lift their hands,
   And cry I know not what towards the leaves,
   Like little children eager and deluded,
Who pray, and he they pray to doth not answer,
   But, to make very keen their appetite,   110
   Holds their desire aloft, and hides it not.
Then they departed as if undeceived;
   And now we came unto the mighty tree

Which prayers and tears so manifold refuses.
"Pass farther onward without drawing near;
    The tree of which Eve ate is higher up,
    And out of that one has this tree been raised."
Thus said I know not who among the branches;
    Whereat Virgilius, Statius, and myself
    Went crowding forward on the side that rises.   120
"Be mindful," said he, "of the accursed ones
    Formed of the cloud-rack, who inebriate
    Combated Theseus with their double breasts;
And of the Jews who showed them soft in drinking,
    Whence Gideon would not have them for companions
    When he tow'rds Midian the hills descended."
Thus, closely pressed to one of the two borders,
    On passed we, hearing sins of gluttony,
    Followed forsooth by miserable gains;
Then set at large upon the lonely road,   130
    A thousand steps and more we onward went,
    In contemplation, each without a word.
"What go ye thinking thus, ye three alone?"
    Said suddenly a voice, whereat I started
    As terrified and timid beasts are wont.
I raised my head to see who this might be,
    And never in a furnace was there seen
    Metals or glass so lucent and so red
As one I saw who said: "If it may please you
    To mount aloft, here it behoves you turn;   140
    This way goes he who goeth after peace."
His aspect had bereft me of my sight,
    So that I turned me back unto my Teachers,
    Like one who goeth as his hearing guides him.
And as, the harbinger of early dawn,
    The air of May doth move and breathe out fragrance,
    Impregnate all with herbage and with flowers,
So did I feel a breeze strike in the midst
    My front, and felt the moving of the plumes
    That breathed around an odour of ambrosia;   150
And heard it said: "Blessed are they whom grace
    So much illumines, that the love of taste
    Excites not in their breasts too great desire,
Hungering at all times so far as is just."

Canto XXV

Now was it the ascent no hindrance brooked,
   Because the sun had his meridian circle
   To Taurus left, and night to Scorpio;
Wherefore as doth a man who tarries not,
   But goes his way, whate'er to him appear,
   If of necessity the sting transfix him,
In this wise did we enter through the gap,
   Taking the stairway, one before the other,
   Which by its narrowness divides the climbers.
And as the little stork that lifts its wing   10
   With a desire to fly, and does not venture
   To leave the nest, and lets it downward droop,
Even such was I, with the desire of asking
   Kindled and quenched, unto the motion coming
   He makes who doth address himself to speak.
Not for our pace, though rapid it might be,
   My father sweet forbore, but said: "Let fly
   The bow of speech thou to the barb hast drawn."
With confidence I opened then my mouth,
   And I began: "How can one meagre grow   20
   There where the need of nutriment applies not?"
"If thou wouldst call to mind how Meleager
   Was wasted by the wasting of a brand,
   This would not," said he, "be to thee so sour;
And wouldst thou think how at each tremulous motion
   Trembles within a mirror your own image;
   That which seems hard would mellow seem to thee.
But that thou mayst content thee in thy wish
   Lo Statius here; and him I call and pray
   He now will be the healer of thy wounds."   30
"If I unfold to him the eternal vengeance,"
   Responded Statius, "where thou present art,
   Be my excuse that I can naught deny thee."
Then he began: "Son, if these words of mine
   Thy mind doth contemplate and doth receive,
   They'll be thy light unto the How thou sayest.
The perfect blood, which never is drunk up
   Into the thirsty veins, and which remaineth
   Like food that from the table thou removest,

Takes in the heart for all the human members   40
    Virtue informative, as being that
    Which to be changed to them goes through the veins
Again digest, descends it where 'tis better
    Silent to be than say; and then drops thence
    Upon another's blood in natural vase.
There one together with the other mingles,
    One to be passive meant, the other active
    By reason of the perfect place it springs from;
And being conjoined, begins to operate,
    Coagulating first, then vivifying   50
    What for its matter it had made consistent.
The active virtue, being made a soul
    As of a plant, (in so far different,
    This on the way is, that arrived already,)
Then works so much, that now it moves and feels
    Like a sea-fungus, and then undertakes
    To organize the powers whose seed it is.
Now, Son, dilates and now distends itself
    The virtue from the generator's heart,
    Where nature is intent on all the members.   60
But how from animal it man becomes
    Thou dost not see as yet; this is a point
    Which made a wiser man than thou once err
So far, that in his doctrine separate
    He made the soul from possible intellect,
    For he no organ saw by this assumed.
Open thy breast unto the truth that's coming,
    And know that, just as soon as in the fœtus
    The articulation of the brain is perfect,
The primal Motor turns to it well pleased   70
    At so great art of nature, and inspires
    A spirit new with virtue all replete,
Which what it finds there active doth attract
    Into its substance, and becomes one soul,
    Which lives, and feels, and on itself revolves.
And that thou less may wonder at my word,
    Behold the sun's heat, which becometh wine,
    Joined to the juice that from the vine distils.
Whenever Lachesis has no more thread,
    It separates from the flesh, and virtually   80

Bears with itself the human and divine;
The other faculties are voiceless all;
   The memory, the intelligence, and the will
   In action far more vigorous than before.
Without a pause it falleth of itself
   In marvellous way on one shore or the other;
   There of its roads it first is cognizant.
Soon as the place there circumscribeth it,
   The virtue informative rays round about,
   As, and as much as, in the living members.   90
And even as the air, when full of rain,
   By alien rays that are therein reflected,
   With divers colours shows itself adorned,
So there the neighbouring air doth shape itself
   Into that form which doth impress upon it
   Virtually the soul that has stood still.
And then in manner of the little flame,
   Which followeth the fire where'er it shifts,
   After the spirit followeth its new form.
Since afterwards it takes from this its semblance,   100
   It is called shade; and thence it organizes
   Thereafter every sense, even to the sight.
Thence is it that we speak, and thence we laugh;
   Thence is it that we form the tears and sighs,
   That on the mountain thou mayhap hast heard.
According as impress us our desires
   And other affections, so the shade is shaped,
   And this is cause of what thou wonderest at."
And now unto the last of all the circles
   Had we arrived, and to the right hand turned,   110
   And were attentive to another care.
There the embankment shoots forth flames of fire,
   And upward doth the cornice breathe a blast
   That drives them back, and from itself sequesters.
Hence we must needs go on the open side,
   And one by one; and I did fear the fire
   On this side, and on that the falling down.
My Leader said: "Along this place one ought
   To keep upon the eyes a tightened rein,
   Seeing that one so easily might err."   120
"*Summæ Deus clementiæ,*" in the bosom

Of the great burning chanted then I heard,
   Which made me no less eager to turn round;
And spirits saw I walking through the flame;
   Wherefore I looked, to my own steps and theirs
   Apportioning my sight from time to time.
After the close which to that hymn is made,
   Aloud they shouted, "*Virum non cognosco;*"
   Then recommenced the hymn with voices low.
This also ended, cried they: "To the wood   130
   Diana ran, and drove forth Helice
   Therefrom, who had of Venus felt the poison."
Then to their song returned they; then the wives
   They shouted, and the husbands who were chaste,
   As virtue and the marriage vow imposes.
And I believe that them this mode suffices,
   For all the time the fire is burning them;
   With such care is it needful, and such food,
That the last wound of all should be closed up.

Canto XXVI

While on the brink thus one before the other
   We went upon our way, oft the good Master
   Said: "Take thou heed! suffice it that I warn thee."
On the right shoulder smote me now the sun,
   That, raying out, already the whole west
   Changed from its azure aspect into white.
And with my shadow did I make the flame
   Appear more red; and even to such a sign
   Shades saw I many, as they went, give heed.
This was the cause that gave them a beginning   10
   To speak of me; and to themselves began they
   To say: "That seems not a factitious body!"
Then towards me, as far as they could come,
   Came certain of them, always with regard
   Not to step forth where they would not be burned.
"O thou who goest, not from being slower
   But reverent perhaps, behind the others,
   Answer me, who in thirst and fire am burning.
Nor to me only is thine answer needful;

For all of these have greater thirst for it   20
   Than for cold water Ethiop or Indian.
Tell us how is it that thou makest thyself
   A wall unto the sun, as if thou hadst not
   Entered as yet into the net of death."
Thus one of them addressed me, and I straight
   Should have revealed myself, were I not bent
   On other novelty that then appeared.
For through the middle of the burning road
   There came a people face to face with these,
   Which held me in suspense with gazing at them.   30
There see I hastening upon either side
   Each of the shades, and kissing one another
   Without a pause, content with brief salute.
Thus in the middle of their brown battalions
   Muzzle to muzzle one ant meets another
   Perchance to spy their journey or their fortune.
No sooner is the friendly greeting ended,
   Or ever the first footstep passes onward,
   Each one endeavours to outcry the other;
The new-come people: "Sodom and Gomorrah!"   40
   The rest: "Into the cow Pasiphae enters,
   So that the bull unto her lust may run!"
Then as the cranes, that to Riphæan mountains
   Might fly in part, and part towards the sands,
   These of the frost, those of the sun avoidant,
One folk is going, and the other coming,
   And weeping they return to their first songs,
   And to the cry that most befitteth them;
And close to me approached, even as before,
   The very same who had entreated me,   50
   Attent to listen in their countenance.
I, who their inclination twice had seen,
   Began: "O souls secure in the possession,
   Whene'er it may be, of a state of peace,
Neither unripe nor ripened have remained
   My members upon earth, but here are with me
   With their own blood and their articulations.
I go up here to be no longer blind;
   A Lady is above, who wins this grace,
   Whereby the mortal through your world I bring.   60

But as your greatest longing satisfied
    May soon become, so that the Heaven may house you
    Which full of love is, and most amply spreads,
Tell me, that I again in books may write it,
    Who are you, and what is that multitude
    Which goes upon its way behind your backs?"
Not otherwise with wonder is bewildered
    The mountaineer, and staring round is dumb,
    When rough and rustic to the town he goes,
Than every shade became in its appearance;   70
    But when they of their stupor were disburdened,
    Which in high hearts is quickly quieted,
"Blessed be thou, who of our border-lands,"
    He recommenced who first had questioned us,
    "Experience freightest for a better life.
The folk that comes not with us have offended
    In that for which once Cæsar, triumphing,
    Heard himself called in contumely, 'Queen.'
Therefore they separate, exclaiming, 'Sodom!'
    Themselves reproving, even as thou hast heard,   80
    And add unto their burning by their shame.
Our own transgression was hermaphrodite;
    But because we observed not human law,
    Following like unto beasts our appetite,
In our opprobrium by us is read,
    When we part company, the name of her
    Who bestialized herself in bestial wood.
Now knowest thou our acts, and what our crime was;
    Wouldst thou perchance by name know who we are,
    There is not time to tell, nor could I do it.   90
Thy wish to know me shall in sooth be granted;
    I'm Guido Guinicelli, and now purge me,
    Having repented ere the hour extreme."
The same that in the sadness of Lycurgus
    Two sons became, their mother re-beholding,
    Such I became, but rise not to such height,
The moment I heard name himself the father
    Of me and of my betters, who had ever
    Practised the sweet and gracious rhymes of love;
And without speech and hearing thoughtfully   100
    For a long time I went, beholding him,

Nor for the fire did I approach him nearer.
When I was fed with looking, utterly
   Myself I offered ready for his service,
   With affirmation that compels belief.
And he to me: "Thou leavest footprints such
   In me, from what I hear, and so distinct,
   Lethe cannot efface them, nor make dim.
But if thy words just now the truth have sworn,
   Tell me what is the cause why thou displayest   110
   In word and look that dear thou holdest me?"
And I to him: "Those dulcet lays of yours
   Which, long as shall endure our modern fashion,
   Shall make for ever dear their very ink!"
"O brother," said he, "he whom I point out,"
   And here he pointed at a spirit in front,
   "Was of the mother tongue a better smith.
Verses of love and proses of romance,
   He mastered all; and let the idiots talk,
   Who think the Lemosin surpasses him.   120
To clamour more than truth they turn their faces,
   And in this way establish their opinion,
   Ere art or reason has by them been heard.
Thus many ancients with Guittone did,
   From cry to cry still giving him applause,
   Until the truth has conquered with most persons.
Now, if thou hast such ample privilege
   'Tis granted thee to go unto the cloister
   Wherein is Christ the abbot of the college,
To him repeat for me a Paternoster,   130
   So far as needful to us of this world,
   Where power of sinning is no longer ours."
Then, to give place perchance to one behind,
   Whom he had near, he vanished in the fire
   As fish in water going to the bottom.
I moved a little tow'rds him pointed out,
   And said that to his name my own desire
   An honourable place was making ready.
He of his own free will began to say:
   Tan m' abellis vostre cortes deman,   140
   Que jeu nom' puesc ni vueill a vos cobrire;
Jeu sui Arnaut, que plor e vai chantan;

> *Consiros vei la passada folor,*
> *E vei jauzen lo jorn qu' esper denan.*
> *Ara vus prec per aquella valor,*
> *Que vus condus al som de la scalina,*
> *Sovenga vus a temprar ma dolor.**

Then hid him in the fire that purifies them.

Canto XXVII

As when he vibrates forth his earliest rays,
    In regions where his Maker shed his blood,
    (The Ebro falling under lofty Libra,
And waters in the Ganges burnt with noon,)
    So stood the Sun; hence was the day departing,
    When the glad Angel of God appeared to us.
Outside the flame he stood upon the verge,
    And chanted forth, "*Beati mundo corde,*"
    In voice by far more living than our own.
Then: "No one farther goes, souls sanctified,   10
    If first the fire bite not; within it enter,
    And be not deaf unto the song beyond."
When we were close beside him thus he said;
    Wherefore e'en such became I, when I heard him,
    As he is who is put into the grave.
Upon my claspëd hands I straightened me,
    Scanning the fire, and vividly recalling
    The human bodies I had once seen burned.
Towards me turned themselves my good Conductors,
    And unto me Virgilius said: "My son,   20
    Here may indeed be torment, but not death.
Remember thee, remember! and if I
    On Geryon have safely guided thee,

---

* So pleases me your courteous demand,
    I cannot and I will not hide me from you.
I am Arnaut, who weep and singing go;
    Contrite I see the folly of the past,
    And joyous see the hoped-for day before me.
Therefore do I implore you, by that power
    Which guides you to the summit of the stairs,
    Be mindful to assuage my suffering!

What shall I do now I am nearer God?
Believe for certain, shouldst thou stand a full
   Millennium in the bosom of this flame,
   It could not make thee bald a single hair.
And if perchance thou think that I deceive thee,
   Draw near to it, and put it to the proof
   With thine own hands upon thy garment's hem.   30
Now lay aside, now lay aside all fear,
   Turn hitherward, and onward come securely;"
   And I still motionless, and 'gainst my conscience!
Seeing me stand still motionless and stubborn,
   Somewhat disturbed he said: "Now look thou, Son,
   'Twixt Beatrice and thee there is this wall."
As at the name of Thisbe oped his lids
   The dying Pyramus, and gazed upon her,
   What time the mulberry became vermilion,
Even thus, my obduracy being softened,   40
   I turned to my wise Guide, hearing the name
   That in my memory evermore is welling.
Whereat he wagged his head, and said: "How now?
   Shall we stay on this side?" then smiled as one
   Does at a child who's vanquished by an apple.
Then into the fire in front of me he entered,
   Beseeching Statius to come after me,
   Who a long way before divided us.
When I was in it, into molten glass
   I would have cast me to refresh myself,   50
   So without measure was the burning there!
And my sweet Father, to encourage me,
   Discoursing still of Beatrice went on,
   Saying: "Her eyes I seem to see already!"
A voice, that on the other side was singing,
   Directed us, and we, attent alone
   On that, came forth where the ascent began.
"*Venite, benedicti Patris mei,*"
   Sounded within a splendour, which was there
   Such it o'ercame me, and I could not look.   60
"The sun departs," it added, "and night cometh;
   Tarry ye not, but onward urge your steps,
   So long as yet the west becomes not dark."
Straight forward through the rock the path ascended

In such a way that I cut off the rays
  Before me of the sun, that now was low.
And of few stairs we yet had made assay,
  Ere by the vanished shadow the sun's setting
  Behind us we perceived, I and my Sages.
And ere in all its parts immeasurable   70
  The horizon of one aspect had become,
  And Night her boundless dispensation held,
Each of us of a stair had made his bed;
  Because the nature of the mount took from us
  The power of climbing, more than the delight.
Even as in ruminating passive grow
  The goats, who have been swift and venturesome
  Upon the mountain-tops ere they were fed,
Hushed in the shadow, while the sun is hot,
  Watched by the herdsman, who upon his staff   80
  Is leaning, and in leaning tendeth them;
And as the shepherd, lodging out of doors,
  Passes the night beside his quiet flock,
  Watching that no wild beast may scatter it,
Such at that hour were we, all three of us,
  I like the goat, and like the herdsmen they,
  Begirt on this side and on that by rocks.
Little could there be seen of things without;
  But through that little I beheld the stars
  More luminous and larger than their wont.   90
Thus ruminating, and beholding these,
  Sleep seized upon me,—sleep, that oftentimes
  Before a deed is done has tidings of it.
It was the hour, I think, when from the East
  First on the mountain Citherea beamed,
  Who with the fire of love seems always burning;
Youthful and beautiful in dreams methought
  I saw a lady walking in a meadow,
  Gathering flowers; and singing she was saying:
"Know whosoever may my name demand   100
  That I am Leah, and go moving round
  My beauteous hands to make myself a garland.
To please me at the mirror, here I deck me,
  But never does my sister Rachel leave
  Her looking-glass, and sitteth all day long.

To see her beauteous eyes as eager is she,
   As I am to adorn me with my hands;
   Her, seeing, and me, doing satisfies."
And now before the antelucan splendours
   That unto pilgrims the more grateful rise,   110
   As, home-returning, less remote they lodge,
The darkness fled away on every side,
   And slumber with it; whereupon I rose,
   Seeing already the great Masters risen.
"That apple sweet, which through so many branches
   The care of mortals goeth in pursuit of,
   To-day shall put in peace thy hungerings."
Speaking to me, Virgilius of such words
   As these made use; and never were there guerdons
   That could in pleasantness compare with these.   120
Such longing upon longing came upon me
   To be above, that at each step thereafter
   For flight I felt in me the pinions growing.
When underneath us was the stairway all
   Run o'er, and we were on the highest step,
   Virgilius fastened upon me his eyes,
And said: "The temporal fire and the eternal,
   Son, thou hast seen, and to a place art come
   Where of myself no farther I discern.
By intellect and art I here have brought thee;   130
   Take thine own pleasure for thy guide henceforth;
   Beyond the steep ways and the narrow art thou.
Behold the sun, that shines upon thy forehead;
   Behold the grass, the flowerets, and the shrubs
   Which of itself alone this land produces.
Until rejoicing come the beauteous eyes
   Which weeping caused me to come unto thee,
   Thou canst sit down, and thou canst walk among them.
Expect no more or word or sign from me;
   Free and upright and sound is thy free-will,   140
   And error were it not to do its bidding;
Thee o'er thyself I therefore crown and mitre!"

Canto XXVIII

Eager already to search in and round
  The heavenly forest, dense and living-green,
  Which tempered to the eyes the new-born day,
Withouten more delay I left the bank,
  Taking the level country slowly, slowly
  Over the soil that everywhere breathes fragrance.
A softly-breathing air, that no mutation
  Had in itself, upon the forehead smote me
  No heavier blow than of a gentle wind,
Whereat the branches, lightly tremulous,   10
  Did all of them bow downward toward that side
  Where its first shadow casts the Holy Mountain;
Yet not from their upright direction swayed,
  So that the little birds upon their tops
  Should leave the practice of each art of theirs;
But with full ravishment the hours of prime,
  Singing, received they in the midst of leaves,
  That ever bore a burden to their rhymes,
Such as from branch to branch goes gathering on
  Through the pine forest on the shore of Chiassi,   20
  When Eolus unlooses the Sirocco.
Already my slow steps had carried me
  Into the ancient wood so far, that I
  Could not perceive where I had entered it.
And lo! my further course a stream cut off,
  Which tow'rd the left hand with its little waves
  Bent down the grass that on its margin sprang.
All waters that on earth most limpid are
  Would seem to have within themselves some mixture
  Compared with that which nothing doth conceal,   30
Although it moves on with a brown, brown current
  Under the shade perpetual, that never
  Ray of the sun lets in, nor of the moon.
With feet I stayed, and with mine eyes I passed
  Beyond the rivulet, to look upon
  The great variety of the fresh may.
And there appeared to me (even as appears
  Suddenly something that doth turn aside
  Through very wonder every other thought)

A lady all alone, who went along   40
   Singing and culling floweret after floweret,
   With which her pathway was all painted over.
"Ah, beauteous lady, who in rays of love
   Dost warm thyself, if I may trust to looks,
   Which the heart's witnesses are wont to be,
May the desire come unto thee to draw
   Near to this river's bank," I said to her,
   "So much that I may hear what thou art singing.
Thou makest me remember where and what
   Proserpina that moment was when lost   50
   Her mother her, and she herself the Spring."
As turns herself, with feet together pressed
   And to the ground, a lady who is dancing,
   And hardly puts one foot before the other,
On the vermilion and the yellow flowerets
   She turned towards me, not in other wise
   Than maiden who her modest eyes casts down;
And my entreaties made to be content,
   So near approaching, that the dulcet sound
   Came unto me together with its meaning.   60
As soon as she was where the grasses are
   Bathed by the waters of the beauteous river,
   To lift her eyes she granted me the boon.
I do not think there shone so great a light
   Under the lids of Venus, when transfixed
   By her own son, beyond his usual custom!
Erect upon the other bank she smiled,
   Bearing full many colours in her hands,
   Which that high land produces without seed.
Apart three paces did the river make us;   70
   But Hellespont, where Xerxes passed across,
   (A curb still to all human arrogance,)
More hatred from Leander did not suffer
   For rolling between Sestos and Abydos,
   Than that from me, because it oped not then.
"Ye are new-comers; and because I smile,"
   Began she, "peradventure, in this place
   Elect to human nature for its nest,
Some apprehension keeps you marvelling;
   But the psalm *Delectasti* giveth light   80

Which has the power to uncloud your intellect.
And thou who foremost art, and didst entreat me,
   Speak, if thou wouldst hear more; for I came ready
   To all thy questionings, as far as needful."
"The water," said I, "and the forest's sound,
   Are combating within me my new faith
   In something which I heard opposed to this."
Whence she: "I will relate how from its cause
   Proceedeth that which maketh thee to wonder,
   And purge away the cloud that smites upon thee.   90
The Good Supreme, sole in itself delighting,
   Created man good, and this goodly place
   Gave him as hansel of eternal peace.
By his default short while he sojourned here;
   By his default to weeping and to toil
   He changed his innocent laughter and sweet play.
That the disturbance which below is made
   By exhalations of the land and water,
   (Which far as may be follow after heat,)
Might not upon mankind wage any war,   100
   This mount ascended tow'rds the heaven so high,
   And is exempt, from there where it is locked.
Now since the universal atmosphere
   Turns in a circuit with the primal motion
   Unless the circle is broken on some side,
Upon this height, that all is disengaged
   In living ether, doth this motion strike
   And make the forest sound, for it is dense;
And so much power the stricken plant possesses
   That with its virtue it impregns the air,   110
   And this, revolving, scatters it around;
And yonder earth, according as 'tis worthy
   In self or in its clime, conceives and bears
   Of divers qualities the divers trees;
It should not seem a marvel then on earth,
   This being heard, whenever any plant
   Without seed manifest there taketh root.
And thou must know, this holy table-land
   In which thou art is full of every seed,
   And fruit has in it never gathered there.   120
The water which thou seest springs not from vein

Restored by vapour that the cold condenses,
   Like to a stream that gains or loses breath;
But issues from a fountain safe and certain,
   Which by the will of God as much regains
   As it discharges, open on two sides.
Upon this side with virtue it descends,
   Which takes away all memory of sin;
   On that, of every good deed done restores it.
Here Lethe, as upon the other side   130
   Eunoë, it is called; and worketh not
   If first on either side it be not tasted.
This every other savour doth transcend;
   And notwithstanding slaked so far may be
   Thy thirst, that I reveal to thee no more,
I'll give thee a corollary still in grace,
   Nor think my speech will be to thee less dear
   If it spread out beyond my promise to thee.
Those who in ancient times have feigned in song
   The Age of Gold and its felicity,   140
   Dreamed of this place perhaps upon Parnassus.
Here was the human race in innocence;
   Here evermore was Spring, and every fruit;
   This is the nectar of which each one speaks."
Then backward did I turn me wholly round
   Unto my Poets, and saw that with a smile
   They had been listening to these closing words;
Then to the beautiful lady turned mine eyes.

Canto XXIX

Singing like unto an enamoured lady
   She, with the ending of her words, continued:
   "*Beati quorum tecta sunt peccata.*"
And even as Nymphs, that wandered all alone
   Among the sylvan shadows, sedulous
   One to avoid and one to see the sun,
She then against the stream moved onward, going
   Along the bank, and I abreast of her,
   Her little steps with little steps attending.
Between her steps and mine were not a hundred,   10

When equally the margins gave a turn,
  In such a way, that to the East I faced.
Nor even thus our way continued far
  Before the lady wholly turned herself
  Unto me, saying, "Brother, look and listen!"
And lo! a sudden lustre ran across
  On every side athwart the spacious forest,
  Such that it made me doubt if it were lightning.
But since the lightning ceases as it comes,
  And that continuing brightened more and more,   20
  Within my thought I said, "What thing is this?"
And a delicious melody there ran
  Along the luminous air, whence holy zeal
  Made me rebuke the hardihood of Eve;
For there where earth and heaven obedient were,
  The woman only, and but just created,
  Could not endure to stay 'neath any veil;
Underneath which had she devoutly stayed,
  I sooner should have tasted those delights
  Ineffable, and for a longer time.   30
While 'mid such manifold first-fruits I walked
  Of the eternal pleasure all enrapt,
  And still solicitous of more delights,
In front of us like an enkindled fire
  Became the air beneath the verdant boughs,
  And the sweet sound as singing now was heard.
O Virgins sacrosanct! if ever hunger,
  Vigils, or cold for you I have endured,
  The occasion spurs me their reward to claim!
Now Helicon must needs pour forth for me,   40
  And with her choir Urania must assist me,
  To put in verse things difficult to think.
A little farther on, seven trees of gold
  In semblance the long space still intervening
  Between ourselves and them did counterfeit;
But when I had approached so near to them
  The common object, which the sense deceives,
  Lost not by distance any of its marks,
The faculty that lends discourse to reason
  Did apprehend that they were candlesticks,   50
  And in the voices of the song "Hosanna!"

Above them flamed the harness beautiful,
   Far brighter than the moon in the serene
   Of midnight, at the middle of her month.
I turned me round, with admiration filled,
   To good Virgilius, and he answered me
   With visage no less full of wonderment.
Then back I turned my face to those high things,
   Which moved themselves towards us so sedately,
   They had been distanced by new-wedded brides.   60
The lady chid me: "Why dost thou burn only
   So with affection for the living lights,
   And dost not look at what comes after them?"
Then saw I people, as behind their leaders,
   Coming behind them, garmented in white,
   And such a whiteness never was on earth.
The water on my left flank was resplendent,
   And back to me reflected my left side,
   E'en as a mirror, if I looked therein.
When I upon my margin had such post   70
   That nothing but the stream divided us,
   Better to see I gave my steps repose;
And I beheld the flamelets onward go,
   Leaving behind themselves the air depicted,
   And they of trailing pennons had the semblance,
So that it overhead remained distinct
   With sevenfold lists, all of them of the colours
   Whence the sun's bow is made, and Delia's girdle.
These standards to the rearward longer were
   Than was my sight; and, as it seemed to me,   80
   Ten paces were the outermost apart.
Under so fair a heaven as I describe
   The four and twenty Elders, two by two,
   Came on incoronate with flower-de-luce.
They all of them were singing: "Blessed thou
   Among the daughters of Adam art, and blessed
   For evermore shall be thy loveliness."
After the flowers and other tender grasses
   In front of me upon the other margin
   Were disencumbered of that race elect,   90
Even as in heaven star followeth after star,
   There came close after them four animals,

Incoronate each one with verdant leaf.
  Plumed with six wings was every one of them,
    The plumage full of eyes; the eyes of Argus
    If they were living would be such as these.
Reader! to trace their forms no more I waste
    My rhymes; for other spendings press me so,
    That I in this cannot be prodigal.
But read Ezekiel, who depicteth them   100
    As he beheld them from the region cold
    Coming with cloud, with whirlwind, and with fire;
And such as thou shalt find them in his pages,
    Such were they here; saving that in their plumage
    John is with me, and differeth from him.
The interval between these four contained
    A chariot triumphal on two wheels,
    Which by a Griffin's neck came drawn along;
And upward he extended both his wings
    Between the middle list and three and three,   110
    So that he injured none by cleaving it.
So high they rose that they were lost to sight;
    His limbs were gold, so far as he was bird,
    And white the others with vermilion mingled.
Not only Rome with no such splendid car
    E'er gladdened Africanus, or Augustus,
    But poor to it that of the Sun would be,—
That of the Sun, which swerving was burnt up
    At the importunate orison of Earth,
    When Jove was so mysteriously just.   120
Three maidens at the right wheel in a circle
    Came onward dancing; one so very red
    That in the fire she hardly had been noted.
The second was as if her flesh and bones
    Had all been fashioned out of emerald;
    The third appeared as snow but newly fallen.
And now they seemed conducted by the white,
    Now by the red, and from the song of her
    The others took their step, or slow or swift.
Upon the left hand four made holiday   130
    Vested in purple, following the measure
    Of one of them with three eyes in her head.
In rear of all the group here treated of

Two old men I beheld, unlike in habit,
   But like in gait, each dignified and grave.
One showed himself as one of the disciples
   Of that supreme Hippocrates, whom nature
   Made for the animals she holds most dear;
Contrary care the other manifested,
   With sword so shining and so sharp, it caused   140
   Terror to me on this side of the river.
Thereafter four I saw of humble aspect,
   And behind all an aged man alone
   Walking in sleep with countenance acute.
And like the foremost company these seven
   Were habited; yet of the flower-de-luce
   No garland round about the head they wore,
But of the rose, and other flowers vermilion;
   At little distance would the sight have sworn
   That all were in a flame above their brows.   150
And when the car was opposite to me
   Thunder was heard; and all that folk august
   Seemed to have further progress interdicted,
There with the vanward ensigns standing still.

Canto XXX

When the Septentrion of the highest heaven
   (Which never either setting knew or rising,
   Nor veil of other cloud than that of sin,
And which made every one therein aware
   Of his own duty, as the lower makes
   Whoever turns the helm to come to port)
Motionless halted, the veracious people,
   That came at first between it and the Griffin,
   Turned themselves to the car, as to their peace.
And one of them, as if by Heaven commissioned,   10
   Singing, "*Veni, sponsa, de Libano*"
   Shouted three times, and all the others after.
Even as the Blessed at the final summons
   Shall rise up quickened each one from his cavern,
   Uplifting light the reinvested flesh,
So upon that celestial chariot

A hundred rose *ad vocem tanti senis,*
  Ministers and messengers of life eternal.
They all were saying, "*Benedictus qui venis,*"
  And, scattering flowers above and round about,   20
  "*Manibus o date lilia plenis.*"
Ere now have I beheld, as day began,
  The eastern hemisphere all tinged with rose,
  And the other heaven with fair serene adorned;
And the sun's face, uprising, overshadowed
  So that by tempering influence of vapours
  For a long interval the eye sustained it;
Thus in the bosom of a cloud of flowers
  Which from those hands angelical ascended,
  And downward fell again inside and out,   30
Over her snow-white veil with olive cinct
  Appeared a lady under a green mantle,
  Vested in colour of the living flame.
And my own spirit, that already now
  So long a time had been, that in her presence
  Trembling with awe it had not stood abashed,
Without more knowledge having by mine eyes,
  Through occult virtue that from her proceeded
  Of ancient love the mighty influence felt.
As soon as on my vision smote the power   40
  Sublime, that had already pierced me through
  Ere from my boyhood I had yet come forth,
To the left hand I turned with that reliance
  With which the little child runs to his mother,
  When he has fear, or when he is afflicted,
To say unto Virgilius: "Not a drachm
  Of blood remains in me, that does not tremble;
  I know the traces of the ancient flame."
But us Virgilius of himself deprived
  Had left, Virgilius, sweetest of all fathers,   50
  Virgilius, to whom I for safety gave me:
Nor whatsoever lost the ancient mother
  Availed my cheeks now purified from dew,
  That weeping they should not again be darkened.
"Dante, because Virgilius has departed
  Do not weep yet, do not weep yet awhile;
  For by another sword thou need'st must weep."

E'en as an admiral, who on poop and prow
   Comes to behold the people that are working
   In other ships, and cheers them to well-doing,   60
Upon the left hand border of the car,
   When at the sound I turned of my own name,
   Which of necessity is here recorded,
I saw the Lady, who erewhile appeared
   Veiled underneath the angelic festival,
   Direct her eyes to me across the river.
Although the veil, that from her head descended,
   Encircled with the foliage of Minerva,
   Did not permit her to appear distinctly,
In attitude still royally majestic   70
   Continued she, like unto one who speaks,
   And keeps his warmest utterance in reserve:
"Look at me well; in sooth I'm Beatrice!
   How didst thou deign to come unto the Mountain?
   Didst thou not know that man is happy here?"
Mine eyes fell downward into the clear fountain,
   But, seeing myself therein, I sought the grass,
   So great a shame did weigh my forehead down.
As to the son the mother seems superb,
   So she appeared to me; for somewhat bitter   80
   Tasteth the savour of severe compassion.
Silent became she, and the Angels sang
   Suddenly, "*In te, Domine, speravi:*"
   But beyond *pedes meos* did not pass.
Even as the snow among the living rafters
   Upon the back of Italy congeals,
   Blown on and drifted by Sclavonian winds,
And then, dissolving, trickles through itself
   Whene'er the land that loses shadow breathes,
   So that it seems a fire that melts a taper;   90
E'en thus was I without a tear or sigh,
   Before the song of those who sing for ever
   After the music of the eternal spheres.
But when I heard in their sweet melodies
   Compassion for me, more than had they said,
   "O wherefore, lady, dost thou thus upbraid him?"
The ice, that was about my heart congealed,
   To air and water changed, and in my anguish

Through mouth and eyes came gushing from my breast.
She, on the right-hand border of the car　　　　　　　100
　　Still firmly standing, to those holy beings
　　Thus her discourse directed afterwards:
"Ye keep your watch in the eternal day,
　　So that nor night nor sleep can steal from you
　　One step the ages make upon their path;
Therefore my answer is with greater care,
　　That he may hear me who is weeping yonder,
　　So that the sin and dole be of one measure.
Not only by the work of those great wheels,
　　That destine every seed unto some end,　　　　　　110
　　According as the stars are in conjunction,
But by the largess of celestial graces,
　　Which have such lofty vapours for their rain
　　That near to them our sight approaches not,
Such had this man become in his new life
　　Potentially, that every righteous habit
　　Would have made admirable proof in him;
But so much more malignant and more savage
　　Becomes the land untilled and with bad seed,
　　The more good earthly vigour it possesses.　　　　120
Some time did I sustain him with my look;
　　Revealing unto him my youthful eyes,
　　I led him with me turned in the right way.
As soon as ever of my second age
　　I was upon the threshold and changed life,
　　Himself from me he took and gave to others.
When from the flesh to spirit I ascended,
　　And beauty and virtue were in me increased,
　　I was to him less dear and less delightful;
And into ways untrue he turned his steps,　　　　　　130
　　Pursuing the false images of good,
　　That never any promises fulfil;
Nor prayer for inspiration me availed,
　　By means of which in dreams and otherwise
　　I called him back, so little did he heed them.
So low he fell, that all appliances
　　For his salvation were already short,
　　Save showing him the people of perdition.
For this I visited the gates of death,

And unto him, who so far up has led him,   140
   My intercessions were with weeping borne.
God's lofty fiat would be violated,
   If Lethe should be passed, and if such viands
   Should tasted be, withouten any scot
Of penitence, that gushes forth in tears."

Canto XXXI

"O thou who art beyond the sacred river,"
   Turning to me the point of her discourse,
   That edgewise even had seemed to me so keen,
She recommenced, continuing without pause,
   "Say, say if this be true; to such a charge,
   Thy own confession needs must be conjoined."
My faculties were in so great confusion,
   That the voice moved, but sooner was extinct
   Than by its organs it was set at large.
Awhile she waited; then she said: "What thinkest?   10
   Answer me; for the mournful memories
   In thee not yet are by the waters injured."
Confusion and dismay together mingled
   Forced such a Yes! from out my mouth, that sight
   Was needful to the understanding of it.
Even as a cross-bow breaks, when 'tis discharged
   Too tensely drawn the bowstring and the bow,
   And with less force the arrow hits the mark,
So I gave way beneath that heavy burden,
   Outpouring in a torrent tears and sighs,   20
   And the voice flagged upon its passage forth.
Whence she to me: "In those desires of mine
   Which led thee to the loving of that good,
   Beyond which there is nothing to aspire to,
What trenches lying traverse or what chains
   Didst thou discover, that of passing onward
   Thou shouldst have thus despoiled thee of the hope?
And what allurements or what vantages
   Upon the forehead of the others showed,
   That thou shouldst turn thy footsteps unto them?"   30
After the heaving of a bitter sigh,

Hardly had I the voice to make response,
  And with fatigue my lips did fashion it.
Weeping I said: "The things that present were
  With their false pleasure turned aside my steps,
  Soon as your countenance concealed itself."
And she: "Shouldst thou be silent, or deny
  What thou confessest, not less manifest
  Would be thy fault, by such a Judge 'tis known.
But when from one's own cheeks comes bursting forth   40
  The accusal of the sin, in our tribunal
  Against the edge the wheel doth turn itself.
But still, that thou mayst feel a greater shame
  For thy transgression, and another time
  Hearing the Sirens thou mayst be more strong,
Cast down the seed of weeping and attend;
  So shalt thou hear, how in an opposite way
  My buried flesh should have directed thee.
Never to thee presented art or nature
  Pleasure so great as the fair limbs wherein   50
  I was enclosed, which scattered are in earth.
And if the highest pleasure thus did fail thee
  By reason of my death, what mortal thing
  Should then have drawn thee into its desire?
Thou oughtest verily at the first shaft
  Of things fallacious to have risen up
  To follow me, who was no longer such.
Thou oughtest not to have stooped thy pinions downward
  To wait for further blows, or little girl,
  Or other vanity of such brief use.   60
The callow birdlet waits for two or three,
  But to the eyes of those already fledged,
  In vain the net is spread or shaft is shot."
Even as children silent in their shame
  Stand listening with their eyes upon the ground,
  And conscious of their fault, and penitent;
So was I standing; and she said: "If thou
  In hearing sufferest pain, lift up thy beard
  And thou shalt feel a greater pain in seeing."
With less resistance is a robust holm   70
  Uprooted, either by a native wind
  Or else by that from regions of Iarbas,

Than I upraised at her command my chin;
   And when she by the beard the face demanded,
   Well I perceived the venom of her meaning.
And as my countenance was lifted up,
   Mine eye perceived those creatures beautiful
   Had rested from the strewing of the flowers;
And, still but little reassured, mine eyes
   Saw Beatrice turned round towards the monster,   80
   That is one person only in two natures.
Beneath her veil, beyond the margent green,
   She seemed to me far more her ancient self
   To excel, than others here, when she was here.
So pricked me then the thorn of penitence,
   That of all other things the one which turned me
   Most to its love became the most my foe.
Such self-conviction stung me at the heart
   O'erpowered I fell, and what I then became
   She knoweth who had furnished me the cause.   90
Then, when the heart restored my outward sense,
   The lady I had found alone, above me
   I saw, and she was saying, "Hold me, hold me."
Up to my throat she in the stream had drawn me,
   And, dragging me behind her, she was moving
   Upon the water lightly as a shuttle.
When I was near unto the blessed shore,
   "*Asperges me*," I heard so sweetly sung,
   Remember it I cannot, much less write it.
The beautiful lady opened wide her arms,   100
   Embraced my head, and plunged me underneath,
   Where I was forced to swallow of the water.
Then forth she drew me, and all dripping brought
   Into the dance of the four beautiful,
   And each one with her arm did cover me.
"We here are Nymphs, and in the Heaven are stars;
   Ere Beatrice descended to the world,
   We as her handmaids were appointed her.
We'll lead thee to her eyes; but for the pleasant
   Light that within them is, shall sharpen thine   110
   The three beyond, who more profoundly look."
Thus singing they began; and afterwards
   Unto the Griffin's breast they led me with them,

Where Beatrice was standing, turned towards us.
"See that thou dost not spare thine eyes," they said;
    "Before the emeralds have we stationed thee,
    Whence Love aforetime drew for thee his weapons."
A thousand longings, hotter than the flame,
    Fastened mine eyes upon those eyes relucent,
    That still upon the Griffin steadfast stayed.   120
As in a glass the sun, not otherwise
    Within them was the twofold monster shining,
    Now with the one, now with the other nature.
Think, Reader, if within myself I marvelled,
    When I beheld the thing itself stand still,
    And in its image it transformed itself.
While with amazement filled and jubilant,
    My soul was tasting of the food, that while
    It satisfies us makes us hunger for it,
Themselves revealing of the highest rank   130
    In bearing, did the other three advance,
    Singing to their angelic saraband.
"Turn, Beatrice, O turn thy holy eyes,"
    Such was their song, "unto thy faithful one,
    Who has to see thee ta'en so many steps.
In grace do us the grace that thou unveil
    Thy face to him, so that he may discern
    The second beauty which thou dost conceal."
O splendour of the living light eternal!
    Who underneath the shadow of Parnassus   140
    Has grown so pale, or drunk so at its cistern,
He would not seem to have his mind encumbered
    Striving to paint thee as thou didst appear,
    Where the harmonious heaven o'ershadowed thee,
When in the open air thou didst unveil?

Canto XXXII

So steadfast and attentive were mine eyes
    In satisfying their decennial thirst,
    That all my other senses were extinct,
And upon this side and on that they had
    Walls of indifference, so the holy smile

Drew them unto itself with the old net;
When forcibly my sight was turned away
   Towards my left hand by those goddesses,
   Because I heard from them a "Too intently!"
And that condition of the sight which is   10
   In eyes but lately smitten by the sun
   Bereft me of my vision some short while;
But to the less when sight re-shaped itself,
   I say the less in reference to the greater
   Splendour from which perforce I had withdrawn,
I saw upon its right wing wheeled about
   The glorious host, returning with the sun
   And with the sevenfold flames upon their faces.
As underneath its shields, to save itself,
   A squadron turns, and with its banner wheels,   20
   Before the whole thereof can change its front,
That soldiery of the celestial kingdom
   Which marched in the advance had wholly passed us
   Before the chariot had turned its pole.
Then to the wheels the maidens turned themselves,
   And the Griffin moved his burden benedight,
   But so that not a feather of him fluttered.
The lady fair who drew me through the ford
   Followed with Statius and myself the wheel
   Which made its orbit with the lesser arc.   30
So passing through the lofty forest, vacant
   By fault of her who in the serpent trusted,
   Angelic music made our steps keep time.
Perchance as great a space had in three flights
   An arrow loosened from the string o'erpassed,
   As we had moved when Beatrice descended.
I heard them murmur altogether, "Adam!"
   Then circled they about a tree despoiled
   Of blooms and other leafage on each bough.
Its tresses, which so much the more dilate   40
   As higher they ascend, had been by Indians
   Among their forests marvelled at for height.
"Blessed art thou, O Griffin, who dost not
   Pluck with thy beak these branches sweet to taste,
   Since appetite by this was turned to evil."
After this fashion round the tree robust

The others shouted; and the twofold creature:
    "Thus is preserved the seed of all the just."
And turning to the pole which he had dragged,
    He drew it close beneath the widowed bough,   50
    And what was of it unto it left bound.
In the same manner as our trees (when downward
    Falls the great light, with that together mingled
    Which after the celestial Lasca shines)
Begin to swell, and then renew themselves,
    Each one with its own colour, ere the Sun
    Harness his steeds beneath another star:
Less than of rose and more than violet
    A hue disclosing, was renewed the tree
    That had erewhile its boughs so desolate.   60
I never heard, nor here below is sung,
    The hymn which afterward that people sang,
    Nor did I bear the melody throughout.
Had I the power to paint how fell asleep
    Those eyes compassionless, of Syrinx hearing,
    Those eyes to which more watching cost so dear,
Even as a painter who from model paints
    I would portray how I was lulled asleep;
    He may, who well can picture drowsihood.
Therefore I pass to what time I awoke,   70
    And say a splendour rent from me the veil
    Of slumber, and a calling: "Rise, what dost thou?"
As to behold the apple-tree in blossom
    Which makes the Angels greedy for its fruit,
    And keeps perpetual bridals in the Heaven,
Peter and John and James conducted were,
    And, overcome, recovered at the word
    By which still greater slumbers have been broken,
And saw their school diminished by the loss
    Not only of Elias, but of Moses,   80
    And the apparel of their Master changed;
So I revived, and saw that piteous one
    Above me standing, who had been conductress
    Aforetime of my steps beside the river,
And all in doubt I said, "Where's Beatrice?"
    And she: "Behold her seated underneath
    The leafage new, upon the root of it.

Behold the company that circles her;
    The rest behind the Griffin are ascending
    With more melodious song, and more profound."   90
And if her speech were more diffuse I know not,
    Because already in my sight was she
    Who from the hearing of aught else had shut me.
Alone she sat upon the very earth,
    Left there as guardian of the chariot
    Which I had seen the biform monster fasten.
Encircling her, a cloister made themselves
    The seven Nymphs, with those lights in their hands
    Which are secure from Aquilon and Auster.
"Short while shalt thou be here a forester,   100
    And thou shalt be with me for evermore
    A citizen of that Rome where Christ is Roman.
Therefore, for that world's good which liveth ill,
    Fix on the car thine eyes, and what thou seest,
    Having returned to earth, take heed thou write."
Thus Beatrice; and I, who at the feet
    Of her commandments all devoted was,
    My mind and eyes directed where she willed.
Never descended with so swift a motion
    Fire from a heavy cloud, when it is raining   110
    From out the region which is most remote,
As I beheld the bird of Jove descend
    Down through the tree, rending away the bark,
    As well as blossoms and the foliage new,
And he with all his might the chariot smote,
    Whereat it reeled, like vessel in a tempest
    Tossed by the waves, now starboard and now larboard.
Thereafter saw I leap into the body
    Of the triumphal vehicle a Fox,
    That seemed unfed with any wholesome food.   120
But for his hideous sins upbraiding him,
    My Lady put him to as swift a flight
    As such a fleshless skeleton could bear.
Then by the way that it before had come,
    Into the chariot's chest I saw the Eagle
    Descend, and leave it feathered with his plumes.
And such as issues from a heart that mourns,
    A voice from Heaven there issued, and it said:

    "My little bark, how badly art thou freighted!"
Methought, then, that the earth did yawn between   130
    Both wheels, and I saw rise from it a Dragon,
    Who through the chariot upward fixed his tail,
And as a wasp that draweth back its sting,
    Drawing unto himself his tail malign,
    Drew out the floor, and went his way rejoicing.
That which remained behind, even as with grass
    A fertile region, with the feathers, offered
    Perhaps with pure intention and benign,
Reclothed itself, and with them were reclothed
    The pole and both the wheels so speedily,   140
    A sigh doth longer keep the lips apart.
Transfigured thus the holy edifice
    Thrust forward heads upon the parts of it,
    Three on the pole and one at either corner.
The first were horned like oxen; but the four
    Had but a single horn upon the forehead;
    A monster such had never yet been seen!
Firm as a rock upon a mountain high,
    Seated upon it, there appeared to me
    A shameless whore, with eyes swift glancing round,   150
And, as if not to have her taken from him,
    Upright beside her I beheld a giant;
    And ever and anon they kissed each other.
But because she her wanton, roving eye
    Turned upon me, her angry paramour
    Did scourge her from her head unto her feet.
Then full of jealousy, and fierce with wrath,
    He loosed the monster, and across the forest
    Dragged it so far, he made of that alone
A shield unto the whore and the strange beast.   160

Canto XXXIII

"*Deus, venerunt gentes,*" alternating
    Now three, now four, melodious psalmody
    The maidens in the midst of tears began;
And Beatrice, compassionate and sighing,
    Listened to them with such a countenance,

That scarce more changed was Mary at the cross.
But when the other virgins place had given
    For her to speak, uprisen to her feet
    With colour as of fire, she made response:
"*Modicum, et non videbitis me;*   10
    Et iterum, my sisters predilect,
    Modicum, et vos videbitis me."
Then all the seven in front of her she placed;
    And after her, by beckoning only, moved
    Me and the lady and the sage who stayed.
So she moved onward; and I do not think
    That her tenth step was placed upon the ground,
    When with her eyes upon mine eyes she smote,
And with a tranquil aspect, "Come more quickly,"
    To me she said, "that, if I speak with thee,   20
    To listen to me thou mayst be well placed."
As soon as I was with her as I should be,
    She said to me: "Why, brother, dost thou not
    Venture to question now, in coming with me?"
As unto those who are too reverential,
    Speaking in presence of superiors,
    Who drag no living utterance to their teeth,
It me befell, that without perfect sound
    Began I: "My necessity, Madonna,
    You know, and that which thereunto is good."   30
And she to me: "Of fear and bashfulness
    Henceforward I will have thee strip thyself,
    So that thou speak no more as one who dreams.
Know that the vessel which the serpent broke
    Was, and is not; but let him who is guilty
    Think that God's vengeance does not fear a sop.
Without an heir shall not for ever be
    The Eagle that left his plumes upon the car,
    Whence it became a monster, then a prey;
For verily I see, and hence narrate it,   .   40
    The stars already near to bring the time,
    From every hindrance safe, and every bar,
Within which a Five-hundred, Ten, and Five,
    One sent from God, shall slay the thievish woman
    And that same giant who is sinning with her.
And peradventure my dark utterance,

Like Themis and the Sphinx, may less persuade thee,
　　Since, in their mode, it clouds the intellect;
But soon the facts shall be the Naiades
　　Who shall this difficult enigma solve,　　　　　　　　　　50
　　Without destruction of the flocks and harvests.
Note thou; and even as by me are uttered
　　These words, so teach them unto those who live
　　That life which is a running unto death;
And bear in mind, whene'er thou writest them,
　　Not to conceal what thou hast seen the plant,
　　That twice already has been pillaged here.
Whoever pillages or shatters it,
　　With blasphemy of deed offendeth God,
　　Who made it holy for his use alone.　　　　　　　　　　60
For biting that, in pain and in desire
　　Five thousand years and more the first-born soul
　　Craved Him, who punished in himself the bite.
Thy genius slumbers, if it deem it not
　　For special reason so pre-eminent
　　In height, and so inverted in its summit.
And if thy vain imaginings had not been
　　Water of Elsa round about thy mind,
　　And Pyramus to the mulberry, their pleasure,
Thou by so many circumstances only　　　　　　　　　　70
　　The justice of the interdict of God
　　Morally in the tree wouldst recognize.
But since I see thee in thine intellect
　　Converted into stone and stained with sin,
　　So that the light of my discourse doth daze thee,
I will too, if not written, at least painted,
　　Thou bear it back within thee, for the reason
　　That cinct with palm the pilgrim's staff is borne."
And I: "As by a signet is the wax
　　Which does not change the figure stamped upon it,　　　　　80
　　My brain is now imprinted by yourself.
But wherefore so beyond my power of sight
　　Soars your desirable discourse, that aye
　　The more I strive, so much the more I lose it?"
"That thou mayst recognize," she said, "the school
　　Which thou hast followed, and mayst see how far
　　Its doctrine follows after my discourse,

And mayst behold your path from the divine
    Distant as far as separated is
    From earth the heaven that highest hastens on."   90
Whence her I answered: "I do not remember
    That ever I estranged myself from you,
    Nor have I conscience of it that reproves me."
"And if thou art not able to remember,"
    Smiling she answered, "recollect thee now
    That thou this very day hast drunk of Lethe;
And if from smoke a fire may be inferred,
    Such an oblivion clearly demonstrates
    Some error in thy will elsewhere intent.
Truly from this time forward shall my words   100
    Be naked, so far as it is befitting
    To lay them open unto thy rude gaze."
And more coruscant and with slower steps
    The sun was holding the meridian circle,
    Which, with the point of view, shifts here and there,
When halted (as he cometh to a halt,
    Who goes before a squadron as its escort,
    If something new he find upon his way)
The ladies seven at a dark shadow's edge,
    Such as, beneath green leaves and branches black,   110
    The Alp upon its frigid border wears.
In front of them the Tigris and Euphrates
    Methought I saw forth issue from one fountain,
    And slowly part, like friends, from one another.
"O light, O glory of the human race!
    What stream is this which here unfolds itself
    From out one source, and from itself withdraws?"
For such a prayer, 'twas said unto me, "Pray
    Matilda that she tell thee;" and here answered,
    As one does who doth free himself from blame,   120
The beautiful lady: "This and other things
    Were told to him by me; and sure I am
    The water of Lethe has not hid them from him."
And Beatrice: "Perhaps a greater care,
    Which oftentimes our memory takes away,
    Has made the vision of his mind obscure.
But Eunoë behold, that yonder rises;
    Lead him to it, and, as thou art accustomed,

Revive again the half-dead virtue in him."
Like gentle soul, that maketh no excuse,   130
  But makes its own will of another's will
  As soon as by a sign it is disclosed,
Even so, when she had taken hold of me,
  The beautiful lady moved, and unto Statius
  Said, in her womanly manner, "Come with him."
If, Reader, I possessed a longer space
  For writing it, I yet would sing in part
  Of the sweet draught that ne'er would satiate me;
But inasmuch as full are all the leaves
  Made ready for this second canticle,   140
  The curb of art no farther lets me go.
From the most holy water I returned
  Regenerate, in the manner of new trees
  That are renewed with a new foliage,
Pure and disposed to mount unto the stars.

NOTES TO PURGATORIO

NOTES TO PURGATORIO

Canto I

1. The Mountain of Purgatory is a vast conical mountain, rising steep and high from the waters of the Southern Ocean, at a point antipodal to Mount Sion in Jerusalem. In Canto III. 14, Dante speaks of it as

> "The hill
> That highest tow'rds the heaven uplifts itself";

and in *Paradiso,* XXVI. 139, as

> "The mount that rises highest o'er the wave."

Around it run seven terraces, on which are punished severally the Seven Deadly Sins. Rough stairways, cut in the rock, lead up from terrace to terrace, and on the summit is the garden of the Terrestrial Paradise.

The Seven Sins punished in the Seven Circles are,—1. Pride; 2. Envy; 3. Anger; 4. Sloth; 5. Avarice and Prodigality; 6. Gluttony; 7. Lust.

The threefold division of the Purgatorio, marked only by more elaborate preludes, or by a natural pause in the action of the poem, is,—1. From Canto I. to Canto IX.; 2. From Canto IX. to Canto XXVIII.; 3. From Canto XXVIII. to the end. The first of these divisions describes the region lying outside the gate of Purgatory; the second, the Seven Circles of the mountain; and the third, the Terrestrial Paradise on its summit.

"Traces of belief in a Purgatory," says Mr. Alger, *Doctrine of a Future Life,* p. 410, "early appear among the Christians. Many of the gravest Fathers of the first five centuries naturally conceived and taught,—as is indeed intrinsically reasonable,—that after death some souls will be punished for their sins until they are cleansed, and then will be released from pain. The Manichæans imagined that all souls, before returning to their native heaven, must be borne first to the moon, where with good waters they would be washed pure from outward filth, and then to the sun, where they would be purged by good fires from every inward stain. After these lunar and solar lustrations, they were fit for the eternal world of light. But the conception of Purgatory as it was held by the early Christians, whether orthodox Fathers or heretical sects, was

merely the just and necessary result of applying to the subject of future pun-
ishment the two ethical ideas that punishment should partake of degrees
proportioned to guilt, and that it should be restorative. . . . .

"Pope Gregory the Great, in the sixth century,—either borrowing some
of the more objectionable features of the Purgatory-doctrine previously held
by the heathen, or else devising the same things himself from a perception
of the striking adaptedness of such notions to secure an enviable power to
the Church,—constructed, established, and gave working efficiency to the
dogmatic scheme of Purgatory ever since firmly defended by the Papal
adherents as an integral part of the Roman Catholic system. The doctrine as
matured and promulgated by Gregory, giving to the representatives of the
Church an almost unlimited power over Purgatory, rapidly grew into favour
with the clergy, and sank with general conviction into the hopes and fears
of the laity."

9. The Muse "of the beautiful voice," who presided over eloquence and
heroic verse.

11. The nine daughters of Pierus, king of Macedonia, called the Pierides.
They challenged the Muses to a trial of skill in singing, and being van-
quished were changed by Apollo into magpies. Ovid, *Met.* V., Maynwaring's
Tr.:—

> "Beneath their nails
> Feathers they feel, and on their faces scales;
> Their horny beaks at once each other scare,
> Their arms are plumed, and on their backs they bear
> Pied wings, and flutter in the fleeting air.
> Chatt'ring, the scandal of the woods, they fly,
> And there continue still their clam'rous cry:
> The same their eloquence, as maids or birds,
> Now only noise, and nothing then but words."

15. The highest heaven.
19. The planet Venus.
20. Chaucer, *Knightes Tale*:—

> "The besy larke, the messager of day,
>   Saleweth in hire song the morwe gray,
>   And firy Phebus riseth up so bright,
>   That all the orient laugheth of the sight."

23. The stars of the Southern Cross. Figuratively the four cardinal vir-
tues, Justice, Prudence, Fortitude, and Temperance. See Canto XXXI.
106:—

> "We here are Nymphs, and in the Heaven are stars."

The next line may be interpreted in the same figurative sense.

Humboldt, *Personal Narrative,* II. 21, Miss Williams's Tr., thus describes his first glimpse of the Southern Cross.

"The pleasure we felt on discovering the Southern Cross was warmly shared by such of the crew as had lived in the colonies. In the solitude of the seas, we hail a star as a friend from whom we have long been separated. Among the Portuguese and Spaniards peculiar motives seem to increase this feeling; a religious sentiment attaches them to a constellation, the form of which recalls the sign of the faith planted by their ancestors in the deserts of the New World.

"The two great stars which mark the summit and the foot of the Cross having nearly the same right ascension, it follows hence, that the constellation is almost perpendicular at the moment when it passes the meridian. This circumstance is known to every nation that lives beyond the tropics, or in the Southern hemisphere. It has been observed at what hour of the night, in different seasons, the Cross of the South is erect or inclined. It is a timepiece that advances very regularly near four minutes a day, and no other group of stars exhibits, to the naked eye, an observation of time so easily made. How often have we heard our guides exclaim in the savannahs of Venezuela, or in the desert extending from Lima to Truxillo, 'Midnight is past, the Cross begins to bend!' How often those words reminded us of that affecting scene, where Paul and Virginia, seated near the source of the river of Lataniers, conversed together for the last time, and where the old man, at the sight of the Southern Cross, warns them that it is time to separate."

24. By the "primal people" Dante does not mean our first parents, but "the early races which inhabited Europe and Asia," says Dr. Barlow, *Study of Dante,* and quotes in confirmation of his view the following passage from Humboldt's *Cosmos,* II.:

"In consequence of the precession of the equinoxes, the starry heavens are continually changing their aspect from every portion of the earth's surface. The early races of mankind beheld in the far north the glorious constellations of the southern hemisphere rise before them, which, after remaining long invisible, will again appear in those latitudes after a lapse of thousands of years. . . . . The Southern Cross began to become invisible in 52° 30' north latitude 2900 years before our era, since, according to Galle, this constellation might previously have reached an altitude of more than 10°. When it disappeared from the horizon of the countries of the Baltic, the great Pyramid of Cheops had already been erected more than 500 years."

30. *Iliad,* XVIII.: "The Pleiades, and the Hyades, and the strength of Orion, and the Bear, which likewise they call by the appellation of the Wain, which there turns round and watches Orion; and it alone is deprived of the baths of Oceanus."

31. Cato of Utica. "Pythagoras escapes, in the fabulous hell of Dante," says Sir Thomas Browne, *Urn Burial,* IV., "among that swarm of philosophers,

wherein, whilst we meet with Plato and Socrates, Cato is found in no lower place than Purgatory."

In the description of the shield of Æneas, *Æneid*, VIII., Cato is represented as presiding over the good in the Tartarean realms: "And the good apart, Cato dispensing laws to them." This line of Virgil may have suggested to Dante the idea of making Cato the warden of Purgatory.

In the *Convito*, IV. 28, he expresses the greatest reverence for him. Marcia returning to him in her widowhood, he says, "symbolizes the noble soul returning to God in old age." And continues: "What man on earth was more worthy to symbolize God, than Cato? Surely none";—ending the chapter with these words: "In his name it is beautiful to close what I have had to say of the signs of nobility, because in him this nobility displays them all through all ages."

Here, on the shores of Purgatory, his countenance is adorned with the light of the four stars, which are the four virtues, Justice, Prudence, Fortitude, and Temperance, and it is foretold of him, that his garments will shine brightly on the last day. And here he is the symbol of Liberty, since, for her sake, to him "not bitter was death in Utica"; and the meaning of Purgatory is spiritual Liberty, or freedom from sin through purification, "the glorious liberty of the children of God." Therefore in thus selecting the "Divine Cato" for the guardian of this realm, Dante shows himself to have greater freedom than the critics, who accuse him of "a perverse theology in saving the soul of an idolater and suicide."

40. The "blind river" is Lethe, which by sound and not by sight had guided them through the winding cavern from the centre of the earth to the surface. *Inf.* XXXIV. 130.

42. His beard. Ford, *Lady's Trial*:

> "Now the down
> Of softness is exchanged for plumes of age."

Dante uses the same expression, *Inf.* XX. 45, and Petrarca, who became gray at an early period, says:

> "In such a tenebrous and narrow cage
> Were we shut up, and the accustomed plumes
> I changed betimes, and my first countenance."

52. Upon this speech of Virgil to Cato, Dr. Barlow, *Study of Dante,* remarks: "The eighth book of the Tesoro of Brunetto Latini is headed *Qui comincia la Rettorica che c' insegna a ben parlare, e di governare città e popoli.* In this art Dante was duly instructed by his loving master, and became the most able orator of his era in Italy. Giov. Villani speaks of him as *retorico perfetto tanto in dittare e versificare come in aringhiera parlare.* But without this record and without acquaintance with the poet's political history, knowing nothing of his influence in

debates and councils, nor of his credit at foreign courts, we might, from the occasional speeches in the Divina Commedia, be fully assured of the truth of what Villani has said, and that Dante's words and manner were always skilfully adapted to the purpose he had in view, and to the persons whom he addressed.

"Virgil's speech to the venerable Cato is a perfect specimen of persuasive eloquence. The sense of personal dignity is here combined with extreme courtesy and respect, and the most flattering appeals to the old man's well-known sentiments, his love of liberty, his love of rectitude, and his devoted attachment to Marcia, are interwoven with irresistible art; but though the resentment of Cato at the approach of the strangers is thus appeased, and he is persuaded to regard them with as much favour as the severity of his character permits, yet he will not have them think that his consent to their proceeding has been obtained by adulation, but simply by the assertion of power vouchsafed to them from on high,—

> Ma se donna del Ciel ti muove e regge,
> Come tu di', non c' è mestier lusinga:
> Bastiti ben, che per lei mi richegge.

In this also the consistency of Cato's character is maintained; he is sensible of the flattery, but disowns its influence."

77. See *Inf.* V. 4.

78. See *Inf.* IV. 128. Also *Convito,* IV. 28: "This the great poet Lucan shadows forth in the second book of his Pharsalia, when he says that Marcia returned to Cato, and besought him and entreated him to take her back in his old age. And by this Marcia is understood the noble soul."

Lucan, *Phars.,* II., Rowe's Tr.:—

> "When lo! the sounding doors are heard to turn,
> Chaste Martia comes from dead Hortensius' urn.
>
> . . . . .
>
> Forth from the monument the mournful dame
> With beaten breasts and locks dishevelled came;
> Then with a pale, dejected, rueful look,
> Thus pleasing to her former lord she spoke.
>
> . . . . .
>
> 'At length a barren wedlock let me prove,
> Give me the name without the joys of love;
> No more to be abandoned let me come,
> That Cato's wife may live upon my tomb.'"

95. A symbol of humility. Ruskin, *Mod. Painters,* III. 232, says: "There is a still deeper significance in the passage quoted, a little while ago, from Homer,

describing Ulysses casting himself down on the *rushes* and the corn-giving land at the river shore,—the rushes and corn being to him only good for rest and sustenance,—when we compare it with that in which Dante tells us he was ordered to descend to the shore of the lake as he entered Purgatory, to gather a *rush,* and gird himself with it, it being to him the emblem not only of rest, but of humility under chastisement, the rush (or reed) being the only plant which can grow there;—'no plant which bears leaves, or hardens its bark, can live on that shore, because it does not yield to the chastisement of its waves.' It cannot but strike the reader singularly how deep and harmonious a significance runs through all these words of Dante,—how every syllable of them, the more we penetrate it, becomes a seed of farther thought! For follow up this image of the girding with the reed, under trial, and see to whose feet it will lead us. As the grass of the earth, thought of as the herb yielding seed, leads us to the place where our Lord commanded the multitude to sit down by companies upon the green grass; so the grass of the waters, thought of as sustaining itself among the waters of affliction, leads us to the place where a stem of it was put into our Lord's hand for his sceptre; and in the crown of thorns, and the rod of reed, was foreshown the everlasting truth of the Christian ages,—that all glory was to be begun in suffering, and all power in humility."

115. Ruskin, *Mod. Painters,* III. 248: "There is only one more point to be noticed in the Dantesque landscape; namely, the feeling entertained by the poet towards the sky. And the love of mountains is so closely connected with the love of clouds, the sublimity of both depending much on their association, that, having found Dante regardless of the Carrara mountains as seen from San Miniato, we may well expect to find him equally regardless of the clouds in which the sun sank behind them. Accordingly, we find that his only pleasure in the sky depends on its 'white clearness,'—that turning into *bianco aspetto di celestro,* which is so peculiarly characteristic of fine days in Italy. His pieces of pure pale light are always exquisite. In the dawn on the purgatorial mountain, first, in its pale white, he sees the *tremolar della marina,*—— trembling of the sea; then it becomes vermilion; and at last, near sunrise, orange. These are precisely the changes of a calm and perfect dawn. The scenery of Paradise begins with 'day added to day,' the light of the sun so flooding the heavens, that 'never rain nor river made lake so wide'; and throughout the Paradise all the beauty depends on spheres of light, or stars, never on clouds. But the pit of the Inferno is at first sight obscure, deep, and so *cloudy* that at its bottom nothing could be seen. When Dante and Virgil reach the marsh in which the souls of those who have been angry and sad in their lives are forever plunged, they find it covered with thick fog; and the condemned souls say to them,

> 'We once were sad,
> In the *sweet air, made gladsome by the sun.*
> Now in these murky settlings are we sad.'

Even the angel crossing the marsh to help them is annoyed by this bitter marsh smoke, *fummo acerbo,* and continually sweeps it with his hand from before his face."

123. Some commentators interpret *Ove adorezza,* by "where the wind blows." But the blowing of the wind would produce an effect exactly opposite to that here described.

135. *Æneid,* VI.: "When the first is torn off, a second of gold succeeds; and a twig shoots forth leaves of the same metal."

Canto II

1. It was sunset at Jerusalem, night on the Ganges, and morning at the Mountain of Purgatory.

The sun being in Aries, the night would "come forth with the scales," or the sign of Libra, which is opposite Aries. These scales fall from the hand of night, or are not above the horizon by night, when the night exceeds, or is longer than the day.

7. Boccaccio, *Decamerone,* Prologue to the Third Day, imitates this passage: "The Aurora, as the sun drew nigh, was already beginning to change from vermilion to orange."

31. Argument used in the sense of means, or appliances, as in *Inf.* XXXI. 55.

44. Cervantes says in *Don Quixote,* Pt. I. ch. 12, that the student Crisostomo "had a face like a benediction."

57. Sackville, in his *Induction* to the *Mirror for Magistrates,* says:

> "Whiles Scorpio dreading Sagittarius' dart
> Whose bow prest bent in fight the string had slipped,
> Down slid into the ocean flood apart."

80. *Odyssey,* XI., Buckley's Tr.: "But I, meditating in my mind, wished to lay hold of the soul of my departed mother. Thrice indeed I essayed it, and my mind urged me to lay hold of it, but thrice it flew from my hands, like unto a shadow, or even to a dream."

And *Æneid,* VI., Davidson's Tr.: "There thrice he attempted to throw his arms around his neck; thrice the phantom, grasped in vain, escaped his hold, like the fleet gales, or resembling most a fugitive dream."

91. Casella was a Florentine musician and friend of Dante, who here speaks to him with so much tenderness and affection as to make us regret that nothing more is known of him. Milton alludes to him in his Sonnet to Mr. H. Lawes:—

> "Dante shall give Fame leave to set thee higher
> Than his Casella, whom he woo'd to sing
> Met in the milder shades of Purgatory."

98. The first three months of the year of Jubilee, 1300. Milman, *Hist. Latin Christ.*, VI. 285, thus describes it: "All Europe was in a frenzy of religious zeal. Throughout the year the roads in the remotest parts of Germany, Hungary, Britain, were crowded with pilgrims of all ages, of both sexes. A Savoyard above one hundred years old determined to see the tombs of the Apostles before he died. There were at times two hundred thousand strangers at Rome. During the year (no doubt the calculations were loose and vague) the city was visited by millions of pilgrims. At one time, so vast was the press both within and without the walls, that openings were broken for ingress and egress. Many people were trampled down, and perished by suffocation. . . . . Lodgings were exorbitantly dear, forage scarce; but the ordinary food of man, bread, meat, wine, and fish, was sold in great plenty and at moderate prices. The oblations were beyond calculation. It is reported by an eyewitness that two priests stood with rakes in their hands sweeping the uncounted gold and silver from the altars. Nor was this tribute, like offerings or subsidies for Crusades, to be devoted to special uses, the accoutrements, provisions, freight of armies. It was entirely at the free and irresponsible disposal of the Pope. Christendom of its own accord was heaping at the Pope's feet this extraordinary custom; and receiving back the gift of pardon and everlasting life."

See also *Inf.* XVIII., Note 29.

100. The sea-shore of Ostia at the mouth of the Tiber, where the souls of those who were saved assembled, and were received by the Celestial Pilot, who transported them to the island of Purgatory. Minutius Felix, a Roman lawyer of the third century, makes it the scene of his *Octavius,* and draws this pleasant picture of the sands and the sea. Reeves's Tr., p. 37:—

"It was vacation-time, and that gave me aloose from my business at the bar; for it was the season after the summer's heat, when autumn promised fair, and put on the face of temperate. We set out, therefore, in the morning early, and as we were walking upon the seashore, and a kindly breeze fanned and refreshed our limbs, and the yielding sand softly submitted to our feet and made it delicious travelling, Cæcilius on a sudden espied the statue of Serapis, and, according to the vulgar mode of superstition, raised his hand to his mouth, and paid his adoration in kisses. Upon which Octavius, addressing himself to me, said: 'It is not well done, my brother Marcus, thus to leave your inseparable companion in the depth of vulgar darkness, and to suffer him, in so clear a day, to stumble upon stones; stones, indeed, of figure, and anointed with oil, and crowned; but stones, however, still they are;—for you cannot but be sensible that your permitting so foul an error in your friend redounds no less to your disgrace than his.' This discourse of his held us through half the city; and now we began to find ourselves upon the free and open shore. There the gently washing waves had spread the extremest sands into the order of an artificial walk; and as the sea always expresses some roughness in his looks, even when the winds are still, although he did not roll in foam and angry surges to the shore, yet were we much delighted, as we walked upon the edges of the water, to see the crisping, frizzly waves glide in snaky folds, one while playing against our feet, and then again retiring and lost in the devouring ocean. Softly, then, and calmly as the sea about us, we travelled on, and kept upon the brim of the gently declining shore, beguiling the way with our stories."

112. This is the first line of the second *canzone* of the *Convito*.

Canto III

15. So in *Paradiso*, XXVI. 139:—

"The mount that rises highest o'er the sea."

27. The tomb of Virgil is on the promontory of Pausilippo, overlooking the Bay of Naples. The inscription upon it is:—

Mantua me genuit: Calabri rapuere: tenet nunc
Parthenope: cecini pascua, rura, duces.

"The epitaph," says Eustace, *Classical Tour*, I. 499, "which, though not genuine, is yet ancient, was inscribed by order of the Duke of Pescolangiano, then proprietor of the place, on a marble slab placed in the side of the rock opposite the entrance of the tomb, where it still remains."

Forsyth, *Italy*, p. 378, says: "*Virgil's tomb* is so called, I believe, on the single authority of Donatus. Donatus places it at the right distance from Naples, but on the wrong side of the city; and even there he omits the grotto of Posilipo, which not being so deep in his time as the two last excavations have left it, must have opened precisely at his tomb. Donatus, too, gives, for Virgil's own composition, an epitaph on the cliff now rejected as a forgery. And who is this Donatus?—an obscure grammarian, or rather his counterfeit. The structure itself resembles a ruined pigeon-house, where the numerous *columbaria* would indicate a family-sepulchre: but who should repose in the tomb of Virgil, but Virgil alone? Visitors of every nation, kings and princes, have scratched their names on the stucco of this apocryphal ruin, but the poet's awful name seems to have deterred them from versifying here."

37. Be satisfied with knowing that a thing is, without asking why it is. These were distinguished in scholastic language as the *Demonstratio quia,* and the *Demonstratio propter quid*.

49. Places on the mountainous seaside road from Genoa to Pisa, known as the *Riviera di Levante*. Of this, Mr. Ruskin, *Mod. Painters*, III. 243, says:—

"The similes by which he illustrates the steepness of that ascent are all taken from the Riviera of Genoa, now traversed by a good carriage road under the name of the Cornice; but as this road did not exist in Dante's time, and the steep precipices and promontories were then probably traversed by footpaths, which, as they necessarily passed in many places over crumbling and slippery limestone, were doubtless not a little dangerous, and as in the manner they commanded the bays of sea below, and lay exposed to the full blaze of the south-eastern sun, they corresponded precisely to the situation of the path by which he ascends above the purgatorial sea, the image could not possibly have been taken from a better source for the fully conveying his idea to the reader: nor, by the way, is there reason to discredit, in *this* place, his powers of climbing; for, with his usual accuracy, he has taken the angle of the path for us, saying it was considerably more than forty-five. Now a continuous mountain-slope of forty-five degrees is already quite unsafe either for ascent or descent, except by zigzag paths; and a greater slope than this could not be climbed, straightforward, but by help of crevices or jags in the rock, and great physical exertion besides."

Mr. Norton, *Travel and Study,* p. 1, thus describes the Riviera: "The Var forms the geographical boundary between France and Italy; but it is not till Nice is left behind, and the first height of the Riviera is surmounted, that the real Italy begins. Here the hills close round at the north, and suddenly, as the road turns at the top of a long ascent, the Mediterranean appears far below, washing the feet of the mountains that form the coast, and stretching away to the Southern horizon. The line of the shore is of extraordinary beauty. Here an abrupt cliff rises from the sea; here bold and broken masses of rock jut out into it; here the hills, their gray sides terraced for vineyards, slope gently down to the water's edge; here they stretch into little promontories covered with orange and olive-trees.

"One of the first of these promontories is that of Capo Sant' Ospizio. A close grove of olives half conceals the old castle on its extreme point. With the afternoon sun full upon it, the trees palely glimmering as their leaves move in the light air, the sea so blue and smooth as to be like a darker sky, and not even a ripple upon the beach, it seems as if this were the very home of summer and of repose. It is remote and secluded from the stir and noise of the world. No road is seen leading to it, and one looks down upon the solitary castle and wonders what stories of enchantment and romance belong to a ruin that appears as if made for their dwelling-place. It is a scene out of that Italy which is the home of the imagination, and which becomes the Italy of memory.

"As the road winds down to the sea, it passes under a high isolated peak, on which stands Esa, built as a city of refuge against pirates and Moors. A little farther on,

> 'Its Roman strength Turbia showed
> In ruins by the mountain road,'—

not only recalling the ancient times, when it was the boundary city of Italy and Gaul, and when Augustus erected his triumphal arch within it, but associated also with Dante and the steep of Purgatory. Beneath lies Monaco, glowing 'like a gem' on its oval rock, the sea sparkling around it, and the long western rays of the sinking sun lingering on its little palace, clinging to its church belfry and its gray wall, as if loath to leave them."

In the Casa Magni, on the sea-shore near Lerici, Shelley once lived. He was returning thither from Leghorn, when he perished in a sudden storm at sea.

67. After they had gone a mile, they were still a stone's throw distant.

82. See *Convito*, I. 10.

112. Manfredi, king of Apulia and Sicily, was a natural son of the Emperor Frederick the Second. He was slain at the battle of Benevento, in 1265; one of the great and decisive battles of the Guelphs and Ghibellines, the Guelph or Papal forces being commanded by Charles of Anjou, and the Ghibellines or Imperialists by Manfredi.

Malispini, *Storia*, ch. 187, thus describes his death and burial: "Manfredi, being left with few followers, behaved like a valiant gentleman who preferred to die in battle rather than to escape with shame. And putting on his helmet, which had on it a silver eagle for a crest, this eagle fell on the saddle-bow before him; and seeing this he was greatly disturbed, and said in Latin to the barons who were near him, '*Hoc est signum Dei;* for this crest I fastened on with my own hands in such a way that it could not fall.' But he was not discouraged, and took heart, and went into battle like any other baron, without the royal insignia, in order not to be recognized. But short while it lasted, for his forces were already in flight; and they were routed and Manfredi slain in the middle of the enemy; and they were driven into the town by the soldiers of King Charles, for it was now night, and they lost the city of Benevento. And many of Manfredi's barons were made prisoners, among whom were the Count Giordano, Messer Piero Asino degli Uberti, and many others, whom King Charles sent captive into Provence, and there had them put to death in prison; and he imprisoned many other Germans in different parts of the kingdom. And a few days afterwards the wife of Manfredi and his children and his sister, who were in Nocera de' Sardini in Apulia, were taken prisoners by Charles; these died in prison. And for more than three days they made search after Manfredi; for he could not be found, nor was it known if he were dead, or a prisoner, or had escaped; because he had not worn his royal robes in the battle. And afterwards he was recognized by one of his own camp-followers, from certain marks upon his person, in the middle of the battle-field; and he threw him across an ass, and came shouting, 'Who will buy Manfredi?' for which a baron of the king beat him with a cane. And the body of Manfredi being brought to King Charles, he assembled all the barons who were prisoners, and asked each one if that was Manfredi; and timidly they answered yes. Count Giordano smote himself in the face with his hands, weeping and crying, 'O my lord!' whereupon he was much commended by the French, and certain Bretons besought that he might have honourable burial. Answered the king and said, 'I would do it willingly, if he were not excommunicated'; and on that account he would not have him laid in consecrated ground, but he was buried at the foot of the bridge of

Benevento, and each one of the army threw a stone upon his grave, so that a great pile was made. But afterwards, it is said, by command of the Pope, the Bishop of Cosenza took him from that grave, and sent him out of the kingdom, because it was Church land. And he was buried by the river Verde, at the confines of the kingdom and the Campagna. This battle was on a Friday, the last day of February, in the year one thousand two hundred and sixty-five."

Villani, who in his account of the battle copies Malispini almost literally, gives in another chapter, VI. 46, the following portrait of Manfredi; but it must be remembered that Villani was a Guelph, and Manfredi a Ghibelline.

"King Manfredi had for his mother a beautiful lady of the family of the Marquises of Lancia in Lombardy, with whom the Emperor had an intrigue, and was beautiful in person, and like his father and more than his father was given to dissipation of all kinds. He was a musician and singer, delighted in the company of buffoons and courtiers and beautiful concubines, and was always clad in green; he was generous and courteous, and of good demeanour, so that he was much beloved and gracious; but his life was wholly epicurean, hardly caring for God or the saints, but for the delights of the body. He was an enemy of holy Church, and of priests and monks, confiscating churches as his father had done; and a wealthy gentleman was he, both from the treasure which he inherited from the Emperor, and from King Conrad, his brother, and from his own kingdom, which was ample and fruitful, and which, so long as he lived, notwithstanding all the wars he had with the Church, he kept in good condition, so that it rose greatly in wealth and power, both by sea and by land."

This battle of Benevento is the same as that mentioned *Inf.* XXVIII. 16:—

> "At Ceperano, where a renegade
> Was each Apulian."

113. Constance, wife of the Emperor Henry the Sixth.

115. His daughter Constance, who was married to Peter of Aragon, and was the mother of Frederic of Sicily and of James of Aragon.

124. The Bishop of Cosenza and Pope Clement the Fourth.

131. The name of the river Verde reminds one of the old Spanish ballad, particularly when one recalls the fact that Manfredi had in his army a band of Saracens:—

> "Rio Verde, Rio Verde,
>   Many a corpse is bathed in thee,
>   Both of Moors and eke of Christians,
>   Slain with swords most cruelly."

132. Those who died "in contumely of holy Church," or under excommunication, were buried with extinguished and inverted torches.

Canto IV

6. Plato's doctrine of three souls: the Vegetative in the liver; the Sensative in the heart; and the Intellectual in the brain. See *Convito,* IV. 7.

15. See *Convito,* II. 14, quoted *Par.* XIV. Note 86.

25. Sanleo, a fortress on a mountain in the duchy of Urbino; Noli, a town in the Genoese territory, by the sea-side; Bismantova, a mountain in the duchy of Modena.

36. Like Christian going up hill Difficulty in Bunyan, *Pilgrim's Progress:* "I looked then after Christian to see him go up the hill, where I perceived he fell from running to going, and from going to clambering upon his hands and knees, because of the steepness of the place."

43. More than forty-five degrees.

61. If the sun were in Gemini, or if we were in the month of May, you would see the sun still farther to the north.

64. *Rubecchio* is generally rendered red or ruddy. But Jacopo dalla Lana says: "*Rubecchio* in the Tuscan tongue signifies an indented mill-wheel." This interpretation certainly renders the image more distinct. The several signs of the Zodiac are so many cogs in the great wheel; and the wheel is an image which Dante more than once applies to the celestial bodies.

71. The Ecliptic. See *Inf.* XVII., Note 107.

73. This, the Mountain of Purgatory; and that, Mount Zion.

83. The Seven Stars of Ursa Major, the North Star.

109. Compare Thomson's description of the "pleasing land of drowsy-head," in the *Castle of Indolence*:—

> "And there a season atween June and May,
> Half prankt with spring, with summer half imbrowned,
> A listless climate made, where, sooth to say,
> No living wight could work, ne cared even for play."

123. "He loved also in life," says Arrivabene, *Commento Storico,* 584, "a certain Belacqua, an excellent maker of musical instruments."

Benvenuto da Imola says of him: "He was a Florentine who made guitars and other musical instruments. He carved and ornamented the necks and heads of the guitars with great care, and sometimes also played. Hence Dante, who delighted in music, knew him intimately." This seems to be all that is known of Belacqua.

133. *Measure for Measure,* II. 2:—

> "True prayers
> That shall be up at heaven, and enter there
> Ere sunrise; prayers from preserved souls,
> From fasting maids, whose minds are dedicate
> To nothing temporal."

Canto V

1. There is an air of reality about this passage, like some personal reminiscence of street gossip, which gives perhaps a little credibility to the otherwise incredible anecdotes of Dante told by Sacchetti and others;—such as those of the ass-driver whom he beat, and the blacksmith whose tools he threw into the street for singing his verses amiss, and the woman who pointed him out to her companions as the man who had been in Hell and brought back tidings of it.

38. Some editions read in this line *mezza notte,* midnight, instead of *prima notte,* early nightfall.

Of meteors Brunetto Latini, *Tresor,* I. pt. 3, ch. 107, writes: "Likewise it often comes to pass that a dry vapour, when it has mounted so high that it takes fire from the heat which is above, falls, when thus kindled, towards the earth, until it is spent and extinguished, whence some people think it is a dragon or a star which falls."

Milton, *Parad. Lost,* IV. 556, describing the flight of Uriel, says:—

> "Swift as a shooting star
> In Autumn thwarts the night, when vapours fired
> Impress the air, and show the mariner
> From what point of his compass to beware
> Impetuous winds."

66. Shakespeare's "war 'twixt will and will not," and "letting I dare not wait upon I would."

67. This is Jacopo del Cassero of Fano, in the region between Romagna and the kingdom of Naples, then ruled by Charles de Valois (Charles Lackland). He was waylaid and murdered at Oriago, between Venice and Padua, by Azzone the Third of Este.

74. *Leviticus,* xvii. 2: "The life of the flesh is in the blood."

75. Among the Paduans, who are called Antenori, because their city was founded by Antenor of Troy. Brunetto Latini, *Tresor,* I. ch. 39, says: "Then Antenor and Priam departed thence, with a great company of people, and went to the Marca Trevisana, not far from Venice, and there they built another city which is called Padua, where lies the body of Antenor, and his sepulchre is still there."

79. La Mira is on the Brenta, or one of its canals, in the fen-lands between Padua and Venice.

88. Buonconte was a son of Guido di Montefeltro, and lost his life in the battle of Campaldino in the Val d'Arno. His body was never found; Dante imagines its fate.

Ruskin, *Mod. Painters,* III. 252, remarks:—

"Observe, Buonconte, as he dies, crosses his arms over his breast, pressing them together, partly in his pain, partly in prayer. His body thus lies by the river shore, as on a sepulchral monument, the arms folded into a cross. The rage of the river, under the influence of the evil demon, *unlooses this cross,* dashing the body supinely away, and rolling it over and over by bank and bottom. Nothing can be truer to the action of a stream in fury than these lines. And how desolate is it all! The lonely flight,—the grisly wound, "pierced in the throat,"—the death, without help or pity,—only the name of Mary on the lips,—and the cross folded over the heart. Then the rage of the demon and the river,—the noteless grave,—and, at last, even she who had been most trusted forgetting him,—

'Giovanna nor none else have care for me.'

There is, I feel assured, nothing else like it in all the range of poetry; a faint and harsh echo of it, only, exists in one Scottish ballad, 'The Twa Corbies.'"

89. The wife of Buonconte.

92. Ampère, *Voyage Dantesque,* p. 241, thus speaks of the battle of Campaldino: "In this plain of Campaldino, now so pleasant and covered with vineyards, took place, on the 11th of June, 1289, a rude combat between the Guelphs of Florence and the *fuorusciti* Ghibellines, aided by the Aretines. Dante fought in the front rank of the Florentine cavalry; for it must needs be that this man, whose life was so complete, should have been a soldier, before being a theologian, a diplomatist, and poet. He was then twenty-four years of age. He himself described this battle in a letter, of which only a few lines remain. 'At the battle of Campaldino,' he says, 'the Ghibelline party was routed and almost wholly slain. I was there, a novice in arms; I had great fear, and at last great joy, on account of the divers chances of the fight.' One must not see in this phrase the confession of cowardice, which could have no place in a soul tempered like that of Alighieri. The only fear he had was lest the battle should be lost. In fact, the Florentines at first seemed beaten; their infantry fell back before the Aretine cavalry; but this first advantage of the enemy was its destruction, by dividing its forces. These were the vicissitudes of the battle to which Dante alludes, and which at first excited his fears, and then caused his joy."

96. The Convent of Camaldoli, thus described by Forsyth, *Italy,* p. 117:—

"We now crossed the beautiful vale of Prato Vecchio, rode round the modest arcades of the town, and arrived at the lower convent of Camaldoli, just at shutting of the gates. The sun was set and every object sinking into repose, except the stream which roared among the rocks, and the convent-bells which were then ringing the *Angelus.*

"This monastery is secluded from the approach of woman in a deep, narrow, woody dell. Its circuit of dead walls, built on the conventual plan, gives it an aspect of confinement and defence; yet this is considered as a privileged retreat, where the rule of the order relaxes its rigour, and no monks can reside but the sick or the superannuated, the dignitary or the steward, the apothecary or the bead-turner. Here we passed the night, and next morning rode up by the steep traverses to the Santo Eremo, where Saint Romualdo lived and established

> de' tacenti cenobiti il coro,
> L'arcane penitenze, ed i digiuni
> Al Camaldoli suo.

"The Eremo is a city of hermits, walled round, and divided into streets of low, detached cells. Each cell consists of two or three naked rooms, built exactly on the plan of the Saint's own tenement, which remains just as Romualdo left it eight hundred years ago; now too sacred and too damp for a mortal tenant.

"The unfeeling Saint has here established a rule which anticipates the pains of Purgatory. No stranger can behold without emotion a number of noble, interesting young men bound to stand erect chanting at choir for eight hours a day; their faces pale, their heads shaven, their beards shaggy, their backs raw, their legs swollen, and their feet bare. With this horrible institute the climate conspires in severity, and selects from society the best constitutions. The sickly novice is cut off in one or two winters, the rest are subject to dropsy, and few arrive at old age."

97. Where the Archiano loses its name by flowing into the Arno.

104. *Epistle of Jude,* 9: "Yet Michael the archangel, when contending with the devil he disputed about the body of Moses, durst not bring against him a railing accusation, but said, The Lord rebuke thee."

And Jeremy Taylor, speaking of the pardon of sin, says: "And while it is disputed between Christ and Christ's enemy who shall be Lord, the pardon fluctuates like the wave, striving to climb the rock, and is washed off like its own retinue, and it gets possession by time and uncertainty, by difficulty and the degrees of a hard progression."

109. Brunetto Latini, *Tresor,* I. ch. 107: "Then arise vapours like unto smoke, and mount aloft in air, where little by little they gather and grow, until they become dark and dense, so that they take away the sight of the sun; and these are the clouds; but they never are so dark as to take away the light of day; for the sun shines through them, as if it were a candle in a lantern, which shines outwardly, though it cannot itself be seen. And when the cloud has waxed great, so that it can no longer support the abundance of water, which is there as vapour, it must needs fall to earth, and that is the rain."

112. In *Ephesians* ii. 2, the evil spirit is called "the prince of the power of the air."

Compare also *Inf.* XXIII. 16,

> "If anger upon evil will be grafted";

and *Inf.* XXXI. 55,

> "For where the argument of intellect
> Is added unto evil will and power,
> No rampart can the people make against it."

116. This Pratomagno is the same as the Prato Vecchio mentioned in Note 96. The "great yoke" is the ridge of the Apennines.

Dr. Barlow, *Study of Dante*, p. 199, has this note on the passage:—

"When rain falls from the upper region of the air, we observe at a considerable altitude a thin light veil, or a hazy turbidness; as this increases, the lower clouds become diffused in it, and form a uniform sheet. Such is the *stratus* cloud described by Dante (v. 115) as covering the valley from Pratomagno to the ridge on the opposite side above Camaldoli. This cloud is a widely extended horizontal sheet of vapour, increasing from below, and lying on or near the earth's surface. It is properly the cloud of night, and first appears about sunset, usually in autumn; it comprehends creeping mists and fogs which ascend from the bottom of valleys, and from the surface of lakes and rivers, in consequence of air colder than that of the surface descending and mingling with it, and from the air over the adjacent land cooling down more rapidly than that over the water, from which increased evaporation is taking place."

118. Milton, *Parad. Lost,* IV. 500:

> "As Jupiter
> On Juno smiles, when he impregns the clouds
> That bring May-flowers."

126. His arms crossed upon his breast.

134. Ampère, *Voyage Dantesque,* 255: "Who was this unhappy and perhaps guilty woman? The commentators say that she was of the family of Tolomei, illustrious at Siena. Among the different versions of her story there is one truly terrible. The outraged husband led his wife to an isolated castle in the Maremma of Siena, and there shut himself up with his victim, waiting his vengeance from the poisoned atmosphere of this solitude. Breathing with her the air which was killing her, he saw her slowly perish. This funeral tête-à-tête found him always impassive, until, according to the expression of Dante, the Maremma had unmade what he had once loved. This melancholy story might well have no other foundation than the enigma of Dante's lines, and the terror with which this enigma may have struck the imaginations of his contemporaries.

"However this may be, one cannot prevent an involuntary shudder, when, showing you a pretty little brick palace [at Siena], they say, 'That is the house of the Pia.'"

Benvenuto da Imola gives a different version of the story, and says that by command of the husband she was thrown from the window of her palace into the street, and died of the fall.

Bandello, the Italian Novelist, Pt. I. Nov. 12, says that the narrative is true, and gives minutely the story of the lovers, with such embellishments as his imagination suggested.

Ugo Foscolo, *Edinb. Review.* XXIX. 458, speaks thus:—

"Shakespeare unfolds the character of his persons, and presents them under all the variety of forms which they can naturally assume. He surrounds them with all the splendour of his imagination, and bestows on them that full and minute reality which his creative genius could alone confer. Of all tragic poets, he most amply developes character. On the other hand, Dante, if compared not only to Virgil, the most sober of poets, but even to Tacitus, will be found never to employ more than a stroke or two of his pencil, which he aims at imprinting almost insensibly on the hearts of his readers. Virgil has related the story of Eurydice in two hundred verses; Dante, in sixty verses, has finished his masterpiece,—the tale of Francesca da Rimini. The history of Desdemona has a parallel in the following passage of Dante. Nello della Pietra had espoused a lady of noble family at Siena, named Madonna Pia. Her beauty was the admiration of Tuscany, and excited in the heart of her husband a jealousy, which, exasperated by false reports and groundless suspicions, at length drove him to the desperate resolution of Othello. It is difficult to decide whether the lady was quite innocent; but so Dante represents her. Her husband brought her into the Maremma, which, then as now, was a district destructive to health. He never told his unfortunate wife the reason of her banishment to so dangerous a country. He did not deign to utter complaint or accusation. He lived with her alone, in cold silence, without answering her questions, or listening to her remonstrances. He patiently waited till the pestilential air should destroy the health of this young lady. In a few months she died. Some chroniclers, indeed, tell us, that Nello used the dagger to hasten her death. It is certain that he survived her, plunged in sadness and perpetual silence. Dante had, in this incident, all the materials of an ample and very poetical narrative. But he bestows on it only four verses."

For a description of the Maremma, see *Inf.* XIII. Note 9.

Also Rogers, *Italy,* near the end:—

> "Where the path
> Is lost in rank luxuriance, and to breathe
> Is to inhale distemper, if not death;
> Where the wild-boar retreats, when hunters chafe,
> And, when the day-star flames, the buffalo-herd
> Afflicted plunge into the stagnant pool,
> Nothing discerned amid the water-leaves,
> Save here and there the likeness of a head,
> Savage, uncouth; where none in human shape
> Come, save the herdsman, levelling his length
> Of lance with many a cry, or Tartar-like
> Urging his steed along the distant hill,
> As from a danger."

Canto VI

1. Zara was a game of chance, played with three dice.

13. Messer Benincasa of Arezzo, who, while Vicario del Podestà, or Judge, in Siena, sentenced to death a brother and a nephew of Ghino di Tacco for highway robbery. He was afterwards an Auditor of the Ruota in Rome, where, says Benvenuto, "one day as he sat in the tribunal, in the midst of a thousand people, Ghino di Tacco appeared like Scævola, terrible and nothing daunted; and having seized Benincasa, he plunged his dagger into his heart, leaped from the balcony, and disappeared in the midst of the crowd stupefied with terror."

14. This terrible Ghino di Tacco was a nobleman of Asinalunga in the territory of Siena; one of those splendid fellows, who, from some real or imaginary wrong done them, take to the mountains and highways to avenge themselves on society. He is the true type of the traditionary stage bandit, the magnanimous melodramatic hero, who utters such noble sentiments and commits such atrocious deeds.

Benvenuto is evidently dazzled and fascinated by him, and has to throw two Romans into the scale to do him justice. His account is as follows:—

"Reader, I would have thee know that Ghino was not, as some write, so infamous as to be a great assassin and highway robber. For this Ghino di Tacco was a wonderful man, tall, muscular, black-haired, and strong; as agile as Scævola, as prudent and liberal as Papirius Cursor. He was of the nobles of La Fratta, in the county of Siena; who, being forcibly banished by the Counts of Santafiore, held the nobly castle of Radicofani against the Pope. With his marauders he made many and great prizes, so that no one could go safely to Rome or elsewhere through those regions. Yet hardly any one fell into his hands, who did not go away contented, and love and praise him. . . . If a merchant were taken prisoner, Ghino asked him kindly how much he was able to give him; and if he said five hundred pieces of gold, he kept three hundred for himself, and gave back two hundred, saying, 'I wish you to go on with your business and to thrive.' If it were a rich and fat priest, he kept his handsome mule, and gave him a wretched horse. And if it were a poor scholar, going to study, he gave him some money, and exhorted him to good conduct and proficiency in learning."

Boccaccio, *Decameron*, X. 2, relates the following adventure of Ghino di Tacco and the Abbot of Cligni.

"Ghino di Tacco was a man famous for his bold and insolent robberies, who being banished from Siena, and at utter enmity with the Counts di Santa Fiore, caused the town of Radicofani to rebel against the Church, and lived there whilst his gang robbed all who passed that way. Now when Boniface the Eighth was Pope, there came to court the Abbot of Cligni, reputed to be one of the richest prelates in the world, and having debauched his stomach with high living, he was advised by his physicians to go to the baths of Siena, as a certain cure. And, having leave from the Pope, he set out with a goodly train of coaches, carriages, horses, and servants, paying no respect to the rumours concerning this robber. Ghino was apprised of his coming, and took his measures accordingly; when, without the loss of a man, he enclosed the Abbot and his whole retinue in a narrow defile, where it was impossible for them to escape. This being done, he sent one of his principal fellows to the Abbot with his service, requesting the favour of him to alight and visit him at his castle. Upon which the Abbot replied, with a great deal of passion, that he had nothing to do with Ghino, but that his resolution was to go on, and he would see who dared to stop him. 'My Lord,' quoth the man, with a great deal of humility, 'you are now in a place where all excommunications are kicked out of doors; then please to oblige my master in this thing; it will be your best way.' Whilst they were talking together, the place was surrounded with highwaymen, and the Abbot, seeing himself a prisoner, went with a great deal of ill-will with the fellow to the castle, followed by his whole retinue, where he dismounted, and was lodged, by Ghino's appointment, in a poor, dark little room, whilst every other person was well accommodated according to his respective station, and the carriages and all the horses taken exact care of. This being done, Ghino went to the Abbot, and said, 'My Lord, Ghino, whose guest you are, requests the favour of you to let him know whither you are going, and upon what account?' The Abbot was wise enough to lay all his haughtiness aside for the present, and satisfied him with regard to both. Ghino went away at hearing this, and, resolving to cure him without a bath, he ordered a great fire to be kept constantly in his room, coming to him no more till next morning, when he brought him two slices of toasted bread, in a fine napkin, and a large glass of his own rich white wine, saying to him, 'My Lord, when Ghino was young, he studied physic, and he declares that the very best medicine for a pain in the stomach is what he has now provided for you, of which these things are to be the beginning. Then take them, and have a good heart.' The Abbot, whose hunger was much greater than was his will to joke, ate the bread, though with a great deal of indignation, and drank the glass of wine; after which he began to talk a little arrogantly, asking many questions, and demanding more particularly to see this Ghino. But Ghino passed over part of what he said as vain, and the rest he answered very courteously, declaring that Ghino meant to make him a visit very soon, and then left him. He saw him no more till next morning, when he brought him as much bread and wine as before, and in the same manner. And thus he continued during many days, till he found the Abbot had eaten some dried beans, which he had left purposely in the chamber, when he inquired of him, as from Ghino, how he found his stomach? The Abbot replied, 'I should be well enough were I out of this man's clutches. There is nothing I want now so much as to eat, for his medicines have had such an effect upon me, that I am fit to die with hunger.' Ghino, then, having furnished a room with the Abbot's own goods, and provided an elegant entertainment, to which many people of the town were invited, as well as the Abbot's own domestics, went the next morning to him, and said, 'My Lord, now you find yourself recovered, it is time for you to quit this infirmary.' So he took him by the hand, and led him into the chamber, leaving him there with his own people; and as he went out to give orders about the feast, the Abbot was giving an account how he had led his life in that place, whilst they declared that they had been used by Ghino with all possible respect. When the time came, they sat down and were nobly entertained, but still without Ghino's making himself known. But after the Abbot had continued some days in that manner, Ghino had all the goods and furniture brought into a large room, and the horses were likewise led into the courtyard which was under it, when he inquired how his Lordship now found himself, or whether he was yet able to ride. The Abbot made answer that he was strong enough, and his stomach perfectly well, and that he only wanted to quit this man. Ghino then brought him into the room where all his goods were, showing him also to the window, that he might take a view of his horses, when he said, 'My Lord, you must understand it was no evil disposition, but his being driven a poor exile from his own house, and persecuted with many enemies, that forced Ghino di Tacco, whom I am, to be a robber upon the highways, and an enemy to the court of Rome. You seem, however, to be a person of honour; as, therefore, I have cured you of your pain in your stomach, I do not mean to treat you as I would do another person that should fall into my hands, that is, to take what I please, but I would have you consider my necessity, and then give me what you will yourself. Here is all that belongs to you; the horses you may see out of the window: take either part or the whole, just as you are disposed, and go or stay, as is most agreeable to you.' The Abbot was surprised to hear a highwayman talk in so courteous a manner, which did not a little please him; so, turning all his former passion and resentment into kindness and goodwill, he ran with a heart full of friendship to embrace him: 'I protest solemnly, that to procure the friendship of such an one as I take you to be, I would undergo more than what you have already made me suffer. Cursed be that evil fortune which has thrown you into this way of life!' So, taking only a few of his most necessary things, and also of his horses, and leaving all the rest, he came back to Rome. The Pope had heard of the Abbot's being a prisoner, and though he was much concerned at it, yet, upon seeing him, he inquired what benefit he had received from the baths? The Abbot replied, with a smile, 'Holy Father, I found a physician much nearer, who has cured me excellently well;' and he told him the manner of it, which made the Pope laugh heartily, when, going on with his story, and moved with a truly generous spirit, he requested of his Holiness one favour. The Pope, imagining he would ask something else, freely consented to grant it. Then said the Abbot, 'Holy Father, what I mean to require is, that you would bestow a free pardon on Ghino di Tacco, my doctor, because, of all people of worth that I ever met with, he certainly is most to be esteemed, and the damage he does is more the fault of fortune than himself. Change but his condition, and give him something to live upon, according to his rank and station, and I dare say you will have the same opinion of him that I have.' The Pope, being of a noble spirit, and a great encourager of merit, promised to do so, if he was such a person as he reported, and, in the mean time, gave letters of safe-conduct for his coming thither. Upon that assurance, Ghino came to court, when the Pope was soon convinced of his worth, and reconciled to him, giving him the priory of an hospital, and creating him a knight. And there he continued as a friend and loyal servant to the Holy Church, and to the Abbot of Cligni, as long as he lived."

15. Cione de' Tarlati of Pietramala, who, according to the *Ottimo*, after the fight at Bibbiena, being pursued by the enemy, endeavoured to ford the Arno, and was drowned. Others interpret the line differently, making him the pursuing party. But as he was an Aretine, and the Aretines were routed in this battle, the other rendering is doubtless the true one.

17. Federigo Novello, son of Ser Guido Novello of Casentino, slain by one of the Bostoli. "A good youth," says Benvenuto, "and therefore Dante makes mention of him."

The Pisan who gave occasion to Marzucco to show his fortitude was Marzucco's own son, Farinata degli Scoringiani. He was slain by Beccio da Caproni, or, as Benvenuto asserts, declaring that Boccaccio told him so, by Count Ugolino. His father, Marzucco, who had become a Franciscan friar, showed no resentment at the murder, but went with the other friars to his son's funeral, and in humility kissed the hand of the murderer, extorting from him the exclamation, "Thy patience overcomes my obduracy." This was an example of Christian forgiveness which even that vindictive age applauded.

19. Count Orso was a son of Napoleone d'Acerbaja, and was slain by his brother-in-law (or uncle) Alberto.

22. Pierre de la Brosse was the secretary of Philip le Bel of France, and suffered at his hands a fate similar to that which befell Pier de la Vigna at the court of Frederick the Second. See *Inf.* XIII. Note 58. Being accused by Marie de Brabant, the wife of Philip, of having written love-letters to her, he was condemned to death by the king in 1276. Benvenuto thinks that during his residence in Paris Dante learned the truth of the innocence of Pierre de la Brosse.

30. In *Æneid*, VI.: "Cease to hope that the decrees of the gods are to be changed by prayers."

37. The *apex juris,* or top of judgment; the supreme decree of God. *Measure for Measure,* II. 2:—

> "How would you be,
> If He who is the top of judgment should
> But judge you as you are?"

51. Virgil's Bucolics, *Eclogue* I.: "And now the high tops of the villages smoke afar, and larger shadows fall from the lofty mountains."

74. This has generally been supposed to be Sordello the Troubadour. But is it he? Is it Sordello the Troubadour, or Sordello the Podestà of Verona?

or are they one and the same person? After much research, it is not easy to decide the question, and to

> "Single out
> Sordello, compassed murkily about
> With ravage of six long sad hundred years."

Yet as far as it is possible to learn it from various conflicting authorities,

> "Who will may hear Sordello's story told."

Dante, in his treatise *De Volgari Eloquio*, I. 15, speaks of Sordello of Mantua as "a man so choice in his language, that not only in his poems, but in whatever way he spoke, he abandoned the dialect of his province." But here there is no question of the Provençal in which Sordello the Troubadour wrote, but only of Italian dialects in comparison with the universal and cultivated Italian, which Dante says "belongs to all the Italian cities, and seems to belong exclusively to none." In the same treatise, II. 13, he mentions a certain Gotto of Mantua as the author of many good songs; and this Gotto is supposed to be Sordello, as Sordello was born at Goïto in the province of Mantua. But would Dante in the same treatise allude to the same person under different names? Is not this rather the Sordel de Goi, mentioned by Raynouard, *Poésies des Troub.*, V. 445?

In the old Provençal manuscript quoted by Raynouard, *Poésies des Troub.*, V. 444, Sordello's biography is thus given:—

"Sordello was a Mantuan of Sirier, son of a poor knight, whose name was Sir El Cort. And he delighted in learning songs and in making them, and rivalled the good men of the court as far as possible, and wrote love-songs and satires. And he came to the court of the Count of Saint Boniface, and the Count honoured him greatly, and by way of pastime (*a forma de solatz*) he fell in love with the wife of the Count, and she with him. And it happened that the Count quarrelled with her brothers, and became estranged from her. And her brothers, Sir Icellis and Sir Albrics, persuaded Sir Sordello to run away with her; and he came to live with them in great content. And afterwards he went into Provence, and received great honour from all good men, and from the Count and Countess, who gave him a good castle and a gentlewoman for his wife."

Citing this passage, Millot, *Hist. Litt. des Troub.*, II. 80, goes on to say:—

"This is all that our manuscripts tell us of Sordello. According to Agnelli and Platina, historians of Mantua, he was of the house of the Visconti of that city; valiant in deeds of arms, famous in jousts and tournaments, he won the love of Beatrice, daughter of Ezzelin da Romano, Lord of the Marca Trevigiana, and married her; he governed Mantua as Podestà and Captain-General; and though son-in-law of the tyrant Ezzelin, he always opposed him, being a great lover of justice.

"We find these facts cited by Crescimbeni, who says that Sordello was the lord of Goïto; but as they are not applicable to our poet, we presume they refer to a warrior of the same name, and perhaps of a different family.

"Among the pieces of Sordello, thirty-four in number, there are some fifteen songs of gallantry, though Nostrodamus says that all his pieces turn only upon philosophic subjects."

Nostrodamus's account, as given by Crescimbeni, *Volgar Poesia,* II. 105, is as follows:—

"Sordello was a Mantuan poet, who surpassed in Provençal song, Calvo, Folchetto of Marseilles, Lanfranco Cicala, Percival Doria, and all the other Genoese and Tuscan poets, who took far greater delight in our Provençal tongue, on account of its sweetness, than in their own maternal language. This poet was very studious, and exceeding eager to know all things, and as much as any one of his nation excellent in learning as well as in understanding and in prudence. He wrote several beautiful songs, not indeed of love, for not one of that kind is found among his works, but on philosophic subjects. Raymond Belinghieri, the last Count of Provence of that name, in the last days of his life, (the poet being then but fifteen years of age,) on account of the excellence of his poetry and the rare invention shown in his productions, took him into his service, as Pietro di Castelnuovo, himself a Provençal poet, informs us. He also wrote various satires in the same language, and among others one in which he reproves all the Christian princes; and it is composed in the form of a funeral song on the death of Blancasso."

In the *Hist. Litt. de la France,* XIX. 452, Eméric-David, after discussing the subject at length, says:—

"Who then is this Sordello, haughty and superb, like a lion in repose,—this Sordello, who, in embracing Virgil, gives rise to this sudden explosion of the patriotic sentiments of Dante? Is it a singer of love and gallantry? Impossible. This Sordello is the old Podestà of Mantua, as decided a Ghibelline as Dante himself; and Dante utters before him sentiments which he well knows the zealous Ghibelline will share. And what still more confirms our judgment is, that Sordello embraces the knees of Virgil, exclaiming, 'O glory of the Latians,' &c. In this admiration, in this love of the Latin tongue, we still see the Podestà, the writer of Latin; we do not see the Troubadour."

Benvenuto calls Sordello a "noble and prudent knight," and "a man of singular virtue in the world, though of impenitent life," and tells a story he has heard of him and Cunizza, but does not vouch for it. "Ezzelino," he says, "had a sister greatly addicted to the pleasures of love, concerning whom much is said in the ninth Canto of Paradiso. She, being enamoured of Sordello, had cautiously contrived that he should visit her at night by a back door near the kitchen of her palace at Verona. And as there was in the street a dirty slough in which the swine wallowed, and puddles of filthy water, so that the place would seem in no way suspicious, he caused himself to be carried by her servant to the door where Cunizza stood ready to receive him. Ezzelino having heard of this, one evening, disguised as a servant, carried Sordello, and brought him back. Which done, he discovered himself to Sordello, and said, 'Enough; abstain in future from doing so foul a deed in so foul a place.' Sordello, terrified, humbly besought pardon; promising never more to return to his sister. But the accursed Cunizza again enticed him into his former error. Wherefore, fearing Ezzelino, the most formidable man of his time, he left the city. But Ezzelino, as some say, afterwards had him put to death."

He says, moreover, that Dante places Sordello alone and separate from the others, like Saladin in *Inf.* IV. 129, on account of his superiority, or because he wrote a book entitled "The Treasure of Treasures"; and that Sordello was a Mantuan of the village of Goïto,—"beautiful of person, valiant of spirit, gentle of manner."

Finally, Quadrio, *Storia d'ogni Poesia,* II. 130, easily cuts the knot which no one can untie; but unfortunately he does not give his authorities. He writes:—

"Sordello, native of Goïto, (Sordel de Goi,) a village in the Mantuan territory, was born in 1184, and was the son of a poor knight named Elcort." He then repeats the story of Count Saint Boniface, and of Sordello's reception by Count Raymond in Provence, and adds: "Having afterwards returned to Italy he governed Mantua with the title of Regent and Captain-General; and was opposed to the tyrant Ezzelino, being a great lover of justice, as Agnelli writes. Finally he died, very old and full of honour, about 1280. He wrote not only in Provençal, but also in our own common Italian tongue; and he was one of those poets who avoided the dialect of his own province, and used the good, choice language, as Dante affirms in his book of *Volgar Eloquenza.*"

If the reader is not already sufficiently confused, he can easily become so by turning to Tiraboschi, *Storia della Lett. Ital.,* IV. 360, where he will find the matter thoroughly discussed, in sixteen solid pages, by the patient librarian of Modena, who finally gives up in despair and calls on the Royal Academy for help;

"But that were overbold;—
Who would has heard Sordello's story told."

76. Before Dante's time Fra Guittone had said, in his famous *Letter to the Florentines*: "O queen of cities, court of justice, school of wisdom, mirror of life, and mould of manners, whose sons were kings, reigning in every land, or were above all others, who art no longer queen but servant, oppressed and subject to tribute! no longer court of justice, but cave of robbers, and school of all folly and madness, mirror of death and mould of felony, whose great strength is stripped and broken, whose beautiful face is covered with foulness and shame; whose sons are no longer kings but vile and wretched servants, held, wherever they go, in opprobrium and derision by others."

See also Petrarca, *Canzone* XVI., Lady Dacre's Tr., beginning:—

"O my own Italy! though words are vain
　　The mortal wounds to close,
　　Unnumbered, that thy beauteous bosom stain,
　　Yet may it soothe my pain
　　To sigh for the Tiber's woes,
　　And Arno's wrongs, as on Po's saddened shore
　　Sorrowing I wander and my numbers pour."

And Filicaja's sonnet:—

"Italy! Italy! thou who'rt doomed to wear
　　The fatal gift of beauty, and possess
　　The dower funest of infinite wretchedness,
　　Written upon thy forehead by despair;
Ah! would that thou wert stronger, or less fair,
　　That they might fear thee more, or love thee less,
　　Who in the splendour of thy loveliness
　　Seem wasting, yet to mortal combat dare!
Then from the Alps I should not see descending
　　Such torrents of armed men, nor Gallic horde,
　　Drinking the wave of Po, distained with gore,
Nor should I see thee girded with a sword
　　Not thine, and with the stranger's arm contending,
　　Victor or vanquished, slave forevermore."

89. Gibbon, *Decline and Fall,* Ch. XLIV., says:—
"The vain titles of the victories of Justinian are crumbled into dust; but the name of the legislator is inscribed on a fair and everlasting monument. Under his reign, and by his care, the civil jurisprudence was digested in the immortal works of the CODE, the PANDECTS, and the INSTITUTES; the public reason of the Romans has been silently or studiously transfused into the domestic institutions of Europe, and the laws of Justinian still command the respect or obedience of independent nations. Wise or fortunate is the prince who connects his own reputation with the honour and interest of a perpetual order of men."

92. Luke xii. 17: "Render to Cæsar the things that are Cæsar's, and to God the things that are God's."
And in the *Vision of Piers Ploughman,* 563:—

"*Reddite Cæsari,* quod God,
　That *Cæsari* bifalleth,
　Et quæ sunt Dei Deo,
　Or ellis ye don ille."

97. Albert, son of the Emperor Rudolph, was the second of the house of Hapsburg who bore the title of King of the Romans. He was elected in 1298,

but never went to Italy to be crowned. He came to an untimely and violent death, by the hand of his nephew John, in 1308. This is the judgment of Heaven to which Dante alludes.

His successor was Henry of Luxembourg, Dante's "divine and triumphant Henry," who, in 1311, was crowned at Milan with the Iron Crown of Lombardy, *il Sacro Chiodo,* as it is sometimes called, from the plate of iron with which the crown is lined, being, according to tradition, made from a nail of the Cross. In 1312, he was again crowned with the Golden Crown at Rome, and died in the following year. "But the end of his career drew on," says Milman, *Latin Christ.,* VI. 520. "He had now advanced, at the head of an army which his enemies dared not meet in the field, towards Siena. He rode still, seemingly in full vigour and activity. But the fatal air of Rome had smitten his strength. A carbuncle had formed under his knee; injudicious remedies inflamed his vitiated blood. He died at Buonconvento, in the midst of his awe-struck army, on the festival of St. Bartholomew. Rumours of foul practice, of course, spread abroad; a Dominican monk was said to have administered poison in the Sacrament, which he received with profound devotion. His body was carried in sad state, and splendidly interred at Pisa.

"So closed that empire, in which, if the more factious and vulgar Ghibellines beheld their restoration to their native city, their triumph, their revenge, their sole administration of public affairs, the nobler Ghibellinism of Dante foresaw the establishment of a great universal monarchy necessary to the peace and civilization of mankind. The ideal sovereign of Dante's famous treatise on Monarchy was Henry of Luxembourg. Neither Dante nor his time can be understood but through this treatise. The attempt of the Pope to raise himself to a great pontifical monarchy had manifestly ignominiously failed: the Ghibelline is neither amazed nor distressed at this event. It is now the turn of the Imperialist to unfold his noble vision. 'An universal monarchy is absolutely necessary for the welfare of the world;' and this is part of his singular reasoning: 'Peace,' (says the weary exile, the man worn out in cruel strife, the wanderer from city to city, each of those cities more fiercely torn by faction than the last,) 'universal Peace is the first blessing of mankind. The angels sang, not riches or pleasures, but peace on earth: peace the Lord bequeathed to his disciples. For peace One must rule. Mankind is most like God when at unity, for God is One; therefore under a monarchy. Where there is parity there must be strife; where strife, judgment; the judge must be a third party intervening with supreme authority.' Without monarchy can be no justice, nor even liberty; for Dante's monarch is no arbitrary despot, but a constitutional sovereign; he is the Roman law impersonated in the Emperor; a monarch who should leave all the nations, all the free Italian cities, in possession of their rights and old municipal institutions."

106. The two noble families of Verona, the Montagues and Capulets, whose quarrels have been made familiar to the English-speaking world by *Romeo and Juliet:*—

> "Three civil brawls, bred of an airy word,
>   By thee, old Capulet and Montague,
>   Have thrice disturbed the quiet of our streets,
>   And made Verona's ancient citizens
>   Cast by their grave beseeming ornaments,
>   To wield old partisans, in hands as old,
>   Cankered with peace, to part your cankered hate."

107. Families of Orvieto.

111. Santafiore is in the neighbourhood of Siena, and much infested with banditti.

112. The state of Rome in Dante's time is thus described by Mr. Norton, *Travel and Study,* pp. 246–248:—

"On the slope of the Quirinal Hill, in the quiet enclosure of the convent of St. Catherine of Siena, stands a square, brick tower, seven stories high. It is a conspicuous object in any general view of Rome; for there are few other towers so tall, and there is not a single spire or steeple in the city. It is the Torre delle Milizie. It was begun by Pope Gregory the Ninth, and finished near the end of the thirteenth century by his vigorous and warlike successor, Boniface the Eighth. Many such towers were built for the purposes of private warfare, in those times when the streets of Rome were the fighting-places of its noble families; but this is, perhaps, the only one that now remains undiminished in height and unaltered in appearance. It was a new building when Dante visited Rome; and it is one of the very few edifices that still preserve the aspect they then presented. The older ruins have been greatly changed in appearance, and most of the structures of the Middle Ages have disappeared, in the vicissitudes of the last few centuries. The Forum was then filled with a confused mass of ruins and miserable dwellings, with no street running through their intricacies. The Capitol was surrounded with uneven battlemented walls, and bore the character and look of an irregular citadel. St. Peter's was a low basilica; the Colosseum had suffered little from the attacks of Popes or princes, neither the Venetian nor the Farnese palace having as yet been built with stones from its walls; and centuries were still to pass before Michael Angelo, Bernini, and Borromini were to stamp its present character upon the face of the modern city. The siege and burning of Rome by Robert Guiscard, in 1084, may be taken as the dividing-line between the city of the Emperors and the city of the Popes, between ancient and modern Rome. . . . . Rome was in a state of too deep depression, its people were too turbulent and unsettled, to have either the spirit or the opportunity for great works. There was no established and recognized authority, no regular course of justice. There was not even any strong force, rarely any overwhelming violence, which for a time at least could subdue opposition, and organize a steady, and consequently a beneficent tyranny. The city was continually distracted by petty personal quarrels, and by bitter family feuds. Its obscure annals are full of bloody civil victories and defeats,—victories which brought no gain to those who won them, defeats which taught no lesson to those who lost them. The breath of liberty never inspired with life the dead clay of Rome; and though for a time it might seem to kindle some vital heat, the glow soon grew cold, and speedily disappeared. The records of Florence, Siena, Bologna, and Perugia are as full of fighting and bloodshed as those of Rome; but their fights were not mere brawls, nor were their triumphs always barren. Even the twelfth and thirteenth centuries, which were like the coming of the spring after a long winter, making the earth to blossom, and gladdening the hearts of men,—the centuries which elsewhere in Italy, and over the rest of Europe, gave birth to the noblest mediæval Art, when every great city was adorning itself with the beautiful works of the new architecture, sculpture, and painting,—even these centuries left scarcely any token of their passage over Rome. The sun, breaking through the clouds that had long hidden it, shone everywhere but here. While Florence was building her Cathedral and her Campanile, and Orvieto her matchless Duomo,—while Pisa was showing her piety and her wealth in her Cathedral, her Camposanto, her Baptistery, and her Tower,—while Siena was beginning a church greater and more magnificent in design than her shifting fortune would permit her to complete,—Rome was building neither cathedral nor campanile, but was selling the marbles of her ancient temples and tombs to the builders of other cities, or quarrying them for her own mean uses."

118. This recalls Pope's *Universal Prayer,*—

> "Father of all! in every age,
> In every clime, adored,
> By saint, by savage, and by sage,
> Jehovah, Jove, or Lord!"

125. Not the great Roman general who took Syracuse, after Archimedes had defended it so long with his engines and burning-glasses, but a descendant of his, who in the civil wars took part with Pompey and was banished by Cæsar. Pope's *Essay on Man,* Ep. IV. 257:—

> "And more true joy Marcellus exiled feels,
> Than Cæsar with a senate at his heels."

127. Of the state of Florence, Napier writes, *Flor. Hist.,* I. 122:—
"It was not the simple movement of one great body against another; not the force of a government in opposition to the people; not the struggle of privilege and democracy, of poverty and riches, or starvation and repletion; but one universal burst of unmitigated anarchy. In the streets, lanes, and squares, in the courts of palaces and humbler dwellings, were heard the clang of arms, the screams of victims, and the gush of blood: the bow of the bridegroom launched its arrows into the very chambers of his young bride's parents and relations, and the bleeding son, the murdered brother, or the

dying husband were the evening visitors of Florentine maids and matrons, and aged citizens. Every art was practised to seduce and deceive, and none felt secure even of their nearest and dearest relatives. In the morning a son left his paternal roof with undiminished love, and returned at evening a corpse, or the most bitter enemy! Terror and death were triumphant; there was no relaxation, no peace by day or night: the crash of the stone, the twang of the bow, the whizzing shaft, the jar of the trembling mangonel from tower and turret, were the dismal music of Florence, not only for hours and days, but months and years. Doors, windows, the jutting galleries and roofs, were all defended, and yet all unsafe: no spot was sacred, no tenement secure: in the dead of night, the most secret chambers, the very hangings, even the nuptial bed itself, were often known to conceal an enemy.

"Florence in those days was studded with lofty towers; most of the noble families possessed one or more, at least two hundred feet in height, and many of them far above that altitude. These were their pride, their family citadels; and jealously guarded; glittering with arms and men, and instruments of war. Every connecting balcony was alive with soldiers; the battle raged above and below, within and without; stones rained in showers, arrows flew thick and fast on every side; the *seraglj,* or barricades, were attacked and defended by chosen bands armed with lances and boar-spears; foes were in ambush at every corner, watching the bold or heedless enemy; confusion was everywhere triumphant, a demon seemed to possess the community, and the public mind, reeling with hatred, was steady only in the pursuit of blood. Yet so accustomed did they at last become to this fiendish life, that one day they fought, the next caroused together in drunken gambols, foe with foe, boasting of their mutual prowess; nor was it until after nearly five years of reciprocal destruction, that, from mere lassitude, they finally ceased thus to mangle each other, and, as it were for relaxation, turned their fury on the neighbouring states."

147. Upon this subject Napier, *Flor. Hist.,* II. 626, remarks:—

"A characteristic, and, if discreetly handled, a wise regulation of the Florentines, notwithstanding Dante's sarcasms, was the periodical revision of their statutes and ordinances, a weeding out, as it were, of the obsolete and contradictory, and a substitution of those which were better adapted to existing circumstances and the forward movement of man. There are certain fundamental laws necessarily permanent and admitted by all communities, as there are certain moral and theological truths acknowledged by all religions; but these broad frames or outlines are commonly filled up with a thick network of subordinate regulations, that cover them like cobwebs, and often impede the march of improvement. The Florentines were early aware of this, and therefore revised their laws and institutions more or less frequently and sometimes factiously, according to the turbulent or tranquil condition of the times; but in 1394, after forty years' omission, an officer was nominated for that purpose, but whether permanently or not is doubtful."

Canto VII

6. See Canto III. Note 7.

28. Limbo, *Inf.* IV. 25, the "foremost circle that surrounds the abyss."

> "There, in so far as I had power to hear,
>   Were lamentations none, but only sighs,
>   Which tremulous made the everlasting air.
>   And this was caused by sorrow without torment
>   Which the crowds had, that many were and great,
>   Of infants and of women and of men."

34. The three Theological Virtues of Faith, Hope, and Charity.

36. The four Cardinal Virtues, Prudence, Justice, Fortitude, and Temperance.

44. John xii. 35: "Then Jesus said unto them, Yet a little while is the light with you. Walk while ye have the light, lest darkness come upon you: for he that walketh in darkness knoweth not whither he goeth."

70. In the Middle Ages the longing for rest and escape from danger, which found its expression in cloisters, is expressed in poetry by descriptions of flowery, secluded meadows, suggesting the classic meadows of Asphodel. Dante has given one already in the Inferno, and gives another here.

Compare with these the following from *The Miracles of Our Lady,* by Gonzalo de Bercéo, a monk of Calahorra, who lived in the thirteenth century, and is the oldest of the Castilian poets whose name has come down to us:—

> "I, Gonzalo de Bercéo, in the gentle summer-tide,
> Wending upon a pilgrimage, came to a meadow's side;
> All green was it and beautiful, with flowers far and wide,
> A pleasant spot, I ween, wherein the traveller might abide.
>
> Flowers with the sweetest odours filled all the sunny air,
> And not alone refreshed the sense, but stole the mind from care;
> On every side a fountain gushed, whose waters pure and fair
> Ice-cold beneath the summer sun, but warm in winter were.
>
> There on the thick and shadowy trees, amid the foliage green,
> Were the fig and the pomegranate, the pear and apple seen,
> And other fruits of various kinds, the tufted leaves between;
> None were unpleasant to the taste and none decayed, I ween.
>
> The verdure of the meadow green, the odour of the flowers,
> The grateful shadows of the trees, tempered with fragrant showers,
> Refreshed me in the burning heat of the sultry noontide hours;
> O, one might live upon the balm and fragrance of those bowers.

> Ne'er had I found on earth a spot that had such power to please,
> Such shadows from the summer sun, such odours on the breeze;
> I threw my mantle on the ground, that I might rest at ease,
> And stretched upon the greensward lay in the shadow of the trees.
>
> There, soft reclining in the shade, all cares beside me flung,
> I heard the soft and mellow notes that through the woodland rung.
> Ear never listened to a strain, from instrument or tongue,
> So mellow and harmonious as the songs above me sung."

See also Brunetto Latini, *Tesoretto,* XIX.; the *Vision of Piers Ploughman;* Gower's *Confessio Amantis,* VIII., &c.

73. Of this description Ruskin, *Modern Painters,* III. 228, remarks:—

"Now, almost in the opening of the Purgatory, as at the entrance of the Inferno, we find a company of great ones resting in a grassy place. But the idea of the grass now is very different. The word now used is not 'enamel,' but 'herb,' and instead of being merely green, it is covered with flowers of many colours. With the usual mediæval accuracy, Dante insists on telling us precisely what these colours were, and how bright; which he does by naming the actual pigments used in illumination,—'Gold, and fine silver, and cochineal, and white lead, and Indian wood, serene and lucid, and fresh emerald, just broken, would have been excelled, as less is by greater, by the flowers and grass of the place.' It is evident that the 'emerald' here means the emerald green of the illuminators; for a fresh emerald is no brighter that one which is not fresh, and Dante was not one to throw away his words thus. Observe, then, we have here the idea of the growth, life, and variegation of the 'green herb,' as opposed to the *smalto* of the Inferno; but the colours of the variegation are illustrated and defined by the reference to actual pigments; and, observe, because the other colours are rather bright, the blue ground (Indian wood, indigo?) is sober; lucid, but serene; and presently two angels enter, who are dressed in the green drapery, but of a paler green than the grass, which Dante marks, by telling us that it was 'the green of leaves just budded.'

"In all this, I wish the reader to observe two things: first, the general carefulness of the poet in defining colour, distinguishing it precisely as a painter would (opposed to the Greek carelessness about it); and, secondly, his regarding the grass for its greenness and variegation, rather than, as a Greek would have done, for its depth and freshness. This greenness or brightness, and variegation, are taken up by later and modern poets, as the things intended to be chiefly expressed by the word 'enamelled;' and, gradually, the term is taken to indicate any kind of bright and interchangeable colouring; there being always this much of propriety about it, when used of greensward, that such sward is indeed, like enamel, a coat of bright colour on a comparatively dark ground; and is thus a sort of natural jewelry and painter's work, different from loose and large vegetation. The word is often awkwardly and falsely used, by the later poets, of all kinds of growth and colour; as by Milton of the flowers of Paradise showing themselves over its wall; but it retains, nevertheless, through all its jaded inanity, some half-unconscious vestige of the old sense, even to the present day."

82. The old church hymn attributed to Arminius or Hermann, Count of Vehringen, in the eleventh century, beginning:—

> "Salve Regina, mater misericordiæ,
> Vita, dulcedo et spes nostra, salve."

94. Rudolph of Hapsburg, first Emperor of the house of Austria, was crowned at Aix-la-Chapelle, in 1273. "It is related," says Voltaire, *Annales de l'Empire,* I. 303, "that, as the imperial sword, which they pretended was that of Charlemagne, could not be found, several lords made this defect in the formalities a pretext for not taking the oath of allegiance. He seized a crucifix; *This is my sceptre,* he said, and all paid homage to him. This single act of firmness made him respected, and the rest of his conduct showed him to be worthy of the Empire."

He would not go to Rome to be crowned, and took so little interest in Italian affairs, that Italy became almost independent of the Empire, which seems greatly to disturb the mind of Dante. He died in 1291.

100. Ottocar the Second, king of Bohemia, who is said to have refused the imperial crown. He likewise refused to pay homage to Rudolph, whom he used to call his *maître d'hôtel,* declaring he had paid his wages and owed him nothing. Whereupon Rudolph attacked and subdued him. According to Voltaire, *Annales de l'Empire,* I. 306, "he consented to pay homage to the Emperor as his liege-lord, in the island of Kamberg in the middle of the Danube, under a tent whose curtains should be closed to spare him public mortification. Ottocar presented himself covered with gold and jewels; Rudolph, by way of superior pomp, received him in his simplest dress; and in the middle of the ceremony the curtains of the tent fell, and revealed to the eyes of the people and of the armies, that lined the Danube, the proud Ottocar on his knees, with his hands clasped in the hands of his conqueror, whom he had often called his *maître d'hôtel,* and whose Grand-Seneschal he now became. This story is accredited, and it is of little importance whether it be true or not."

But the wife was not quiet under this humiliation, and excited him to revolt against Rudolph. He was again overcome, and killed in battle in 1278.

101. This Winceslaus, says the *Ottimo,* was "most beautiful among all men; but was not a man of arms; he was a meek and humble ecclesiastic, and did not live long." Why Dante accuses him of living in luxury and ease does not appear.

103. Philip the Third of France, surnamed the Bold (1270–1285). Having invaded Catalonia, in a war with Peter the Third of Aragon, both by land and sea, he was driven back, and died at Perpignan during the retreat.

104. He with the benign aspect, who rests his cheek upon his hand, is Henry of Navarre, surnamed the Fat, and brother of "Good King Thibault,"

Inf. XXII. 52. An old French chronicle quoted by Philalethes says, that, "though it is a general opinion that fat men are of a gentle and benign nature, nevertheless this one was very harsh."

109. Philip the Fourth of France, surnamed the Fair, son of Philip the Third, and son-in-law of Henry of Navarre (1285–1314).

112. Peter the Third of Aragon (1276–1285), the enemy of Charles of Anjou and competitor with him for the kingdom of Sicily. He is counted among the Troubadours, and when Philip the Bold invaded his kingdom, Peter launched a song against him, complaining that the "flower-de-luce kept him sorrowing in his house," and calling on the Gascons for aid.

113. Charles of Anjou, king of Sicily and Naples (1265). Villani, VII. 1, thus describes him: "This Charles was wise and prudent, and valiant in arms, and rough, and much feared and redoubted by all the kings of the world; magnanimous and of a high spirit; steadfast in carrying on every great enterprise, firm in every adversity, and true to every promise, speaking little and doing much. He laughed but little; was chaste as a monk, catholic, harsh in judgment, and of a fierce countenance; large and muscular in person, with an olive complexion and a large nose, and looked the king more than any other lord. He sat up late at night, and slept little, and was in the habit of saying that a great deal of time was lost in sleeping. He was generous to his knights, but eager to acquire land, lordship, and money wherever he could, to furnish means for his enterprises and wars. In courtiers, minstrels, and players he never took delight."

Yet this is the monarch whose tyranny in Sicily brought about the bloody revenge of the Sicilian Vespers; which in turn so roused the wrath of Charles, that he swore that, "if he could live a thousand years, he would go on razing the cities, burning the lands, torturing the rebellious slaves. He would leave Sicily a blasted, barren, uninhabited rock, as a warning to the present age, an example to the future."

116. Philip the Third of Aragon left four sons, Alfonso, James, Frederick, and Peter. Whether the stripling here spoken of is Alfonso or Peter does not appear.

121. Chaucer, *Wif of Bathes Tale*:—

> "Wel can the wise poet of Florence,
> That highte Dant, speken of this sentence:
> Lo, in swiche maner rime is Dantes tale.
>   Ful selde up riseth by his branches smale
> Prowesse of man, for God of his goodnesse
> Wol that we claime of him our gentillesse:
> For of our elders may we nothing claime
> But temporel thing, that man may hurt and maime."

124. It must be remembered that these two who are singing together in this Valley of Princes were deadly foes on earth; and one had challenged the other to determine their quarrel by single combat.

"The wager of battle between the kings," says Milman, *Latin Christianity,* VI. 168, "which maintained its solemn dignity up almost to the appointed time, ended in a pitiful comedy, in which Charles of Anjou had the ignominy of practising base and disloyal designs against his adversary; Peter, that of eluding the contest by craft, justifiable only as his mistrust of his adversary was well or ill grounded, but much too cunning for a frank and generous knight. He had embarked with his knights for the South of France; he was cast back by tempests on the shores of Spain. He set off with some of his armed companions, crossed the Pyrenees undiscovered, appeared before the gates of Bordeaux, and summoned the English Seneschal. To him he proclaimed himself to be the king of Aragon, demanded to see the lists, rode down them in slow state, obtained an attestation that he had made his appearance within the covenanted time, and affixed his solemn protest against the palpable premeditated treachery of his rival, which made it unsafe for him to remain longer at Bordeaux. Charles, on his part, was furious that Peter had thus broken through the spider's web of his policy. He was in Bordeaux when Peter appeared under the walls, and had challenged him in vain. Charles presented himself in full armour on the appointed day, summoned Peter to appear, and proclaimed him a recreant and a dastardly craven, unworthy of the name of knight."

Charles of Anjou, Peter the Third of Aragon, and Philip the Third of France, all died in the same year, 1285.

126. These kingdoms being badly governed by his son and successor, Charles the Second, called the Lame.

128. Daughters of Raymond Berenger the Fifth, Count of Provence; the first married to St. Louis of France, and the second to his brother, Charles of Anjou.

129. Constance, daughter of Manfredi of Apulia, and wife of Peter the Third of Aragon.

131. Henry the Third (1216–1272,) of whom Hume says: "This prince was noted for his piety and devotion, and his regular attendance on public worship; and a saying of his on that head is much celebrated by ancient writers. He was engaged in a dispute with Louis the Ninth of France, concerning the preference between sermons and masses; he maintained the superiority of the latter, and affirmed that he would rather have one hour's conversation with a friend, than hear twenty of the most elaborate discourses pronounced in his praise."

Dickens, *Child's History of England,* Ch. XV., says of him: "He was as much of a king in death as he had ever been in life. He was the mere pale shadow of a king at all times."

His "better issue" was Edward the First, called, on account of his amendment and establishment of the laws, the English Justinian, and less respectfully Longshanks, on account of the length of his legs. "His legs had need to be strong," says the authority just quoted, "however long, and this they were; for they had to support him through many difficulties on the fiery sands of Syria, where his small force of soldiers fainted, died, deserted, and seemed to melt away. But his prowess made light of it, and he said, 'I will go on, if I go on with no other follower than my groom.'"

134. The Marquis of Monferrato, a Ghibelline, was taken prisoner by the people of Alessandria in Piedmont, in 1290, and, being shut up in a wooden cage, was exhibited to the public like a wild beast. This he endured for eighteen months, till death released him. A bloody war was the consequence between Alessandria and the Marquis's provinces of Monferrato and Canavese.

135. The city of Alessandria is in Piedmont, between the Tanaro and the Bormida, and not far from their junction. It was built by the Lombard League, to protect the country against the Emperor Frederick, and named in honour of Pope Alexander the Third, a protector of the Guelphs. It is said to have been built in a single year, and was called in derision, by the Ghibellines, Alessandria della Paglia (of the Straw); either from the straw used in the bricks, or more probably from the supposed insecurity of a city built in so short a space of time.

Canto VIII

1. Apollonius Rhodius, *Argonautica,* III. 302:—

> "It was the hour when every traveller
> And every watchman at the gate of towns
> Begins to long for sleep, and drowsiness
> Is falling even on the mother's eyes
> Whose child is dead."

Also Byron, *Don Juan,* III. 108:—

> "Soft hour! which wakes the wish and melts the heart
>   Of those who sail the seas, on the first day
> When they from their sweet friends are torn apart;
>   Or fills with love the pilgrim on his way,
> As the far bell of vesper makes him start,
>   Seeming to weep the dying day's decay.
> Is this a fancy which our reason scorns?
> Ah! surely nothing dies but something mourns!"

4. The word "pilgrim" is here used by Dante in a general sense, meaning any traveller.

6. Gray, *Elegy:*—

> "The curfew tolls the knell of parting day."

13. An evening hymn of the Church, sung at Complines, or the latest service of the day:—

> "Te lucis ante terminum,
> Rerum creator, poscimus
> Ut pro tua clementia
> Sis presul ad custodiam.
>
> Procul recedant somnia
> Et noxium phantasmata,
> Hostemque nostrum comprime,
> Ne polluantur corpora.
>
> Presta, Pater piissime,
> Patrique compar Unice,
> Cum Spiritu Paraclito
> Regnans per omne sæculum."

This hymn would seem to have no great applicability to disembodied spirits; and perhaps may have the same reference as the last petition in the Lord's Prayer, Canto XI. 19:—

> "Our virtue, which is easily o'ercome,
>   Put not to proof with the old Adversary,
>   But thou from him who spurs it so, deliver.
> This last petition verily, dear Lord,
>   Not for ourselves is made, who need it not,
>   But for their sake who have remained behind us."

Dante seems to think his meaning very easy to penetrate. The commentators have found it uncommonly difficult.

26. Genesis iii. 24: "And he placed at the east of the garden of Eden cherubims, and a flaming sword which turned every way, to keep the way of the tree of life."

27. Justice tempered with mercy, say the commentators.

28. Green, the colour of hope, which is the distinguishing virtue of Purgatory. On the symbolism of colours, Mrs. Jameson, *Sacred and Legendary Art, Introd.*, says:—

"In very early Art we find colours used in a symbolical or mystic sense, and, until the ancient principles and traditions were wholly worn out of memory or set aside by the later painters, certain colours were appropriated to certain subjects and personages, and could not arbitrarily be applied or misapplied. In the old specimens of stained glass we find these significations scrupulously attended to. Thus:—

"WHITE, represented by the diamond or silver, was the emblem of light, religious purity, innocence, virginity, faith, joy, and life. Our Saviour wears white after his resurrection. In the judge it indicated integrity; in the rich man, humility; in the woman, chastity. It was the colour consecrated to the Virgin, who, however, never wears white except in pictures of the Assumption.

"RED, the ruby, signified fire, divine love, the Holy Spirit, heat, or the creative power, and royalty. White and red roses expressed love and innocence, or love and wisdom, as in the garland with which the angel crowns St. Cecilia. In a bad sense, red signified blood, war, hatred, and punishment. Red and black combined were the colours of purgatory and the Devil.

"BLUE, or the sapphire, expressed heaven, the firmament, truth, constancy, fidelity. Christ and the Virgin wear the red tunic and the blue mantle, as signifying heavenly love and heavenly truth.* The same colours were given to St. John the Evangelist, with this difference,—that he wore the blue tunic and the red mantle; in later pictures the colours are sometimes red and green.

"YELLOW, or gold, was the symbol of the sun; of the goodness of God; initiation, or marriage; faith, or fruitfulness. St. Joseph, the husband of the Virgin, wears yellow. In pictures of the Apostles, St. Peter wears a yellow mantle over a blue tunic. In a bad sense, yellow signifies inconstancy, jealousy, deceit; in this sense it is given to the traitor Judas, who is generally habited in dirty yellow.

"GREEN, the emerald, is the colour of spring; of hope, particularly hope in immortality; and of victory, as the colour of the palm and the laurel.

"VIOLET, the amethyst, signified love and truth; or, passion and suffering. Hence it is the colour often worn by the martyrs. In some instances our Saviour, after his resurrection, is habited in a violet, instead of a blue mantle. The Virgin also wears violet after the crucifixion. Mary Magdalene, who as patron saint wears the red robe, as penitent wears violet and blue, the colours of sorrow and of constancy. In the devotional representation of her by Timoteo della Vite, she wears red and green, the colours of love and hope.

"GRAY, the colour of ashes, signified mourning, humility, and innocence accused; hence adopted as the dress of the Franciscans (the Gray Friars); but it has since been changed for a dark rusty brown.

"BLACK expressed the earth, darkness, mourning, wickedness, negation, death; and was appropriate to the Prince of Darkness. In some old illuminated MSS., Jesus, in the Temptation, wears a black robe. White and black together signified purity of life, and mourning or humiliation; hence adopted by the Dominicans and the Carmelites."

50. It was not so dark that on a near approach he could not distinguish objects indistinctly visible at a greater distance.

---

* In the Spanish schools the colour of our Saviour's mantle is generally a deep rich violet.

53. Nino de' Visconti of Pisa, nephew of Count Ugolino, and Judge of Gallura in Sardinia. Dante had known him at the siege of Caprona, in 1290, where he saw the frightened garrison march out under safeguard. *Inf.* XXI. 95. It was this "gentle Judge," who hanged Friar Gomita for peculation. *Inf.* XXII. 82.

71. His daughter, still young and innocent.

75. His widow married Galeazzo de' Visconti of Milan, "and much discomfort did this woman suffer with her husband," says the *Ottimo,* "so that many a time she wished herself a widow."

79. *Hamlet,* IV. 5:—

> "His obscure funeral,
> No trophy, sword, or hatchment o'er his grave."

80. The Visconti of Milan had for their coat of arms a viper; and being on the banner, it led the Milanese to battle.

81. The arms of Gallura. "According to Fara, a writer of the sixteenth century," says Valery, *Voyage en Corse et en Sardaigne,* II. 37, "the elegant but somewhat chimerical historian of Sardinia, Gallura is a Gallic colony; its arms are a cock; and one might find some analogy between the natural vivacity of its inhabitants and that of the French." Nino thinks it would look better on a tombstone than a viper.

89. These three stars are the *Alphæ* of Euridanus, of the Ship, and of the Golden Fish; allegorically, if any allegory be wanted, the three Theological Virtues, Faith, Hope, and Charity. The four morning stars, the Cardinal Virtues of active life, are already set; these announce the evening and the life contemplative.

100. Compare this with Milton's description of the serpent, *Parad. Lost,* IX. 434–496:—

> "Nearer he drew, and many a walk traversed
> Of stateliest covert, cedar, pine, or palm;
> Then voluble and bold, now hid, now seen,
> Among thick-woven arborets, and flowers
> Imbordered on each bank.
>
> . . . . .
>
> Not with indented wave,
> Prone on the ground, as since; but on his rear,
> Circular base of rising folds, that towered
> Fold above fold, a surging maze! his head
> Crested aloft, and carbuncle his eyes:
> With burnished neck of verdant gold, erect
> Amidst his circling spires, that on the grass
> Floated redundant: pleasing was his shape
> And lovely; never since of serpent-kind

> Lovelier, not those that in Illyria changed
> Hermione and Cadmus, or the god
> In Epidaurus; nor to which transformed
> Ammonian Jove or Capitoline was seen,—
> He with Olympias, this with her who bore
> Scipio, the height of Rome. With track oblique
> At first, as one who sought access, but feared
> To interrupt, sidelong he works his way.
> As when a ship, by skilful steersman wrought
> Nigh river's mouth or foreland, where the wind
> Veers oft, as oft so steers, and shifts her sail;
> So varied he, and of his tortuous train
> Curled many a wanton wreath in sight of Eve.
> .   .   .   .   .   Oft he bowed
> His turret crest, and sleek enamelled neck,
> Fawning; and licked the ground whereon she trod."

114. In the original *al sommo smalto,* to the highest enamel; referring either to the Terrestrial Paradise, enamelled with flowers, or to the highest heaven enamelled with stars. The azure-stone, *pierre d'azur,* or lapis lazuli, is perhaps a fair equivalent for the *smalto,* particularly if the reference be to the sky.

116. The valley in Lunigiana, through which runs the Magra, dividing the Genoese and Tuscan territories. *Par.* IX. 89:—

> "The Magra, that with journey short
> Doth from the Tuscan part the Genoese."

118. Currado or Conrad Malaspina, father of Marcello Malaspina, who six years later sheltered Dante in his exile, as foreshadowed in line 136. It was from the convent of the Corvo, overlooking the Gulf of Spezia, in Lunigiana, that Frate Ilario wrote the letter describing Dante's appearance in the cloister. See Illustrations at the end of *Inferno.*

131. Pope Boniface the Eighth.

134. Before the sun shall be seven times in Aries, or before seven years are passed.

137. *Ecclesiastes,* xii. 11: "The words of the wise are as goads, and as nails fastened by the masters of assemblies."

139. With this canto ends the first day in Purgatory, as indicated by the description of evening at the beginning, and the rising of the stars in line 89. With it closes also the first subdivision of this part of the poem, indicated, as the reader will not fail to notice, by the elaborate introduction of the next canto.

Canto IX

1. "Dante begins this canto," says Benvenuto da Imola, "by saying a thing that was never said or imagined by any other poet, which is, that the aurora of the moon is the concubine of Tithonus. Some maintain that he means the aurora of the sun; but this cannot be, if we closely examine the text." This point is elaborately discussed by the commentators. I agree with those who interpret the passage as referring to a lunar aurora. It is still evening; and the hour is indicated a few lines lower down.

To Tithonus was given the gift of immortality, but not of perpetual youth. As Tennyson makes him say:—

> "The woods decay, the woods decay and fall,
>   The vapours weep their burthen to the ground,
>   Man comes and tills the field and lies beneath,
>   And after many a summer dies the swan.
>   Me only cruel immortality
>   Consumes: I wither slowly in thine arms,
>   Here at the quiet limit of the world,
>   A white-haired shadow roaming like a dream
>   The ever silent spaces of the East,
>   Far-folded mists, and gleaming halls of morn."

2. *Don Quixote*, I. 2: "Scarcely had ruddy Phœbus spread the golden tresses of his beauteous hair over the face of the wide and spacious earth, and scarcely had the painted little birds, with the sweet and mellifluous harmony of their serrated tongues, saluted the approach of rosy Aurora, when, quitting the soft couch of her jealous husband, she disclosed herself to mortals through the gates and balconies of the Manchegan horizon."

. 5. As the sun was in Aries, and it was now the fourth day after the full moon, the Scorpion would be rising in the dawn which precedes the moon.

8. This indicates the time to be two hours and a half after sunset, or half past eight o'clock. Two hours of the ascending night are passed, and the third is half over.

This circumstantial way of measuring the flight of time is Homeric. *Iliad*, X. 250: "Let us be going, then, for the night declines fast, and the morning is near. And the stars have already far advanced, and the greater portion of the night, by two parts, has gone by, but the third portion still remains."

10. Namely, his body.

12. Virgil, Sordello, Dante, Nino, and Conrad. And here Dante falls upon the grass and sleeps till dawn. There is a long pause of rest and sleep between this line and the next, which makes the whole passage doubly beautiful. The narrative recommences like the twitter of early birds just beginning to stir in the woods.

14. For the tragic story of Tereus, changed to a lapwing, Philomela to a nightingale, and Procne to a swallow, see Ovid, *Metamorph.*, VI.:—

> "Now, with drawn sabre and impetuous speed,
> In close pursuit he drives Pandion's breed;
> Whose nimble feet spring with so swift a force
> Across the fields, they seem to wing their course.
> And now, on real wings themselves they raise,
> And steer their airy flight by different ways;
> One to the woodland's shady covert hies,
> Around the smoky roof the other flies;
> Whose feathers yet the marks of murder stain,
> Where stamped upon her breast the crimson spots remain.
> Tereus, through grief and haste to be revenged,
> Shares the like fate, and to a bird is changed;
> Fixed on his head the crested plumes appear,
> Long is his beak, and sharpened like a spear;
> Thus armed, his looks his inward mind display,
> And, to a lapwing turned, he fans his way."

See also Gower, *Confes. Amant.*, V.:—

> "And of her suster Progne I finde
> How she was torned out of kinde
> Into a swalwe swift of wing,
> Which eke in winter lith swouning
> There as she may no thing be sene,
> And whan the worlde is woxe grene
> And comen is the somer tide,
> Then fleeth she forth and ginneth to chide
> And chitereth out in her langage
> What falshede is in mariage,
> And telleth in a maner speche
> Of Tereus the spouse breche."

18. Pope, *Temple of Fame*, 7:—

> "What time the morn mysterious visions brings,
> While purer slumbers spread their golden wings."

22. Mount Ida.

30. To the region of fire. Brunetto Latini, *Tresor*, Ch. CXIII., says: "After the environment of the air is seated the fourth element: this is an orb of fire, which extends to the moon and surrounds this atmosphere in which we are.

And know that above the fire is in the first place the moon, and the other stars, which are all of the nature of fire."

37. To prevent Achilles from going to the siege of Troy, his mother Thetis took him from Chiron, the Centaur, and concealed him in female attire in the court of Lycomedes, king of Scyros.

53. As Richter says: "The hour when sleep is nigh unto the soul."

55. Lucia, the Enlightening Grace of heaven. *Inf.* II. 97.

58. Nino and Conrad.

63. Ovid uses a like expression:—

> "Sleep and the god together went away."

94. The first stair is Confession; the second, Contrition; and the third, Penance.

97. Purple and black. See *Inf.* V. Note 89.

105. The gate of Paradise is thus described by Milton, *Parad. Lost,* III. 501:—

> "Far distant he descries,
> Ascending by degrees magnificent
> Up to the wall of heaven, a structure high;
> At top whereof, but far more rich, appeared
> The work as of a kingly palace gate,
> With frontispiece of diamond and gold
> Imbellished; thick with sparkling orient gems
> The portal shone, inimitable on earth
> By model or by shading pencil drawn.
> The stairs were such as whereon Jacob saw
> Angels, ascending and descending, bands
> Of guardians bright, when he from Esau fled
> To Padan-Aram in the field of Luz,
> Dreaming by night under the open sky,
> And waking cried, 'This is the gate of heaven.'
> Each stair mysteriously was meant, nor stood
> There always, but drawn up to heaven sometimes
> Viewless; and underneath a bright sea flowed
> Of jasper, or of liquid pearl, whereon
> Who after came from earth sailing arrived,
> Wafted by angels; or flew o'er the lake,
> Rapt in a chariot drawn by fiery steeds."

112. The Seven Sins, which are punished in the seven circles of Purgatory; Pride, Envy, Anger, Sloth, Avarice, Gluttony, Lust.

118. The golden key is the authority of the confessor; the silver, his knowledge.

132. *Luke* ix. 62: "No man having put his hand to the plough, and look-ing back, is fit for the kingdom of God." And xvii. 32: "Remember Lot's wife."

Boëthius, *Cons. Phil.,* Lib. III. *Met.* 12:—

> "Heu! noctis prope terminos
> Orpheus Eurydicen suam
> Vidit, perdidit, occidit.
> Vos hæc fabula respicit,
> Quicumque in superum diem
> Mentem ducere quæritis,
> Nam qui Tartareum in specus
> Victus lumina flexerit,
> Quicquid præcipuum trahit,
> Perdit, dum videt inferos."

136. Milton, *Parad. Lost,* II. 879:—

> "On a sudden open fly
> With impetuous recoil and jarring sound
> The infernal doors, and on their hinges grate
> Harsh thunder."

138. When Cæsar robbed the Roman treasury on the Tarpeian hill, the tribune Metellus strove to defend it; but Cæsar, drawing his sword, said to him, "It is easier to do this than to say it."

Lucan, *Phars.,* III.:—

> "The tribune with unwilling steps withdrew,
> While impious hands the rude assault renew:
> The brazen gates with thundering strokes resound,
> And the Tarpeian mountain rings around.
> At length the sacred storehouse, open laid,
> The hoarded wealth of ages past displayed;
> There might be seen the sums proud Carthage sent,
> Her long impending ruin to prevent.
> There heaped the Macedonian treasures shone,
> What great Flaminius and Æmilius won
> From vanquished Philip and his hapless son.
> There lay, what flying Pyrrhus lost, the gold
> Scorned by the patriot's honesty of old:
> Whate'er our parsimonious sires could save,
> What tributary gifts rich Syria gave;
> The hundred Cretan cities' ample spoil;
> What Cato gathered from the Cyprian isle.

> Riches of captive kings by Pompey borne,
> In happier days, his triumph to adorn,
> From utmost India and the rising morn;
> Wealth infinite, in one rapacious day,
> Became the needy soldier's lawless prey:
> And wretched Rome, by robbery laid low,
> Was poorer than the bankrupt Cæsar now."

140. The hymn of St. Ambrose, universally known in the churches as the *Te Deum*.

144. Thomson, *Hymn*:—

> "In swarming cities vast
> Assembled men to the deep organ join
> The long-resounding voice, oft breaking clear
> At solemn pauses through the swelling bass,
> And, as each mingling flame increases each,
> In one united ardour rise to heaven."

Canto X

1. In this canto is described the First Circle of Purgatory, where the sin of Pride is punished.

14. It being now Easter Monday, and the fourth day after the full moon, the hour here indicated would be four hours after sunrise. And as the sun was more than two hours high when Dante found himself at the gate of Purgatory (Canto IX. 44), he was an hour and a half in this needle's eye.

30. Which was so steep as to allow of no ascent; *dritto di salita* being used in the sense of right of way.

32. Polycletus, the celebrated Grecian sculptor, among whose works one, representing the body-guard of the king of Persia, acquired such fame for excellence as to be called "the Rule."

33. With this description of the sculptures on the wall of Purgatory compare that of the shield which Vulcan made for Achilles, *Iliad*, XVIII. 484, Buckley's Tr.:—

"On it he wrought the earth, and the heaven, and the sea, the unwearied sun, and the full moon. On it also he represented all the constellations with which the heaven is crowned, the Pleiades, the Hyades, and the strength of Orion, and the Bear, which they also call by the appellation of the Wain, which there revolves, and watches Orion; but it alone is free from the baths of the ocean.

"In it likewise he wrought two fair cities of articulate speaking men. In the one, indeed, there were marriages and feasts; and they were conducting the brides from their chambers through the city with brilliant torches, and many a bridal song was raised. The youthful dancers were wheeling round, and among them pipes and lyres uttered a sound; and the women standing, each at her portals, admired. And people were crowded together in an assembly, and there a contest had arisen; for two men contended for the ransom-money of a slain man: the one affirmed that he had paid all, appealing to the people; but the other denied, averring that he had received naught: and both wished to find an end of the dispute before a judge. The people were applauding both, supporters of either party, and the heralds were keeping back the people; but the elders sat upon polished stones, in a sacred circle, and the pleaders held in their hands the staves of the clear-voiced heralds; with these then they arose, and alternately pleaded their cause. Moreover, in the midst lay two talents of gold, to give to him who should best establish his claim among them. But round the other city sat two armies of people glittering in arms; and one of two plans was agreeable to them, either to waste it, or to divide all things into two parts,—the wealth, whatever the pleasant city contained within it. They, however, had not yet complied, but were secretly arming themselves for an ambuscade. Meanwhile, their beloved wives and young children kept watch, standing above, and among them the men whom old age possessed. But they (the younger men) advanced; but Mars was their leader, and Pallas Minerva, both golden, and clad in golden dresses, beautiful and large, along with their armour, radiant all round, and indeed like gods; but the people were of humbler size. But when they now had reached a place where it appeared fit to lay an ambuscade, by a river, where there was a watering-place for all sorts of cattle, there then they settled, clad in shining steel. There, apart from the people, sat two spies, watching when they might perceive the sheep and crooked-horned oxen. These, however, soon advanced, and two shepherds accompanied them, amusing themselves with their pipes, for they had not yet perceived the stratagem. Then they, discerning them, ran in upon them, and immediately slaughtered on all sides the herds of oxen, and the beautiful flocks of snow-white sheep; and slew the shepherds besides. But they, when they heard the great tumult among the oxen, previously sitting in front of the assembly, mounting their nimble-footed steeds, pursued; and soon came up with them. Then, having marshalled themselves, they fought a battle on the banks of the river, and wounded one another with their brazen spears. Among them mingled Discord and Tumult, and destructive Fate, holding one alive recently wounded, another unwounded, but a third, slain, she drew by the feet through the battle; and had the garment around her shoulders crimsoned with the gore of men. But they turned about, like living mortals, and fought, and drew away the slaughtered bodies of each other.

"On it he also placed a soft fallow field, rich glebe, wide, thrice-ploughed; and in it many ploughmen drove hither and thither, turning round their teams. But when, returning, they reached the end of the field, then a man, advancing, gave into their hands a cup of very sweet wine; but they turned themselves in series, eager to reach the other end of the deep fallow. But it was all black behind, similar to ploughed land, which indeed was a marvel beyond all others.

"On it likewise he placed a field of deep corn, where reapers were cutting, having sharp sickles in their hands. Some handfuls fell one after the other upon the ground along the furrow, and the binders of sheaves tied others with bands. Three binders followed the reapers, while behind them boys gathering the handfuls, and bearing them in their arms, continually supplied them; and among them the master stood by the swath in silence, holding a sceptre, delighted in heart. But apart, beneath an oak, servants were preparing a banquet, and, sacrificing a huge ox, they ministered; while women sprinkled much white barley on the meat, as a supper for the reapers.

"On it likewise he placed a vineyard, heavily laden with grapes, beautiful, golden; but the clusters throughout were black; and it was supported throughout by silver poles. Round it he drew an azure trench, and about it a hedge of tin; but there was only one path to it, by which the gatherers went when they collected the vintage. Young virgins and youths, of tender minds, bore the luscious fruit in woven baskets, in the midst of whom a boy played sweetly on a shrill harp; and with tender voice sang gracefully to the chord; while they, beating the ground in unison with dancing and shouts, followed, skipping with their feet.

"In it he also wrought a herd of oxen with horns erect. But the kine were made of gold and of tin, and rushed out with a lowing from the stall to the pasture, beside a murmuring stream, along the breeze-waving reeds. Four golden herdsmen accompanied the oxen, and nine dogs, swift of foot, followed. But two terrible lions detained the bull, roaring among the foremost oxen, and he was dragged away, loudly bellowing, and the dogs and youths followed for a rescue. They indeed, having torn off the skin of the great ox, lapped up his entrails and black blood; and the shepherds vainly pressed upon them, urging on their fleet dogs. These however refused to bite the lions, but, standing very near, barked, and shunned them.

"On it illustrious Vulcan also formed a pasture in a beautiful grove full of white sheep, and folds, and covered huts and cottages.

"Illustrious Vulcan likewise adorned it with a dance, like unto that which, in wide Gnossus, Dædalus contrived for fair-haired Ariadne. There danced youths and alluring virgins, holding each other's hands at the wrist. These wore fine linen robes, but those were dressed in well-woven tunics, shining as with oil; these also had beautiful garlands, and those wore golden swords, hanging from silver belts. Sometimes, with skilful feet, they nimbly bounded round; as when a potter, sitting, shall make trial of a wheel fitted to his hands, whether it will run: and at other times again they ran back to their places through one another. But a great crowd surrounded the pleasing dance, amusing themselves; and among them two tumblers, beginning their songs, spun round through the midst.

"But in it he also formed the vast strength of the river Oceanus, near the last border of the well-formed shield."

Notes

See also Virgil's description of the Shield of Æneas, *Æneid*, VIII., and of the representations on the walls of the Temple of Juno at Carthage, *Æneid,* I. Also the description of the Temple of Mars, in Statius, *Thebaid,* VII., and that of the tomb of the Persian queen in the *Alexandreis* of Philip Gaultier, noticed in Mr. Sumner's article, *Atlantic Monthly,* XVI. 754. And finally "the noble kerving and the portreitures" of the Temples of Venus, Mars, and Diana, in Chaucer's *Knightes Tale*:—

> "Why shulde I not as wel eke tell you all
> The portreiture that was upon the wall
> Within the temple of mighty Mars the Rede?
>
> . . . . .
>
> "First on the wall was peinted a forest,
> In which ther wonneth neyther man ne best;
> With knotty, knarry, barrein trees old,
> Of stubbes sharpe, and hidous to behold;
> In which ther ran a romble and a swough,
> As though a storme shuld bresten every bough.
> And, dounward from an hill, under a bent,
> Ther stood the temple of Mars Armipotent,
> Wrought all of burned stele; of which th' entree
> Was longe and streite, and gastly for to see;
> And therout came a rage and swiche a vise,
> That it made all the gates for to rise.
> The northern light in at the dore shone;
> For window, on the wall, ne was ther none,
> Thurgh which men mighten any light discerne.
> The dore was all of athamant eterne;
> Yclenched, overthwart and endelong,
> With yren tough. And, for to make it strong,
> Every piler the temple to sustene
> Was tonne-gret, of yren bright and shene.
> "Ther saw I, first, the derke imagining
> Of felonie, and alle the compassing;
> The cruel ire, red as any glede;
> The pikepurse; and eke the pale drede;
> The smiler, with the knif under the cloke;
> The shepen brenning, with the blake smoke;
> The treson of the mordring in the bedde;
> The open werre, with woundes all bebledde;
> Conteke, with blody knif and sharp menace:
> All full of chirking was that sory place.
> The sleer of himself, yet, saw I there,
> His herte-blood hath bathed all his here,
> The naile ydriven in the shode anyght,
> The colde deth, with mouth gaping upright."

40. *Luke* i. 28: "And the angel came in unto her and said, Hail, thou that art highly favoured, the Lord is with thee."

44. *Luke* i. 38: "And Mary said, Behold the handmaid of the Lord."

57. *2 Samuel* vi. 6, 7: "And when they came to Nachon's threshing-floor, Uzzah put forth his hand to the ark of God, and took hold of it; for the oxen shook it. And the anger of the Lord was kindled against Uzzah, and God smote him there for his error; and there he died by the ark of God."

65. *2 Samuel* vi. 14: "And David danced before the Lord with all his might; and David was girded with a linen ephod."

68. *2 Samuel* vi. 16: "And as the ark of the Lord came into the city of David, Michal, Saul's daughter, looked through a window and saw King David leaping and dancing before the Lord;. and she despised him in her heart."

73. This story of Trajan is told in nearly the same words, though in prose, in the *Fiore di Filosofi,* a work attributed to Brunetto Latini. See Nannucci, *Manuale della Letteratura del Primo Secolo,* III. 291. It may be found also in the *Legenda Aurea,* in the *Cento Novelle Antiche,* Nov. 67, and in the *Life of St. Gregory,* by Paulus Diaconus.

As told by Ser Brunetto the story runs thus: "Trajan was a very just Emperor, and one day, having mounted his horse to go into battle with his cavalry, a woman came and seized him by the foot, and, weeping bitterly, asked him and besought him to do justice upon those who had without cause put to death her son, who was an upright young man. And he answered and said, 'I will give thee satisfaction when I return.' And she said, 'And if thou dost not return?' And he answered, 'If I do not return, my successor will give thee satisfaction.' And she said, 'How do I know that? and suppose he do it, what is it to thee if another do good? Thou art my debtor, and according to thy deeds shalt thou be judged; it is a fraud for a man not to pay what he owes; the justice of another will not liberate thee, and it will be well for thy successor if he shall liberate himself.' Moved by these words the Emperor alighted, and did justice, and consoled the widow, and then mounted his horse, and went to battle, and routed his enemies. A long time afterwards St. Gregory, hearing of this justice, saw his statue, and had him disinterred, and found that he was all turned to dust, except his bones and his tongue, which was like that of a living man. And by this St. Gregory knew his justice, for this tongue had always spoken it; so that when he wept very piteously through compassion, praying God that he would take this soul out of Hell, knowing that he had been a Pagan. Then God, because of these prayers, drew that soul from pain, and put it into glory. And thereupon the angel spoke to St. Gregory, and told him never to make such a prayer again, and God laid upon him as a penance either to be two days in Purgatory, or to be always ill with fever and side-ache. St. Gregory as the lesser punishment chose the fever and side-ache (*male di fianco*)."

75. Gregory's "great victory" was saving the soul of Trajan by prayer.

124. Jeremy Taylor says: "As the silk-worm eateth itself out of a seed to become a little worm; and there feeding on the leaves of mulberries, it grows

till its coat be off, and then works itself into a house of silk; then, casting its pearly seeds for the young to breed, it leaveth its silk for man, and dieth all white and winged in the shape of a flying creature: so is the progress of souls."

127. Gower, *Confes. Amant.,* I.:—

> "The proude vice of veingloire
> Remembreth nought of purgatoire."

And Shakespeare, *King Henry the Eighth,* III. 2.:—

> "I have ventured,
> Like little wanton boys that swim on bladders,
> This many summers in a sea of glory."

Canto XI

3. The angels, the first creation or effects of the divine power.

6. *Wisdom of Solomon,* vii. 25: "For she is the breath of the power of God, and a pure influence flowing from the glory of the Almighty." In the Vulgate: *Vapor est enim virtutis Dei.*

45. See *Inf.* XII. Note 2.

58. Or Italian. The speaker is Omberto Aldobrandeschi, Count of Santafiore, in the Maremma of Siena. "The Counts of Santafiore were, and are, and almost always will be at war with the Sienese," says the *Ottimo.* In one of these wars Omberto was slain, at the village of Campagnatico. "The author means," continues the same commentator, "that he who cannot carry his head high should bow it down like a bulrush."

79. Vasari, *Lives of the Painters,* Mrs. Foster's Tr., I. 103, says:—

"At this time there lived in Rome—to omit nothing relative to art that may be worthy of commemoration—a certain Oderigi of Agobbio, an excellent miniature-painter of those times, with whom Giotto lived on terms of close friendship; and who was therefore invited by the Pope to illuminate many books for the library of the palace: but these books have in great part perished in the lapse of time. In my book of ancient drawings I have some few remains from the hand of this artist, who was certainly a clever man, although much surpassed by Franco of Bologna, who executed many admirable works in the same manner, for the same Pontiff (and which were also destined for the library of the palace), at the same time with those of Oderigi. From the hand of Franco also, I have designs, both in painting and illuminating, which may be seen in my book above cited; among others are an eagle, perfectly well done, and a lion tearing up a tree, which is most beautiful."

81. The art of illuminating manuscripts, which was called in Paris *alluminare,* was in Italy called *miniare.* Hence Oderigi is called by Vasari a *miniatore,* or miniature-painter.

83. Franco Bolognese was a pupil of Oderigi, who perhaps alludes to this fact in claiming a part of the honour paid to the younger artist.

94. Of Cimabue, Vasari, *Lives of the Painters,* Mrs. Foster's Tr., I. 35, says:—

"The overwhelming flood of evils by which unhappy Italy has been submerged and devastated had not only destroyed whatever could properly be called buildings, but, a still more deplorable consequence, had totally exterminated the artists themselves, when, by the will of God, in the year 1240, Giovanni Cimabue, of the noble family of that name, was born, in the city of Florence, to give the first light to the art of painting. This youth, as he grew up, being considered by his father and others to give proof of an acute judgment and a clear understanding, was sent to Santa Maria Novella to study letters under a relation, who was then master in grammar to the novices of that convent. But Cimabue, instead of devoting himself to letters, consumed the whole day in drawing men, horses, houses, and other various fancies, on his books and different papers,—an occupation to which he felt himself impelled by nature; and this natural inclination was favoured by fortune, for the governors of the city had invited certain Greek painters to Florence, for the purpose of restoring the art of painting, which had not merely degenerated, but was altogether lost. These artists, among other works, began to paint the Chapel of the Gondi, situate next the principal chapel, in Santa Maria Novella, the roof and walls of which are now almost entirely destroyed by time,—and Cimabue, often escaping from the school, and having already made a commencement in the art he was so fond of, would stand watching those masters at their work, the day through. Judging from these circumstances, his father, as well as the artists themselves, concluded him to be well endowed for painting, and thought that much might be hoped from his future efforts, if he were devoted to that art. Giovanni was accordingly, to his no small satisfaction, placed with those masters. From this time he laboured incessantly, and was so far aided by his natural powers that he soon greatly surpassed his teachers both in design and colouring. For these masters, caring little for the progress of art, had executed their works as we now see them, not in the excellent manner of the ancient Greeks, but in the rude modern style of their own day. Wherefore, though Cimabue imitated his Greek instructors, he very much improved the art, relieving it greatly from their uncouth manner, and doing honour to his country by the name he acquired, and by the works he performed. Of this we have evidence in Florence from the pictures which he painted there; as, for example, the front of the altar of Santa Cecilia, and a picture of the Virgin, in Santa Croce, which was, and is still, attached to one of the pilasters on the right of the choir."

95. Shakespeare, *Troil. and Cres.,* III. 3:—

> "The present eye praises the present object:
> Then marvel not, thou great and complete man,
> That all the Greeks begin to worship Ajax;

> Since things in motion sooner catch the eye
> Than what not stirs. The cry went once on thee;
> And still it might, and yet it may again,
> If thou wouldst not entomb thyself alive,
> And case thy reputation in thy tent."

Cimabue died in 1300. His epitaph is:

> "Credidit ut Cimabos picturæ castra tenere,
>   Sic tenuit vivens, nunc tenet astra poli."

Vasari, *Lives of the Painters,* I. 93:—

"The gratitude which the masters in painting owe to Nature,—who is ever the truest model of him who, possessing the power to select the brightest parts from her best and loveliest features, employs himself unweariedly in the reproduction of these beauties,—this gratitude, I say, is due, in my judgment, to the Florentine painter Giotto, seeing that he alone,—although born amidst incapable artists, and at a time when all good methods in art had long been entombed beneath the ruins of war,—yet, by the favour of Heaven, he, I say, alone succeeded in resuscitating Art, and restoring her to a path that may be called the true one. And it was in truth a great marvel, that from so rude and inapt an age Giotto should have had strength to elicit so much, that the art of design, of which the men of those days had little, if any knowledge, was by his means effectually recalled into life. The birth of this great man took place in the hamlet of Vespignano, fourteen miles from the city of Florence, in the year 1276. His father's name was Bondone, a simple husbandman, who reared the child, to whom he had given the name of Giotto, with such decency as his condition permitted. The boy was early remarked for extreme vivacity in all his childish proceedings, and for extraordinary promptitude of intelligence; so that he became endeared, not only to his father, but to all who knew him in the village and around it. When he was about ten years old, Bondone gave him a few sheep to watch, and with these he wandered about the vicinity,—now here and now there. But, induced by Nature herself to the arts of design, he was perpetually drawing on the stones, the earth, or the sand, some natural object that came before him, or some fantasy that presented itself to his thoughts. It chanced one day that the affairs of Cimabue took him from Florence to Vespignano, when he perceived the young Giotto, who, while his sheep fed around him, was occupied in drawing one of them from the life, with a stone slightly pointed, upon a smooth, clean piece of rock,—and that without any teaching whatever but such as Nature herself had imparted. Halting in astonishment, Cimabue inquired of the boy if he would accompany him to his home, and the child replied, he would go willingly, if his father were content to permit it. Cimabue therefore requesting the consent of Bondone, the latter granted it readily, and suffered the artist to conduct his son to Florence, where, in a short time, instructed by Cimabue and aided by Nature, the boy not only equalled his master in his own manner, but became so good an imitator of Nature that he totally banished the rude Greek manner, restoring art to the better path adhered to in modern times, and introducing the custom of accurately drawing living persons from nature, which had not been used for more than two hundred years. Or, if some had attempted it, as said above, it was not by any means with the success of Giotto. Among the portraits by this artist, and which still remain, is one of his contemporary and intimate friend, Dante Alighieri, who was no less famous as a poet than Giotto as a painter, and whom Messer Giovanni Boccaccio has lauded so highly in the introduction to his story of Messer Forese da Rabatta, and of Giotto the painter himself. This portrait is in the chapel of the palace of the Podestà in Florence; and in the same chapel are the portraits of Ser Brunetto Latini, master of Dante, and of Messer Corso Donati, an illustrious citizen of that day."

Pope Benedict the Ninth, hearing of Giotto's fame, sent one of his courtiers to Tuscany, to propose to him certain paintings for the Church of St. Peter. "The messenger," continues Vasari, "when on his way to visit Giotto, and to inquire what other good masters there were in Florence, spoke first with many artists in Siena,—then, having received designs from them, he proceeded to Florence, and repaired one morning to the workshop where Giotto was occupied with his labours. He declared the purpose of the Pope, and the manner in which that Pontiff desired to avail himself of his assistance; and, finally, requested to have a drawing, that he might send it to his Holiness. Giotto, who was very courteous, took a sheet of paper and a pencil dipped in a red colour, then, resting his elbow on his side, to form a sort of compass, with one turn of the hand he drew a circle, so perfect and exact that it was a marvel to behold. This done, he turned smiling to the courtier, saying, 'Here is your drawing.' 'Am I to have nothing more than this?' inquired the latter, conceiving himself to be jested with. 'That is enough and to spare,' returned Giotto; 'send it with the rest, and you will see if it will be recognised.' The messenger, unable to obtain anything more, went away very ill satisfied, and fearing that he had been fooled. Nevertheless, having despatched the other drawings to the Pope, with the names of those who had done them, he sent that of Giotto also, relating the mode in which he had made his circle, without moving his arm and without compasses; from which the Pope, and such of the courtiers as were well versed in the subject, perceived how far Giotto surpassed all the other painters of his time. This incident, becoming known, gave rise to the proverb, still used in relation to people of dull wits,—*Tu sei più tondo che l'O di Giotto;* the significance of which consists in the double meaning of the word 'tondo,' which is used in the Tuscan for slowness of intellect and heaviness of comprehension, as well as for an exact circle. The proverb has besides an interest from the circumstance which gave it birth. . . . .

"It is said that Giotto, when he was still a boy, and studying with Cimabue, once painted a fly on the nose of a figure on which Cimabue himself was employed, and this so naturally, that, when the master returned to continue his work, he believed it to be real, and lifted his hand more than once to drive it away before he should go on with the painting."

Boccaccio, *Decameron,* VI. 5, tells this tale of Giotto:—

"As it often happens that fortune hides under the meanest trades in life the greatest virtues, which has been proved by Pampinea; so are the greatest geniuses found frequently lodged by Nature in the most deformed and misshapen bodies, which was verified in two of our own citizens, as I am now going to relate. For the one, who was called Forese da Rabatta, being a little deformed mortal, with a flat Dutch face, worse than any of the family of the Baronci, yet was he esteemed by most men a repository of the civil law. And the other, whose name was Giotto, had such a prodigious fancy, that there was nothing in Nature, the parent of all things, but he could imitate it with his pencil so well, and draw it so like, as to deceive our very senses, imagining that to be the very thing itself which was only his painting: therefore, having brought that art again to light, which had lain buried for many ages under the errors of such as aimed more to captivate the eyes of the ignorant, than to please the understandings of those who were really judges, he may be deservedly called one of the lights and glories of our city, and the rather as being master of his art, notwithstanding his modesty would never suffer himself to be so esteemed; which honour, though rejected by him, displayed itself in him with the greater lustre, as it was so eagerly usurped by others less knowing than himself, and by many also who had all their knowledge from him. But though his excellence in his profession was so wonderful, yet as to his person and aspect he had no way the advantage of Signor Forese. To come then to my story. These two worthies had each his country-seat at Mugello, and Forese being gone thither in the vacation time, and riding upon an unsightly steed, chanced to meet there with Giotto; who was no better equipped than himself, when they returned together to Florence. Travelling slowly along, as they were able to go no faster, they were overtaken by a great shower of rain, and forced to take shelter in a poor man's house, who was well known to them both; and, as there was no appearance of the weather's clearing up, and each being desirous of getting home that night, they borrowed two old, rusty cloaks, and two rusty hats, and they proceeded on their journey. After they had gotten a good part of their way, thoroughly wet, and covered with dirt and mire, which their two shuffling steeds had thrown upon them, and which by no means improved their looks, it began to clear up at last, and they, who had hitherto said but little to each other, now turned to discourse together; whilst Forese, riding along and listening to Giotto, who was excellent at telling a story, began at last to view him attentively from head to foot, and, seeing him in that wretched, dirty pickle, without having any regard to himself he fell a laughing, and said, 'Do you suppose, Giotto, if a stranger were to meet with you now, who had never seen you before, that he would imagine you to be the best painter in the world, as you really are?' Giotto readily replied, 'Yes, sir, I believe he might think so, if, looking at you at the same time, he would ever conclude that you had learned your

A, B, C.' At this Forese was sensible of his mistake, finding himself well paid in his own coin."

Another story of Giotto may be found in Sacchetti, Nov. 75.

97. Probably Dante's friend, Guido Cavalcanti, *Inf.* X. Note 63; and Guido Guinicelli, *Purg.* XXVI. Note 92, whom he calls

> "The father
> Of me and of my betters, who had ever
> Practised the sweet and gracious rhymes of love."

99. Some commentators suppose that Dante here refers to himself. He more probably is speaking only in general terms, without particular reference to any one.

103. Ben Jonson, *Ode on the Death of Sir H. Morison:*—

> "It is not growing like a tree
>   In bulk doth make men better be,
> Or standing long an oak, three hundred year,
> To fall a log at last, dry, bald, and sear;
>   A lily of a day
>   Is fairer far in May,
>   Although it fall and die that night:
>   It was the plant and flower of light."

105. The babble of childhood; *pappo* for *pane,* bread, and *dindi* for *danari,* money.

Halliwell, *Dic. of Arch. and Prov. Words*: "DINDERS, small coins of the Lower Empire, found at Wroxeter."

108. The revolution of the fixed stars, according to the Ptolemaic theory, which was also Dante's, was thirty-six thousand years.

109. "Who goes so slowly," interprets the *Ottimo.*

112. At the battle of Monte Aperto. See *Inf.* X. Note 86.

118. Henry Vaughan, *Sacred Poems*:

> "O holy hope and high humility,
>   High as the heavens above;
> These are your walks, and you have showed them me
>   To kindle my cold love!"

And Milton, *Sams. Agon.,* 185:—

> "Apt words have power to swage
> The tumours of a troubled mind."

121. A haughty and ambitious nobleman of Siena, who led the Sienese troops at the battle of Monte Aperto. Afterwards, when the Sienese were

routed by the Florentines at the battle of Colle in the Val d'Elsa, (*Purg.* XIII. Note 115,) he was taken prisoner "and his head was cut off," says Villani, VII. 31, "and carried through all the camp fixed upon a lance. And well was fulfilled the prophecy and revelation which the devil had made to him, by means of necromancy, but which he did not understand; for the devil, being constrained to tell how he would succeed in that battle, mendaciously answered, and said: 'Thou shalt go forth and fight, thou shalt conquer not die in the battle, and thy head shall be highest in the camp.' And he, believing from these words that he should be victorious, and believing that he should be lord over all, did not put a stop after 'not' (*vincerai no, morrai,* thou shalt conquer not, thou shalt die). And therefore it is great folly to put faith in the devil's advice. This Messer Provenzano was a great man in Siena after his victory at Monte Aperto, and led the whole city, and all the Ghibelline party of Tuscany made him their chief, and he was very presumptuous in his will."

The humility which saved him was his seating himself at a little table in the public square of Siena, called the Campo, and begging money of all passers to pay the ransom of a friend who had been taken prisoner by Charles of Anjou, as here narrated by Dante.

138. Spenser, *Faery Queene,* VI. c. 7, st. 22:—

> "He, therewith much abashed and affrayd,
>   Began to tremble every limbe and vaine."

141. A prophecy of Dante's banishment and poverty and humiliation.

Canto XII

1. In the first part of this canto the same subject is continued, with examples of pride humbled, sculptured on the pavement, upon which the proud are doomed to gaze as they go with their heads bent down beneath their heavy burdens,

> "So that they may behold their evil ways."

Iliad, XIII. 700: "And Ajax, the swift son of Oïleus, never at all stood apart from the Telamonian Ajax; but as in a fallow field two dark bullocks, possessed of equal spirit, drag the compacted plough, and much sweat breaks out about the roots of their horns, and the well-polished yoke alone divides them, stepping along the furrow, and the plough cuts up the bottom of the soil, so they, joined together, stood very near to each other."

3. In Italy a pedagogue is not only a teacher, but literally a leader of children, and goes from house to house collecting his little flock, which he brings home again after school.

Galatians iii. 24: "The law was our schoolmaster (Paidagogos) to bring us unto Christ."

17. Tombs under the pavement in the aisles of churches, in contradistinction to those built aloft against the walls.

25. The reader will not fail to mark the artistic structure of the passage from this to the sixty-third line. First there are four stanzas beginning, "I saw;" then four beginning, "O;" then four beginning, "Displayed;" and then a stanza which resumes and unites them all.

27. *Luke* x. 18: "I beheld Satan as lightning fall from heaven."
Milton, *Parad. Lost*, I. 44:—

> "Him the Almighty Power
> Hurled headlong flaming from the ethereal sky
> With hideous ruin and combustion, down
> To bottomless perdition, there to dwell
> In adamantine chains and penal fire,
> Who durst defy the Omnipotent to arms."

28. *Iliad*, I. 403: "Him of the hundred hands, whom the gods call Briareus, and all men Ægæon." *Inf.* XXI. Note 98.

He was struck by the thunderbolt of Jove, or by a shaft of Apollo, at the battle of Flegra. "Ugly medley of sacred and profane, of revealed truth and fiction!" exclaims Venturi.

31. Thymbræus, a surname of Apollo, from his temple in Thymbra.

34. Nimrod, who "began to be a mighty one in the earth," and his "tower whose top may reach unto heaven."
Genesis xi. 8: "So the Lord scattered them abroad from thence upon the face of all the earth; and they left to build the city. Therefore is the name of it called Babel; because the Lord did there confound the language of all the earth, and from thence did the Lord scatter them abroad upon the face of all the earth."

See also *Inf.* XXXI. Note 77.

36. Lombardi proposes in this line to read "together" instead of "proud;" which Biagioli thinks is "changing a beautiful diamond for a bit of lead; and stupid is he who accepts the change."

37. Among the Greek epigrams is one on Niobe, which runs as follows:—

> "This sepulchre within it has no corse;
> This corse without here has no sepulchre,
> But to itself is sepulchre and corse."

Ovid, *Metamorph.*, VI., Croxall's Tr.:—

> "Widowed and childless, lamentable state!
> A doleful sight, among the dead she sate;

> Hardened with woes, a statue of despair,
> To every breath of wind unmoved her hair;
> Her cheek still reddening, but its colour dead,
> Faded her eyes, and set within her head.
> No more her pliant tongue its motion keeps,
> But stands congealed within her frozen lips.
> Stagnate and dull, within her purple veins,
> Its current stopped, the lifeless blood remains.
> Her feet their usual offices refuse,
> Her arms and neck their graceful gestures lose:
> Action and life from every part are gone,
> And even her entrails turn to solid stone;
> Yet still she weeps, and whirled by stormy winds,
> Borne through the air, her native country finds;
> There fixed, she stands upon a bleaky hill,
> There yet her marble cheeks eternal tears distil."

39. Homer, *Iliad,* XXIV. 604, makes them but twelve. "Twelve children perished in her halls, six daughters and six blooming sons; these Apollo slew from his silver bow, enraged with Niobe; and those Diana, delighting in arrows, because she had deemed herself equal to the beautiful-cheeked Latona. She said that Latona had borne only two, but she herself had borne many; nevertheless those, though but two, exterminated all these."

But Ovid, *Metamorph.,* VI., says:—

> "Seven are my daughters of a form divine,
> With seven fair sons, an indefective line."

40. 1 *Samuel* xxxi. 4, 5: "Then said Saul unto his armour-bearer, Draw thy sword and thrust me through therewith, lest these uncircumcised come and thrust me through and abuse me. But his armour-bearer would not, for he was sore afraid; therefore Saul took a sword, and fell upon it. And when his armour-bearer saw that Saul was dead, he fell likewise upon his sword, and died with him."

42. 2 *Samuel* i. 21: "Ye mountains of Gilboa, let there be no dew, neither let there be rain upon you."

43. Arachne, daughter of Idmon the dyer of Colophon. Ovid, *Metamorph.,* VI.:—

> "One at the loom so excellently skilled,
>   That to the goddess she refused to yield
>   Low was her birth, and small her native town,
>   She from her art alone obtained renown.
>
>   . . . . .
>
>   Nor would the work, when finished, please so much,
>   As, while she wrought, to view each graceful touch;

> Whether the shapeless wool in balls she wound,
> Or with quick motion turned the spindle round,
> Or with her pencil drew the neat design,
> Pallas her mistress shone in every line.
> This the proud maid with scornful air denies,
> And even the goddess at her work defies;
> Disowns her heavenly mistress every hour,
> Nor asks her aid, nor deprecates her power.
> Let us, she cries, but to a trial come,
> And if she conquers, let her fix my doom."

It was rather an unfair trial of skill, at the end of which Minerva, getting angry, struck Arachne on the forehead with her shuttle of box-wood.

> "The unhappy maid, impatient of the wrong,
> Down from a beam her injured person hung;
> When Pallas, pitying her wretched state,
> At once prevented and pronounced her fate:
> 'Live; but depend, vile wretch!' the goddess cried,
> 'Doomed in suspense for ever to be tied;
> That all your race, to utmost date of time,
> May feel the vengeance and detest the crime.'
>   Then, going off, she sprinkled her with juice
> Which leaves of baneful aconite produce.
> Touched with the poisonous drug, her flowing hair
> Fell to the ground and left her temples bare;
> Her usual features vanished from their place,
> Her body lessened all, but most her face.
> Her slender fingers, hanging on each side
> With many joints, the use of legs supplied;
> A spider's bag the rest, from which she gives
> A thread, and still by constant weaving lives."

46. In the revolt of the Ten Tribes. 1 *Kings* xii. 18: "Then King Rehoboam sent Adoram, who was over the tribute; and all Israel stoned him with stones, that he died; therefore King Rehoboam made speed to get him up to his chariot, to flee to Jerusalem."

50. Amphiaraüs, the soothsayer, foreseeing his own death if he went to the Theban war, concealed himself, to avoid going. His wife Eriphyle, bribed by a "golden necklace set with diamonds," betrayed to her brother Adrastus his hiding-place, and Amphiaraüs, departing, charged his son Alcmeon to kill Eriphyle as soon as he heard of his death.

Ovid, *Metamorph.,* IX.:—

> "The son shall bathe his hands in parent's blood,
> And in one act be both unjust and good."

Statius, *Theb.*, II. 355, Lewis's Tr.:—

> "Fair Eriphyle the rich gift beheld,
>   And her sick breast with secret envy swelled.
>   Not the late omens and the well-known tale
>   To cure her vain ambition aught avail.
>   O had the wretch by self-experience known
>   The future woes and sorrows not her own!
>   But fate decrees her wretched spouse must bleed,
>   And the son's frenzy clear the mother's deed."

53. *Isaiah* xxxvii. 38: "And it came to pass, as he was worshipping in the house of Nisroch his god, that Adrammelech and Sharezer, his sons, smote him with the sword; and they escaped into the land of Armenia, and Esarhaddon, his son, reigned in his stead."

56. *Herodotus,* Book I. Ch. 214, Rawlinson's Tr.: "Tomyris, when she found that Cyrus paid no heed to her advice, collected all the forces of her kingdom, and gave him battle. Of all the combats in which the barbarians have engaged among themselves, I reckon this to have been the fiercest. . . . . The greater part of the army of the Persians was destroyed, and Cyrus himself fell, after reigning nine and twenty years. Search was made among the slain, by order of the queen, for the body of Cyrus, and when it was found, she took a skin, and filling it full of human blood, she dipped the head of Cyrus in the gore, saying, as she thus insulted the corse, 'I live and have conquered thee in fight, and yet by thee am I ruined; for thou tookest my son with guile; but thus I make good my threat, and give thee thy fill of blood.' Of the many different accounts which are given of the death of Cyrus, this which I have followed appears to be the most worthy of credit."

59. After Judith had slain Holofernes. *Judith* xv. 1: "And when they that were in the tents heard, they were astonished at the thing that was done. And fear and trembling fell upon them, so that there was no man that durst abide in the sight of his neighbour, but, rushing out altogether, they fled into every way of the plain and of the hill country. . . . . Now when the children of Israel heard it, they all fell upon them with one consent, and slew them unto Chobai."

61. This tercet unites the "I saw," "O," and "Displayed," of the preceding passage, and binds the whole as with a selvage.

67. Ruskin, *Mod. Painters,* III. 19: "There was probably never a period in which the influence of art over the minds of men seemed to depend less on its merely *imitative* power, than the close of the thirteenth century. No painting or sculpture at that time reached more than a rude resemblance of reality. Its despised perspective, imperfect chiaroscuro, and unrestrained flights of fantastic imagination, separated the artist's work from nature by an interval which there was no attempt to disguise, and little to diminish. And yet, at this very period, the greatest poet of that, or perhaps of any other age, and the attached friend of its greatest painter, who must over and over again have

held full and free conversation with him respecting the objects of his art, speaks in the following terms of painting, supposed to be carried to its highest perfection:—

> 'Qual di pennel fu maestro, e di stile
>   Che ritraesse l'ombre, e i tratti, ch' ivi
>   Mirar farieno uno ingegno sottile.
> Mori li morti, e i vivi parean vivi:
>   Non vide me' di me, chi vide il vero,
>   Quant' io calcai, fin che chinato givi.'

Dante has here clearly no other idea of the highest art than that it should bring back, as in a mirror or vision, the aspect of things passed or absent. The scenes of which he speaks are, on the pavement, for ever represented by angelic power, so that the souls which traverse this circle of the rock may see them, as if the years of the world had been rolled back, and they again stood beside the actors in the moment of action. Nor do I think that Dante's authority is absolutely necessary to compel us to admit that such art as this *might* indeed be the highest possible. Whatever delight we may have been in the habit of taking in pictures, if it were but truly offered to us to remove at our will the canvas from the frame, and in lieu of it to behold, fixed for ever, the image of some of those mighty scenes which it has been our way to make mere themes for the artist's fancy,—if, for instance, we could again behold the Magdalene receiving her pardon at Christ's feet, or the disciples sitting with him at the table of Emmaus,—and this not feebly nor fancifully, but as if some silver mirror, that had leaned against the wall of the chamber, had been miraculously commanded to retain for ever the colours that had flashed upon it for an instant,—would we not part with our picture, Titian's or Veronese's though it might be?"

81. The sixth hour of the day, or noon of the second day.

102. Florence is here called ironically "the well guided" or well governed. Rubaconte is the name of the most easterly of the bridges over the Arno, and takes its name from Messer Rubaconte, who was Podestà of Florence in 1236, when this bridge was built. Above it on the hill stands the church of San Miniato. This is the hill which Michael Angelo fortified in the siege of Florence. In early times it was climbed by stairways.

105. In the good old days, before any one had falsified the ledger of the public accounts, or the standard of measure. In Dante's time a certain Messer Niccola tore out a leaf from the public records, to conceal some villany of his; and a certain Messer Durante, a custom-house officer, diminished the salt-measure by one stave. This is again alluded to, *Par.* XVI. 105.

110. *Matthew* v. 3: "Blessed are the poor in spirit: for theirs is the kingdom of heaven."

It must be observed that all the Latin lines in Dante should be chanted with an equal stress on each syllable, in order to make them rhythmical.

Canto XIII

1. The Second Circle, or Cornice, where is punished the sin of Envy; of which St. Augustine says: "Envy is the hatred of another's felicity; in respect of superiors, because they are not equal to them; in respect of inferiors, lest they should be equal to them; in respect of equals, because they are equal to them. Through envy proceeded the fall of the world, and the death of Christ."

9. The livid colour of Envy.

14. The military precision with which Virgil faces to the right is Homeric. Biagioli says that Dante expresses it "after his own fashion, that is, entirely new and different from mundane custom."

16. Boëthius, *Cons. Phil.,* V. Met. 2:

> "Him the Sun, then, rightly call,—
> God who sees and lightens all."

29. *John* ii. 3: "And when they wanted wine, the mother of Jesus saith unto him, They have no wine."

Examples are first given of the virtue opposite the vice here punished. These are but "airy tongues that syllable men's names;" and it must not be supposed that the persons alluded to are actually passing in the air.

33. The name of Orestes is here shouted on account of the proverbial friendship between him and Pylades. When Orestes was condemned to death, Pylades tried to take his place, exclaiming, "I am Orestes."

36. *Matthew* v. 44: "But I say unto you, Love your enemies, bless them that curse you, do good to them that hate you, and pray for them which despitefully use you and persecute you."

39. See Canto XIV. 147.

42. The next stairway leading from the second to the third circle.

51. The Litany of All Saints.

92. Latian for Italian.

109. A Sienese lady living in banishment at Colle, where from a tower she witnessed the battle between her townsmen and the Florentines. "Sapia hated the Sienese," says Benvenuto, "and placed herself at a window not far from the field of battle, waiting the issue with anxiety, and desiring the rout and ruin of her own people. Her desires being verified by the entire discomfiture of the Sienese, and the death of their captain," (Provenzan Salvani, see Canto XI. Note 121,) "exultant and almost beside herself, she lifted her bold face to heaven, and cried, 'Now, O God, do with me what thou wilt, do me all the harm thou canst; now my prayers are answered, and I die content.'"

110. Gower, *Confes. Amant.,* II.:—

> "Whan I have sene another blithe
> Of love and hadde a goodly chere,
> Ethna, which brenneth yere by yere,

> Was thanne nought so hote as I
> Of thilke sore which prively
> Mine hertes thought withinne brenneth."

114. *Convito,* IV. 23: "Every effect, in so far as it is effect, receiveth the likeness of its cause, as far as it can retain it. Therefore, inasmuch as our life, as has been said, and likewise that of every living creature here below, is caused by the heavens, and the heavens reveal themselves to all these effects, not in complete circle, but in part thereof, so must its movement needs be above; and as an arch retains all lives nearly, (and, I say, retains those of men as well as of other living creatures,) ascending and curving, they must be in the similitude of an arch. Returning then to our life, of which it is now question, I say that it proceeds in the image of this arch, ascending and descending."

122. The warm days near the end of January are still called in Lombardy *I giorni della merla,* the days of the blackbird; from an old legend, that once in the sunny weather a blackbird sang, "I fear thee no more, O Lord, for the winter is over."

128. Peter Pettignano, or Pettinajo, was a holy hermit, who saw visions and wrought miracles at Siena. Forsyth, *Italy,* 149, describing the festival of the Assumption in that city in 1802, says:—

"The Pope had reserved for this great festival the Beatification of Peter, a Sienese comb-maker, whom the Church had neglected to canonize till now. Poor Peter was honoured with all the solemnity of music, high-mass, and officiating cardinal, a florid panegyric, pictured angels bearing his tools to heaven, and combing their own hair as they soared; but he received five hundred years ago a greater honour than all, a verse of praise from Dante."

138. Dante's besetting sin was not envy, but pride.

144. On the other side of the world.

153. The vanity of the Sienese is also spoken of *Inf.* XXIX. 123.

152. Talamone is a seaport in the Maremma, "many times abandoned by its inhabitants," says the *Ottimo,* "on account of the malaria. The town is utterly in ruins; but as the harbour is deep, and would be of great utility if the place were inhabited, the Sienese have spent much money in repairing it many times, and bringing in inhabitants; it is of little use, for the malaria prevents the increase of population."

Talamone is the ancient Telamon, where Marius landed on his return from Africa.

153. The Diana is a subterranean river, which the Sienese were in search of for many years to supply the city with water. "They never have been able to find it," says the *Ottimo,* "and yet they still hope." In Dante's time it was evidently looked upon as an idle dream. To the credit of the Sienese be it said, they persevered, and finally succeeded in obtaining the water so patiently sought for. The *Pozzo Diana,* or Diana's Well, is still to be seen at the Convent of the Carmen.

154. The admirals who go to Talamone to superintend the works will lose there more than their hope, namely, their lives.

Canto XIV

1. The subject of the preceding canto is here continued. Compare the introductory lines with those of Canto V.

7. These two spirits prove to be Guido del Duca and Rinieri da Calboli.

17. A mountain in the Apennines, north-east of Florence, from which the Arno takes its rise. Ampère, *Voyage Dantesque,* p. 246, thus describes this region of the Val d'Arno. "Farther on is another tower, the tower of *Porciano,* which is said to have been inhabited by Dante. From there I had still to climb the summits of the Falterona. I started towards midnight in order to arrive before sunrise. I said to myself, How many times the poet, whose footprints I am following, has wandered in these mountains! It was by these little alpine paths that he came and went, on his way to friends in Romagna or friends in Urbino, his heart agitated with a hope that was never to be fulfilled. I figured to myself Dante walking with a guide under the light of the stars, receiving all the impressions produced by wild and weather-beaten regions, steep roads, deep valleys, and the accidents of a long and difficult route, impressions which he would transfer to his poem. It is enough to have read this poem to be certain that its author has travelled much, has wandered much. Dante really walks with Virgil. He fatigues himself with climbing, he stops to take breath, he uses his hands when feet are insufficient. He gets lost, and asks the way. He observes the height of the sun and stars. In a word, one finds the habits and souvenirs of the traveller in every verse, or rather at every step of his poetic pilgrimage.

"Dante has certainly climbed the top of the Falterona. It is upon this summit, from which all the Valley of the Arno is embraced, that one should read the singular imprecation which the poet has uttered against this whole valley. He follows the course of the river, and as he advances marks every place he comes to with fierce invective. The farther he goes, the more his hate redoubles in violence and bitterness. It is a piece of topographical satire, of which I know no other example."

32. The Apennines, whose long chain ends in Calabria, opposite Cape Peloro in Sicily. *Æneid,* III. 410, Davidson's Tr.:—

"But when, after setting out, the wind shall waft you to the Sicilian coast, and the straits of narrow Pelorus shall open wider to the eye, veer to the land on the left, and to the sea on the left, by a long circuit; fly the right both sea and shore. These lands, they say, once with violence and vast desolation convulsed, (such revolutions a long course of time is able to produce,) slipped asunder; when in continuity both lands were one, the sea rushed impetuously between, and by its waves tore the Italian side from that of Sicily; and with a narrow frith runs between the fields and cities separated by the shores. Scylla guards the right side, implacable Charybdis the left, and thrice with the deepest eddies of its gulf swallows up the vast billows, headlong in, and again spouts them out by turns high into the air, and lashes the stars with the waves."

And Lucan, *Phars.*, II.:—

> "And still we see on fair Sicilia's sands
> Where part of Apennine Pelorus stands."

And Shelley, *Ode to Liberty:*—

> "O'er the lit waves every Æolian isle
> From Pithecusa to Pelorus
> Howls, and leaps, and glares in chorus."

40. When Dante wrote this invective against the inhabitants of the Val d'Arno, he probably had in mind the following passage of Boëthius, *Cons. Phil.*, IV. Pros. 3, Ridpath's Tr.:—

"Hence it again follows, that every thing which strays from what is good ceases to be; the wicked therefore must cease to be what they were; but that they were formerly men, their human shape, which still remains, testifies. By degenerating into wickedness, then, they must cease to be men. But as virtue alone can exalt a man above what is human, so it is on the contrary evident, that vice, as it divests him of his nature, must sink him below humanity; you ought therefore by no means to consider him as a man whom vice has rendered vicious. Tell me, What difference is there betwixt a wolf who lives by rapine, and a robber whom the desire of another's wealth stimulates to commit all manner of violence? Is there anything that bears a stronger resemblance to a wrathful dog who barks at passengers, than a man whose dangerous tongue attacks all the world? What is liker to a fox than a cheat, who spreads his snares in secret to undermine and ruin you? to a lion, than a furious man who is always ready to devour you? to a deer, than a coward who is afraid of his own shadow? to an ass, than a mortal who is slow, dull, and indolent? to the birds of the air, than a man volatile and inconstant? and what, in fine, is a debauchee who is immersed in the lowest sensual gratifications, but a hog who wallows in the mire? Upon the whole, it is an unquestionable truth that a man who forsakes virtue ceases to be a man; and, as it is impossible that he can ascend in the scale of beings, he must of necessity degenerate and sink into a beast."

43. The people of Casentino. Forsyth, *Italy*, p. 126:—

"On returning down to the Casentine, we could trace along the Arno the mischief which followed a late attempt to clear some Apennines of their woods. Most of the soil, which was then loosened from the roots and washed down by the torrents, lodged in this plain; and left immense beds of sand and large rolling stones on the very spot where Dante describes

'Li ruscelletti che de' verdi colli
Del Casentin discendon giuso in Arno,
Facendo i lor canali e freddi e molli.'

"I was surprised to find so large a town as Bibbiena in a country devoid of manufactures, remote from public roads, and even deserted by its landholders; for the Niccolini and Vecchietti, who possess most of this district, prefer the obscurer pleasures of Florence to their palaces and pre-eminence here. The only commodity which the Casentines trade in is pork. Signore Baglione, a gentleman at whose house I slept here, ascribed the superior flavour of their hams, which are esteemed the best in Italy and require no cooking, to the dryness of the air, the absence of stagnant water, and the quantity of chestnuts given to their hogs. Bibbiena has been long renowned for its chestnuts, which the peasants dry in a kiln, grind into a sweet flour, and then convert into bread, cakes, and *polenta*."

46. The people of Arezzo. Forsyth, *Italy,* p. 128:—

"The Casentines were no favourites with Dante, who confounds the men with their hogs. Yet, following the *divine poet* down the Arno, we came to a race still more forbidding. The Aretine peasants seem to inherit the coarse, surly visages of their ancestors, whom he styles *Bottoli*. Meeting one girl, who appeared more cheerful than her neighbours, we asked her how far it was from Arezzo, and received for answer, '*Quanto c'è.*'

"The valley widened as we advanced, and when Arezzo appeared, the river left us abruptly, wheeling off from its environs at a sharp angle, which Dante converts into a snout, and points disdainfully against the currish race. . . . .

"On entering the Val di Chiana, we passed through a peasantry more civil and industrious than their Aretine neighbours. One poor girl, unlike the last whom we accosted, was driving a laden ass, bearing a billet of wood on her head, spinning with the rocca, and singing as she went on. Others were returning with their sickles from the fields which they had reaped in the Maremma, to their own harvest on the hills. That contrast which struck me in the manners of two cantons so near as Cortona to Arezzo, can only be a vestige of their ancient rivalry while separate republics. Men naturally dislike the very virtues of their enemies, and affect qualities as remote from theirs as they can well defend."

50. The Florentines.

53. The Pisans.

57. At the close of these vituperations, perhaps to soften the sarcasm by making it more general, Benvenuto appends this note: "What Dante says of the inhabitants of the Val d'Arno might he said of the greater part of the Italians, nay, of the world. Dante, being once asked why he had put more Christians than Gentiles into Hell, replied, 'Because I have known the Christians better.'"

58. Messer Fulcieri da Calboli of Forlì, nephew of Rinieri. He was Podestà of Florence in 1302, and, being bribed by the Neri, had many of the Bianchi put to death.

64. Florence, the habitation of these wolves, left so stripped by Fulcieri, on his retiring from office, that it will be long in recovering its former prosperity.

81. Guido del Duca of Brettinoro, near Forlì, in Romagna; nothing remains but the name. He and his companion Rinieri were "gentlemen of worth, if they had not been burned up with envy."

87. On worldly goods, where selfishness excludes others; in contrast with the spiritual, which increase by being shared. See Canto XV. 45.

88. Rinieri da Calboli. "He was very famous," says the *Ottimo,* and history says no more. In the *Cento Novelle Antiche,* Nov. 44, Roscoe's Tr., he figures thus:—

"A certain knight was one day entreating a lady whom he loved to smile upon his wishes, and among other delicate arguments which he pressed upon her was that of his own superior wealth, elegance, and accomplishments, especially when compared with the merits of her own liege-lord, 'whose extreme ugliness, madam,' he continued, 'I think I need not insist upon.' Her husband, who overheard this compliment from the place of his concealment, immediately replied, 'Pray, sir, mend your own manners, and do not vilify other people.' The name of the plain gentleman was Lizio di Valbona, and Messer Rinieri da Calvoli that of the other."

92. In Romagna, which is bounded by the Po, the Apennines, the Adriatic, and the river Reno, that passes near Bologna.

93. For study and pleasure.

97. Of Lizio and Manardi the *Ottimo* says: "Messer Lizio di Valbona, a courteous gentleman, in order to give a dinner at Forlì, sold half his silken bedquilt for sixty florins. Arrigo Manardi was of Brettinoro; he was a gentleman full of courtesy and honour, was fond of entertaining guests, made presents of robes and horses, loved honourable men, and all his life was devoted to largess and good living."

The marriage of Riccardo Manardi with Lizio's daughter Caterina is the subject of one of the tales of the *Decameron,* V. 4. Pietro Dante says, that, when Lizio was told of the death of his dissipated son, he replied, "It is no news to me, he never was alive."

98. Of Pier Traversaro the *Ottimo* says: "He was of Ravenna, a man of most gentle blood;" and of Guido di Carpigna: "He was of Montefeltro. . . . . . Most of the time he lived at Brettinoro, and surpassed all others in generosity, loved for the sake of loving, and lived handsomely."

100. "This Messer Fabbro," says the *Ottimo,* "was born of low parents, and lived so generously that the author (Dante) says there never was his like in Bologna."

101. The *Ottimo* again: "This Messer Bernardino, son of Fosco, a farmer, and of humble occupation, became so excellent by his good works, that he was an honour to Faenza; and he was named with praise, and the old grandees were not ashamed to visit him, to see his magnificence, and to hear his pleasant jests."

104. Guido da Prata, from the village of that name, between Faenza and Forlì, and Ugolin d'Azzo of Faenza, according to the same authority, though "of humble birth, rose to such great honour, that, leaving their native places, they associated with the noblemen before mentioned."

106. Frederick Tignoso was a gentleman of Rimini, living in Brettinoro. "A man of great mark," says Buti, "with his band of friends." According to Benvenuto, "he had beautiful blond hair, and was called *tignoso* (the scurvy fellow) by way of antiphrase." The *Ottimo* speaks of him as follows: "He avoided the city as much as possible, as a place hostile to gentlemen, but when he was in it, he kept open house."

107. Ancient and honourable families of Ravenna. There is a story of them in the *Decameron,* Gior. V. Nov. 8, which is too long to quote. Upon this tale is founded Dryden's poem of *Theodore and Honoria.*

109. Ariosto, *Orlando Furioso,* I. 1:—

> "The dames, the cavaliers, the arms, the loves,
>   The courtesies, the daring deeds I sing."

112. Brettinoro, now Bertinoro, is a small town in Romagna, between Forlì and Cesena, in which lived many of the families that have just been mentioned. The hills about it are still celebrated for their wines, as its inhabitants were in old times for their hospitality. The following anecdote is told of them by the *Ottimo,* and also in nearly the same words in the *Cento Novelle Antiche,* Nov. 89:—

"Among other laudable customs of the nobles of Brettinoro was that of hospitality, and their not permitting any man in the town to keep an inn for money. But there was a stone column in the middle of the town," (upon which were rings or knockers, as if all the front-doors were there represented), "and to this, as soon as a stranger made his appearance, he was conducted, and to one of the rings hitched his horse or hung his hat upon it; and thus, as chance decreed, he was taken to the house of the gentleman to whom the ring belonged, and honoured according to his rank. This column and its rings were invented to remove all cause of quarrel among the noblemen, who used to run to get possession of a stranger, as now-a-days they almost run away from him."

115. Towns in Romagna. "Bagnacavallo, and Castrocaro, and Conio," says the *Ottimo,* "were all habitations of courtesy and honour." Now in Bagnacavallo the Counts are extinct; and he (Dante) says it does well to produce no more of them because they had degenerated like those of Conio and Castrocaro.

118. The Pagani were Lords of Faenza and Imola. The head of the family, Mainardo, was surnamed "the Devil."—See *Inf.* XXVII. Note 49. His bad repute will always be a reproach to the family.

121. A nobleman of Faenza, who died without heirs, and thus his name was safe.

132. Milton, *Comus*:—

> "Of calling shapes and beckoning shadows dire,
>   And airy tongues that syllable men's names."

These voices in the air proclaim examples of envy.

133. *Genesis* iv. 13, 14: "And Cain said unto the Lord, ... Every one that findeth me shall slay me."

139. Aglauros through envy opposed the interview of Mercury with her sister Herse, and was changed by the god into stone. Ovid, *Metamorph.*, I., Addison's Tr.:—

> " 'Then keep thy seat for ever,' cries the god,
>   And touched the door, wide opening to his rod.
>   Fain would she rise and stop him, but she found
>   Her trunk too heavy to forsake the ground;
>   Her joints are all benumbed, her hands are pale,
>   And marble now appears in every nail.
>   As when a cancer in the body feeds,
>   And gradual death from limb to limb proceeds,
>   So does the chillness to each vital part
>   Spread by degrees, and creeps into her heart;
>   Till hardening everywhere, and speechless grown,
>   She sits unmoved, and freezes to a stone.
>   But still her envious hue and sullen mien
>   Are in the sedentary figure seen."

147. The falconer's call or lure, which he whirls round in the air to attract the falcon on the wing.

148. Ovid, *Metamorph.*, I., Dryden's Tr.:—

> "Thus, while the mute creation downward bend
>   Their sight, and to their earthly mother tend,
>   Man looks aloft; and with erected eyes
>   Beholds his own hereditary skies."

150. Beaumont and Fletcher, *The Laws of Candy,* IV. 1:—

> "Seldom despairing men look up to heaven,
>   Although it still speaks to 'em in its glories;
>   For when sad thoughts perplex the mind of man,
>   There is a plummet in the heart that weighs
>   And pulls us, living, to the dust we came from."

Canto XV

1. In this canto is described the ascent to the Third Circle of the mountain. The hour indicated by the peculiarly Dantesque introduction is three hours before sunset, or the beginning of that division of the canonical day called Vespers. Dante states this simple fact with curious circumlocution, as if he would imitate the celestial sphere in this *scherzoso* movement. The beginning of the day is sunrise; consequently the end of the third hour, three hours after sunrise, is represented by an arc of the celestial sphere measuring forty-five degrees. The sun had still an equal space to pass over before his setting. This would make it afternoon in Purgatory, and midnight in Tuscany, where Dante was writing the poem.

20. From a perpendicular.

38. *Matthew* v. 7: "Blessed are the merciful, for they shall obtain mercy;"—sung by the spirits that remained behind. See Canto XII. Note 110.

39. Perhaps an allusion to "what the Spirit saith unto the churches," *Revelation* ii. 7: "To him that overcometh will I give to eat of the tree of life, which is in the midst of the paradise of God." And also the "hidden manna," and the "morning star," and the "white raiment," and the name not blotted "out of the book of life."

55. Milton, *Par. Lost,* V. 71:—

> "Since good the more
> Communicated, more abundant grows."

67. *Convito,* IV. 20: "According to the Apostle, 'Every good gift and every perfect gift is from above, and cometh down from the Father of lights.' He says then that God only giveth this grace to the soul of him whom he sees to be prepared and disposed in his person to receive this divine act. . . . . Whence if the soul is imperfectly placed, it is not disposed to receive this blessed and divine infusion; as when a pearl is badly disposed, or is imperfect, it cannot receive the celestial virtue, as the noble Guido Guinizzelli says in an ode of his, beginning,

> 'To noble heart love doth for shelter fly.'

The soul, then, may be ill placed in the person through defect of temperament, or of time; and in such a soul this divine radiance never shines. And of those whose souls are deprived of this light it may be said that they are like valleys turned toward the north, or like subterranean caverns, where the light of the sun never falls, unless reflected from some other place illuminated by it."

The following are the first two stanzas of Guido's *Ode*:—

> "To noble heart love doth for shelter fly,
> As seeks the bird the forest's leafy shade;

Love was not felt till noble heart beat high,
   Nor before love the noble heart was made;
   Soon as the sun's broad flame
Was formed, so soon the clear light filled the air,
   Yet was not till he came;
So love springs up in noble breasts, and there
   Has its appointed space,
As heat in the bright flame finds its allotted place.

"Kindles in noble heart the fire of love,
   As hidden virtue in the precious stone;
This virtue comes not from the stars above,
   Till round it the ennobling sun has shone;
But when his powerful blaze
Has drawn forth what was vile, the stars impart
   Strange virtue in their rays;
And thus when nature doth create the heart
   Noble, and pure, and high,
Like virtue from the star, love comes from woman's eye."

70. *Par.* XIV. 40:—

"Its brightness is proportioned to the ardour,
   The ardour to the vision, and the vision
   Equals what grace it has above its merit."

89. *Luke* ii. 48: "And his mother said unto him, Son, why hast thou thus dealt with us? behold, thy father and I have sought thee sorrowing."

97. The contest between Neptune and Minerva for the right of naming Athens, in which Minerva carried the day by the vote of the women. This is one of the subjects which Minerva wrought in her trial of skill with Arachne. Ovid, *Metamorph.*, VI.:—

"Pallas in figures wrought the heavenly powers,
   And Mars's hill among the Athenian towers.
   On lofty thrones twice six celestials sate,
   Jove in the midst, and held their warm debate;
   The subject weighty, and well known to fame,
   From whom the city should receive its name.
   Each god by proper features was expressed,
   Jove with majestic mien excelled the rest.
   His three-forked mace the dewy sea-god shook,
   And, looking sternly, smote the ragged rock;
   When from the stone leapt forth a sprightly steed,
   And Neptune claims the city for the deed.
   Herself she blazons, with a glittering spear,

And crested helm that veiled her braided hair,
With shield, and scaly breastplate, implements of war.
Struck with her pointed lance, the teeming earth
Seemed to produce a new, surprising birth;
When from the glebe the pledge of conquest sprung,
A tree pale-green with fairest olives hung."

101. Pisistratus, the tyrant of Athens, who used his power so nobly as to make the people forget the usurpation by which he had attained it. Among his good deeds was the collection and preservation of the Homeric poems, which but for him might have perished. He was also the first to found a public library in Athens. This anecdote is told by Valerius Maximus, *Fact. ac Dict.*, VI. 1.

106. The stoning of Stephen. *Acts* vii. 54: "They gnashed on him with their teeth. But he, being full of the Holy Ghost, looked up steadfastly into heaven. . . . . Then they cried out with a loud voice, and stopped their ears, and ran upon him with one accord, and cast him out of the city, and stoned him. . . . . And he kneeled down, and cried with a loud voice, Lord, lay not this sin to their charge! And when he had said this, he fell asleep."

117. He recognizes it to be a vision, but not false, because it symbolized the truth.

Canto XVI

1. The Third Circle of Purgatory, and the punishment of the Sin of Pride.
2. Poor, or impoverished of its stars by clouds. The same expression is applied to the Arno, Canto XIV. 45, to indicate its want of water.
19. In the *Litany of the Saints:*—
"Lamb of God, who takest away the sins of the world, spare us, O Lord.
"Lamb of God, who takest away the sins of the world, graciously hear us, O Lord.
"Lamb of God, who takest away the sins of the world, have mercy on us!"
27. Still living the life temporal, where time is measured by the calendar.
46. Marco Lombardo, was a Venetian nobleman, a man of wit and learning and a friend of Dante. "Nearly all that he gained," says the *Ottimo,* "he spent in charity. . . . . He visited Paris, and, as long as his money lasted, he was esteemed for his valour and courtesy. Afterwards he depended upon those richer than himself, and lived and died honourably." There are some anecdotes of him in the *Cento Novelle Antiche,* Nov. 41, 52, hardly worth quoting.

It is doubtful whether the name of Lombardo is a family name, or only indicates that Marco was an Italian, after the fashion then prevalent among the French of calling all Italians Lombards. See Note 124.

Benvenuto says of him that he "was a man of noble mind, but disdainful, and easily moved to anger."

Buti's portrait is as follows: "This Marco was a Venetian, called Marco Daca; and. was a very learned man, and had many political virtues, and was very courteous, giving to poor noblemen all that he gained, and he gained much; for he was a courtier, and was much beloved for his virtue, and much was given him by the nobility; and as he gave to those who were in need, so he lent to all who asked. So that, coming to die, and having much still due to him, he made a will, and among other bequests this, that whoever owed him should not be held to pay the debt, saying, 'Whoever has, may keep.'"

Portarelli thinks that this Marco may be Marco Polo the traveller; but this is inadmissible, as he was still living at the time of Dante's death.

57. What Guido del Duca has told him of the corruption of Italy, in Canto XIV.

64. Ovid, *Metamorph.,* X., Ozell's Tr.:—

> "The god upon its leaves
> The sad expression of his sorrow weaves,
> And to this hour the mournful purple wears
> *Ai, ai,* inscribed in funeral characters."

67. See the article *Cabala,* at the end of *Paradiso.*

69. Boëthius, *Cons. Phil.,* V. Prosa 29 Ridpath's Tr.:—

" 'But in this indissoluble chain of causes, can we preserve the liberty of the will? Does this fatal Necessity restrain the motions of the human soul?'— 'There is no reasonable being,' replied she, 'who has not freedom of will: for every being distinguished with this faculty is endowed with judgment to perceive the differences of things; to discover what he is to avoid or pursue. Now what a person esteems desirable, he desires; but what he thinks ought to be avoided, he shuns. Thus every rational creature hath a liberty of choosing and rejecting. But I do not assert that this liberty is equal in all beings. Heavenly substances, who are exalted above us, have an enlightened judgment, an incorruptible will, and a power ever at command effectually to accomplish their desires. With regard to man, his immaterial spirit is also free; but it is most at liberty when employed in the contemplation of the Divine mind; it becomes less so when it enters into a body; and is still more restrained when it is imprisoned in a terrestrial habitation, composed of members of clay; and is reduced, in fine, to the most extreme servitude when, by plunging into the pollutions of vice, it totally departs from reason: for the soul no sooner turns her eye from the radiance of supreme truth to dark and base objects, but she is involved in a mist of ignorance, assailed by impure desires; by yielding to which she increases her thraldom, and thus the freedom which she derives from nature becomes in some measure the cause of her slavery. But the eye of Providence, which sees everything from eternity, perceives all this; and that same Providence disposes everything she has predestinated, in the order it deserves. As Homer says of the sun, It sees everything and hears everything.'"

Also Milton, *Parad. Lost,* II. 557:—

> "Others apart sat on a hill retired,
>   In thoughts more elevate, and reasoned high
>   Of providence, foreknowledge, will and fate,
>   Fixed fate, free will, foreknowledge absolute,
>   And found no end, in wandering mazes lost."

See also *Par.* XVII. Note 40.

70. Boëthius, *Cons. Phil.,* V. Prosa 3, Ridpath's Tr.:—

"But I shall now endeavour to demonstrate, that, in whatever way the chain of causes is disposed, the event of things which are foreseen is necessary; although prescience may not appear to be the necessitating cause of their befalling. For example, if a person sits, the opinion formed of him that he is seated is of necessity true; but by inverting the phrase, if the opinion is true that he is seated, he must necessarily sit. In both cases, then, there is a necessity; in the latter, that the person sits; in the former, that the opinion concerning him is true: but the person doth not sit, because the opinion of his sitting is true, but the opinion is rather true because the action of his being seated was antecedent in time. Thus, though the truth of the opinion may be the effect of the person taking a seat, there is, nevertheless, a necessity common to both. The same method of reasoning, I think, should be employed with regard to the prescience of God, and future contingencies; for, allowing it to be true that events are foreseen because they are to happen, and that they do not befall because they are foreseen, it is still necessary that what is to happen must be foreseen by God, and that what is foreseen must take place. This then is of itself sufficient to destroy all idea of human liberty."

78. Ptolemy says, "The wise man shall control the stars;" and the Turkish proverb, "Wit and a strong will are superior to Fate."

79. Though free, you are subject to the divine power which has immediately breathed into you the soul, and the soul is not subject to the influence of the stars, as the body is.

84. Shakespeare, *Lear,* V. 3:—

> "And take upon's the mystery of things,
>   As if we were God's spies."

92. *Convito,* IV. 12: "The supreme desire of everything, and that first given by nature, is to return to its source; and since God is the source of our souls, and maker of them in his own likeness, as is written, 'Let us make man in our image, after our likeness,' to him this soul chiefly desireth to return. And like as a pilgrim, who goeth upon a road on which he never was before,

thinketh every house he seeth afar off to be an inn, and not finding it so, directeth his trust to the next, and thus from house to house until he reacheth the inn; in like manner our soul, presently as she entereth the new and untravelled road of this life, turneth her eyes to the goal of her supreme good; and therefore whatever thing she seeth that seemeth to have some good in it, she believeth to be that. And because her knowledge at first is imperfect, not being experienced nor trained, small goods seem great, and therefore with them beginneth her desire. Hence we see children desire exceedingly an apple; and then, going farther, desire a little bird; and farther still, a beautiful dress; and then a horse; and then a woman; and then wealth not very great, and then greater, and then greater still. And this cometh to pass, because she findeth not in any of these things that which she is seeking, and trusteth to find it farther on."

96. Henry Vaughan, *Sacred Poems:*—

> "They are indeed our pillar-fires,
>   Seen as we go;
> They are that city's shining spires
>   We travel to."

99. *Leviticus* xi. 4: "The camel because he cheweth the cud, but divideth not the hoof: he is unclean to you." Dante applies these words to the Pope as temporal sovereign.

101. Worldly goods. As in the old French satirical verses:—

> "Au temps passé du siècle d'or,
>   Crosse de bois, évêque d'or;
> Maintenant changent les lois,
>   Crosse d'or, évêque de bois."

107. The Emperor and the Pope; the temporal and spiritual power.

115. Lombardy and Romagna.

117. The dissension and war between the Emperor Frederick the Second and Pope Gregory the Ninth. Milman, *Hist. Lat. Christ.,* Book X. Ch. 3, says:—

"The Empire and the Papacy were now to meet in their last mortal and implacable strife; the two first acts of this tremendous drama, separated by an interval of many years, were to be developed during the pontificate of a prelate who ascended the throne of St. Peter at the age of eighty. Nor was this strife for any specific point in dispute, like the right of investiture, but avowedly for supremacy on one side, which hardly deigned to call itself independence; for independence, on the other, which remotely at least aspired after supremacy. Cæsar would bear no superior, the successor of St. Peter no equal. The contest could not have begun under men more strongly contrasted, or more determinedly oppugnant in character, than Gregory the Ninth and

Frederick the Second. Gregory retained the ambition, the vigour, almost the activity of youth, with the stubborn obstinacy, and something of the irritable petulance, of old age. He was still master of all his powerful faculties; his knowledge of affairs, of mankind, of the peculiar interests of almost all the nations in Christendom, acquired by long employment in the most important negotiations both by Innocent the Third and by Honorius the Third; eloquence which his own age compared to that of Tully; profound erudition in that learning which, in the mediæval churchman, commanded the highest admiration. No one was his superior in the science of the canon law; the Decretals, to which he afterwards gave a more full and authoritative form, were at his command, and they were to him as much the law of God as the Gospels themselves, or the primary principles of morality. The jealous reverence and attachment of a great lawyer to his science strengthened the lofty pretensions of the churchman.

"Frederick the Second, with many of the noblest qualities which could captivate the admiration of his own age, in some respects might appear misplaced, and by many centuries prematurely born. Frederick having crowded into his youth adventures, perils, successes, almost unparalleled in history, was now only expanding into the prime of manhood. A parentless orphan, he had struggled upward into the actual reigning monarch of his hereditary Sicily; he was even then rising above the yoke of the turbulent magnates of his realm, and the depressing tutelage of the Papal See; he had crossed the Alps a boyish adventurer, and won so much through his own valour and daring that he might well ascribe to himself his conquest, the kingdom of Germany, the imperial crown; he was in undisputed possession of the Empire, with all its rights in Northern Italy; King of Apulia, Sicily, and Jerusalem. He was beginning to be at once the Magnificent Sovereign, the knight, the poet, the lawgiver, the patron of arts, letters, and science; the Magnificent Sovereign, now holding his court in one of the old barbaric and feudal cities of Germany among the proud and turbulent princes of the Empire, more often on the sunny shores of Naples or Palermo, in southern and almost Oriental luxury; the gallant Knight and troubadour Poet, not forbidding himself those amorous indulgences which were the reward of chivalrous valour and of the 'gay science;' the Lawgiver, whose far-seeing wisdom seemed to anticipate some of those views of equal justice, of the advantages of commerce, of the cultivation of the arts of peace, beyond all the toleration of adverse religions, which even in a more dutiful son of the Church would doubtless have seemed godless indifference. Frederick must appear before us in the course of our history in the full development of all these shades of character; but besides all this, Frederick's views of the temporal sovereignty were as imperious and autocratic as those of the haughtiest churchman of the spiritual supremacy. The ban of the Empire ought to be at least equally awful with that of the Church; disloyalty to the Emperor was as heinous a sin as infidelity to the head of Christendom; the independence of the Lombard republics was as a great and punishable political heresy. Even in Rome itself, as head of the Roman

Empire, Frederick aspired to a supremacy which was not less unlimited because vague and undefined, and irreconcilable with that of the Supreme Pontiff. If ever Emperor might be tempted by the vision of a vast hereditary monarchy to be perpetuated in his house, the princely house of Hohenstaufen, it was Frederick. He had heirs of his greatness; his eldest son was King of the Romans; from his loins might yet spring an inexhaustible race of princes; the failure of his imperial line was his last fear. The character of the man seemed formed to achieve and to maintain this vast design; he was at once terrible and popular, courteous, generous, placable to his foes; yet there was a depth of cruelty in the heart of Frederick towards revolted subjects, which made him look on the atrocities of his allies, Eccelin di Romano, and the Salinguerras, but as legitimate means to quell insolent and stubborn rebellion. . . . .

"It is impossible to conceive a contrast more strong or more irreconcilable than the octogenarian Gregory, in his cloister palace, in his conclave of stern ascetics, with all but severe imprisonment within conventual walls, completely monastic in manners, habits, views, in corporate spirit, in celibacy, in rigid seclusion from the rest of mankind, in the conscientious determination to enslave, if possible, all Christendom to its inviolable unity of faith, and to the least possible latitude of discipline; and the gay and yet youthful Frederick, with his mingled assemblage of knights and ladies, of Christians, Jews, and Mohammedans, of poets, and men of science, met, as it were, to enjoy and minister to enjoyment,—to cultivate the pure intellect,—where, if not the restraints of religion, at least the awful authority of churchmen was examined with freedom, sometimes ridiculed with sportive wit."

See also *Inf.* X. Note 119.

124. Currado (Conrad) da Palazzo of Brescia; Gherardo da Camino of Treviso; and Guido da Castello of Reggio. Of these three the *Ottimo* thus speaks:—

"Messer Currado was laden with honour during his life, delighted in a fine retinue, and in political life in the government of cities, in which he acquired much praise and fame.

"Messer Guido was assiduous in honouring men of worth, who passed on their way to France, and furnished many with horses and arms, who came hitherward from France. To all who had honourably consumed their property, and returned more poorly furnished than became them, he gave, without hope of return, horses, arms, and money.

"Messer Gherardo da Camino delighted not in one, but in all noble things, keeping constantly at home."

He farther says, that his fame was so great in France that he was there spoken of as the "simple Lombard," just as, "when one says the City, and no more, one means Rome." Benvenuto da Imola says that all Italians were called Lombards by the French. In the *Histoire et Cronique du petit Jehan de Saintré,* fol. 219, ch. iv., the author remarks: "The fifteenth day after Saintré's return, there came to Paris two young, noble, and brave Italians, whom we call Lombards."

132. *Deuteronomy* xviii. 2: "Therefore shall they have no inheritance among their brethren: the Lord is their inheritance, as he hath said unto them."

140. "This Gherardo," says Buti, "had a daughter, called, on account of her beauty, Gaja; and so modest and virtuous was she, that through all Italy was spread the fame of her beauty and modesty."

The *Ottimo,* who preceded Buti in point of time, gives a somewhat different and more equivocal account. He says: "Madonna Gaia was the daughter of Messer Gherardo da Camino: she was a lady of such conduct in amorous delectations, that her name was notorious throughout all Italy; and therefore she is thus spoken of here."

Canto XVII

1. The trance and vision of Dante, and the ascent to the Fourth Circle, where the sin of Sloth is punished.

2. *Iliad,* III. 10: "As the south wind spreads a mist upon the brow of a mountain, by no means agreeable to the shepherd, but to the robber better than night, in which a man sees only as far as he can cast a stone."

19. In this vision are represented some of the direful effects of anger, beginning with the murder of Itys by his mother, Procne, and her sister, Philomela. Ovid, VI.:—

> "Now, at her lap arrived, the flattering boy
> Salutes his parent with a smiling joy;
> About her neck his little arms are thrown,
> And he accosts her in a prattling tone.
>
> . . . . . .
>
> When Procne, on revengeful mischief bent,
> Home to his heart a piercing poniard sent.
> Itys, with rueful cries, but all too late,
> Holds out his hands, and deprecates his fate;
> Still at his mother's neck he fondly aims,
> And strives to melt her with endearing names;
> Yet still the cruel mother perseveres,
> Nor with concern his bitter anguish hears.
> This might suffice; but Philomela too
> Across his throat a shining cutlass drew."

Or perhaps the reference is to the Homeric legend of Philomela, *Odyssey,* XIX. 518: "As when the daughter of Pandarus, the swarthy nightingale, sings beautifully when the spring newly begins, sitting in the thick branches of trees, and she, frequently changing, pours forth her much-sounding voice, lamenting her dear Itylus, whom once she slew with the brass through ignorance."

25. *Esther* vii. 9, 10: "And Harbonah, one of the chamberlains, said before the king, Behold also, the gallows, fifty cubits high, which Haman had made for Mordecai, who had spoken good for the king, standeth in the house of Haman. Then the king said, Hang him thereon. So they hanged Haman on the gallows that he had prepared for Mordecai. Then was the king's wrath pacified."

34. Lavinia, daughter of King Latinus and Queen Amata, betrothed to Turnus. Amata, thinking Turnus dead, hanged herself in anger and despair. *Æneid*, XII. 875, Dryden's Tr.:—

> "Mad with her anguish, impotent to bear
> The mighty grief, she loathes the vital air.
> She calls herself the cause of all this ill,
> And owns the dire effects of her ungoverned will;
> She raves against the gods, she beats her breast,
> She tears with both her hands her purple vest;
> Then round a beam a running noose she tied,
> And, fastened by the neck, obscenely died.
>
> "Soon as the fatal news by fame was blown,
> And to her dames and to her daughters known,
> The sad Lavinia rends her yellow hair
> And rosy cheeks; the rest her sorrow share;
> With shrieks the palace rings, and madness of despair."

53. See *Par.* V. 134:—

> "Even as the sun, that doth conceal himself
> By too much light."

And Milton, *Parad. Lost,* III. 380:—

> "Dark with excessive bright thy skirts appear."

68. *Matthew* v. 9: "Blessed are the peacemakers: for they shall be called the children of God."

85. Sloth. See *Inf.* VII. Note 115. And Brunetto Latini, *Tesoretto,* XXI. 145:—

> "In ira nasce e posa
> Accidia niquitosa."

97. The first, the object; the second, too much or too little vigour.

124. The sins of Pride, Envy, and Anger. The other is Sloth, or lukewarmness in well-doing, punished in this circle.

136. The sins of Avarice, Gluttony, and Lust.

Canto XVIII

1. The punishment of the sin of Sloth.

27. Bound or taken captive by the image of pleasure presented to it. See Canto XVII. 91.

22. Milton, *Parad. Lost,* V. 100:—

> "But know that in the soul
> Are many lesser faculties, that serve
> Reason as chief; among these Fancy next
> Her office holds; of all external things,
> Which the five watchful senses represent,
> She forms imaginations, aery shapes,
> Which Reason joining or disjoining frames
> All what we affirm or what deny, and call
> Our knowledge or opinion; then retires
> Into her private cell, when Nature rests."

30. The region of Fire. Brunetto Latini, *Tresor.* Ch. CVIII.: "After the zone of the air is placed the fourth element. This is an orb of fire without any moisture, which extends as far as the moon, and surrounds this atmosphere in which we are. And know that above the fire is first the moon, and the other stars, which are all of the nature of fire."

44. If the soul follows the *appetitus naturalis,* or goes not with another foot than that of nature.

49. In the language of the Scholastics, Form was the passing from the potential to the actual. "Whatever is Act," says Thomas Aquinas, *Summa Theol.,* Quæst. LXVI. Art. 1, "whatever is Act is Form; *quod est actus est forma.*" And again Form was divided into Substantial Form, which caused a thing to be; and Accidental Form, which caused it to be in a certain way, "as heat makes its subject not simply to be, but to be hot."

"The soul," says the same Angelic Doctor, Quæst. LXXVI. Art. 4, "is the substantial form of man; *anima est forma substantialis hominis.*" It is segregate or distinct from matter, though united with it.

61. "This" refers to the power that counsels, or the faculty of Reason.

66. Accepts, or rejects like chaff.

73. Dante makes Beatrice say, *Par.* V. 19:—

> "The greatest gift that in his largess God
>   Creating made, and unto his own goodness
>   Nearest conformed, and that which he doth prize
> Most highly, is the freedom of the will,
>   Wherewith the creatures of intelligence
>   Both all and only were and are endowed."

76. Near midnight of the Second Day of Purgatory.

80. The moon was rising in the sign of the Scorpion, it being now five days after the full; and when the sun is in this sign, it is seen by the inhabitants of Rome to sit between the islands of Corsica and Sardinia.

83. Virgil, born at Pietola, near Mantua.

84. The burden of Dante's doubts and questions, laid upon Virgil.

91. Rivers of Bœotia, on whose banks the Thebans crowded at night to invoke the aid of Bacchus to give them rain for their vineyards.

94. The word *falcare,* in French *faucher,* here translated "curve," is a term of equitation, describing the motion of the outer fore-leg of a horse in going round in a circle. It is the sweep of a mower's scythe.

100. *Luke* i. 39: "And Mary arose in those days and went into the hill-country with haste."

101. Cæsar on his way to subdue Ilerda, now Lerida, in Spain, besieged Marseilles, leaving there part of his army under Brutus to complete the work.

118. Nothing is known of this Abbot, not even his name. Finding him here, the commentators make bold to say that he was "slothful and deficient in good deeds." This is like some of the definitions in the *Crusca,* which, instead of the interpretation of a Dantesque word, give you back the passage in which it occurs.

119. This is the famous Emperor Frederick Barbarossa, who, according to the German popular tradition, is still sitting in a cave in the Kipphaüser mountains, waiting for something to happen, while his beard has grown through the stone-table before him. In 1162 he burned and devastated Milan, Brescia, Piacenza, and Cremona. He was drowned in the Salef in Armenia, on his crusade in 1190, endeavouring to ford the river on horseback in his impatience to cross. His character is thus drawn by Milman, *Lat. Christ.,* Book VIII. Ch. 7, and sufficiently explains why Dante calls him "the good Barbarossa":—

"Frederick was a prince of intrepid valour, consummate prudence, unmeasured ambition, justice which hardened into severity, the ferocity of a barbarian somewhat tempered with a high chivalrous gallantry; above all, with a strength of character which subjugated alike the great temporal and ecclesiastical princes of Germany; and was prepared to assert the Imperial rights in Italy to the utmost. Of the constitutional rights of the Emperor, of his unlimited supremacy, his absolute independence of, his temporal superiority over, all other powers, even that of the Pope, Frederick proclaimed the loftiest notions. He was to the Empire what Hildebrand and Innocent were to the Popedom. His power was of God alone; to assert that it was bestowed by the successor of St. Peter was a lie, and directly contrary to the doctrine of St. Peter."

121. Alberto della Scala, Lord of Verona. He made his natural son, whose qualifications for the office Dante here enumerates, and the commentators repeat, Abbot of the Monastery of San Zeno.

132. See *Inf.* VII. Note 115.

135. *Numbers* xxxii. 11, 12: "Surely none of the men that came out of Egypt, from twenty years old and upward, shall see the land which I sware unto Abraham, unto Isaac, and unto Jacob; because they have not wholly followed me: save Caleb the son of Jephunneh the Kenezite, and Joshua the son of Nun; for they have wholly followed the Lord."

137. The Trojans who remained with Acestes in Sicily, instead of following Æneas to Italy. *Æneid,* V.: "They enroll the matrons for the city, and set on shore as many of the people as were willing,—souls that had no desire of high renown."

145. The end of the Second Day.

Canto XIX

1. The ascent to the Fifth Circle, where Avarice is punished. It is the dawn of the Third Day.

3. Brunetto Latini, *Tresor.* Ch. CXI. "Saturn, who is sovereign over all, is cruel and malign and of a cold nature."

4. Geomancy is divination by points in the ground, or pebbles arranged in certain figures, which have peculiar names. Among these is the figure called the *Fortuna Major,* which is thus drawn:—

```
  ★     ★
  ★     ★
  ★     ★
     ★
     ★
```

and which by an effort of imagination can also be formed out of some of the last stars of Aquarius, and some of the first of Pisces.

Chaucer, *Troil. and Cres.,* III., 1415:—

> "But whan the cocke, commune astrologer,
>   Gan on his brest to bete and after crowe,
>   And Lucifer, the dayes messanger,
>   Gan for to rise and out his bemes throwe,
>   And estward rose, to him that could it knowe,
>   *Fortuna Major.*"

6. Because the sun is following close behind.

7. This "stammering woman" of Dante's dream is Sensual Pleasure, which the imagination of the beholder adorns with a thousand charms. The "lady saintly and alert" is Reason, the same that tied Ulysses to the mast, and

stopped the ears of his sailors with wax that they might not hear the song of the Sirens.

Gower, *Conf. Amant.*, I.:—

> "Of such nature
> They ben, that with so swete a steven
> Like to the melodie of heven
> In womannishe vois they singe
> With notes of so great likinge,
> Of suche mesure, of suche musike,
> Whereof the shippes they beswike
> That passen by the costes there.
> For whan the shipmen lay an ere
> Unto the vois, in here airs
> They wene it be a paradis,
> Which after is to hem an helle."

51. "That is," says Buti, "they shall have the gift of comforting their souls." *Matthew* v. 4: "Blessed are they that mourn: for they shall be comforted."

59. The three remaining sins to be purged away are Avarice, Gluttony, and Lust.

61. See Canto XIV. 148.

73. *Psalms* cxix. 25: "My soul cleaveth unto the dust: quicken thou me according to thy word."

99. Know that I am the successor of Peter. It is Pope Adrian the Fifth who speaks. He was of the family of the Counts of Lavagna, the family taking its title from the river Lavagna, flowing between Siestri and Chiaveri, towns on the Riviera di Genova. He was Pope only thirty-nine days, and died in 1276. When his kindred came to congratulate him on his election, he said, "Would that ye came to a Cardinal in good health, and not to a dying Pope."

134. *Revelation* xix. 10: "And I fell at his feet to worship him. And he said unto me, See thou do it not, I am thy fellow-servant."

137. *Matthew* xxii. 30: "For in the resurrection they neither marry, nor are given in marriage, but are as the angels in heaven." He reminds Dante that here all earthly distinctions and relations are laid aside. He is no longer "the Spouse of the Church."

141. Penitence; line 92:—

> "In whom weeping ripens
> That without which to God we cannot turn."

142. Madonna Alagia was the wife of Marcello Malespini, that friend of Dante with whom, during his wanderings he took refuge in the Lunigiana, in 1307.

Canto XX

1. In this canto the subject of the preceding is continued, namely, the punishment of Avarice and Prodigality.

2. To please the speaker, Pope Adrian the Fifth, (who, Canto XIX. 139, says,

> "Now go, no longer will I have thee linger,")

Dante departs without further question, though not yet satisfied.

13. See the article *Cabala* at the end of *Paradiso*.

15. This is generally supposed to refer to Can Grande della Scala. See *Inf.* I. Note 101.

23. The inn at Bethlehem.

25. The Roman Consul who rejected with disdain the bribes of Pyrrhus, and died so poor that he was buried at the public expense, and the Romans were obliged to give a dowry to his daughters. Virgil, *Æneid,* VI. 844, calls him "powerful in poverty." Dante also extols him in the *Convito,* IV. 5.

31. Gower, *Conf. Amant.,* V. 13:—

> "Betwene the two extremites
> Of vice stont the propertes
> Of vertue, and to prove it so
> Take avarice and take also
> The vice of prodegalite,
> Betwene hem liberalite,
> Which is the vertue of largesse
> Stant and governeth his noblesse."

32. This is St. Nicholas, patron saint of children, sailors, and travellers. The incident here alluded to is found in the *Legenda Aurea* of Jacobus de Voragine, the great storehouse of mediæval wonders.

It may be found also in Mrs. Jameson's *Sacred and Legendary Art,* II. 62, and in her version runs thus:—

"Now in that city there dwelt a certain nobleman who had three daughters, and, from being rich, he became poor; so poor that there remained no means of obtaining food for his daughters but by sacrificing them to an infamous life; and oftentimes it came into his mind to tell them so, but shame and sorrow held him dumb. Meantime the maidens wept continually, not knowing what to do, and not having bread to eat; and their father became more and more desperate. When Nicholas heard of this, he thought it a shame that such a thing should happen in a Christian land; therefore one night, when the maidens were asleep, and their father alone sat watching and weeping, he took a handful of gold, and, tying it up in a handkerchief, he repaired to the dwelling of the poor man. He considered how he might bestow it without making himself known, and, while he stood irresolute, the moon coming from behind a cloud showed him a window open; so he threw it in, and it fell at the feet of the father, who, when he found it, returned thanks, and with it he portioned his eldest daughter. A second time Nicholas provided a similar sum, and again he threw it in by night; and with it the nobleman married his second daughter. But he greatly desired to know who it was that came to his aid; therefore he determined to watch, and when the good saint came for the third time, and prepared to throw in the third portion, he was discovered, for the nobleman seized him by the skirt of his robe, and flung himself at his feet, saying, 'O Nicholas! servant of God! why seek to hide thyself?' and he kissed his feet and his hands. But Nicholas made him promise that he would tell no man. And many other charitable works did Nicholas perform in his native city."

43. If we knew from what old chronicle, or from what Professor of the Rue du Fouarre, Dante derived his knowledge of French history, we might possibly make plain the rather difficult passage which begins with this line. The spirit that speaks is not that of the King Hugh Capet, but that of his father, Hugh Capet, Duke of France and Count of Paris. He was son of Robert the Strong. Pasquier, *Rech. de la France,* VI. 1, describes him as both valiant and prudent, and says that, "although he was never king, yet was he a maker and unmaker of kings," and then goes on to draw an elaborate parallel between him and Charles Martel.

The "malignant plant" is Philip the Fair, whose character is thus drawn by Milman, *Lat. Christ.,* Book XI. Ch. 8:—

"In Philip the Fair the gallantry of the French temperament broke out on rare occasions; his first Flemish campaigns were conducted with bravery and skill, but Philip ever preferred the subtle negotiation, the slow and wily encroachment; till his enemies were, if not in his power, at least at great disadvantage, he did not venture on the usurpation or invasion. In the slow systematic pursuit of his object he was utterly without scruple, without remorse. He was not so much cruel as altogether obtuse to human suffering, if necessary to the prosecution of his schemes; not so much rapacious as, finding money indispensable to his aggrandizement, seeking money by means of which he hardly seemed to discern the injustice or the folly. Never was man or monarch so intensely selfish as Philip the Fair: his own power was his ultimate scope; he extended so enormously the royal prerogative, the influence of France, because he was King of France. His rapacity, which persecuted the Templars, his vindictiveness, which warred on Boniface after death as through life, was this selfishness in other forms."

He was defeated at the battle of Courtray, 1302, known in history as the battle of the Spurs of Gold, from the great number found on the field after the battle. This is the vengeance imprecated upon him by Dante.

50. For two centuries and a half, that is, from 1060 to 1316, there was either a Louis or a Philip on the throne of France. The succession was as follows:—

52. It is doubtful whether this passage is to be taken literally or figuratively.
Pasquier, *Rech. de la France,* Liv. VI. Ch. I (thinking it is the King Hugh Capet
that speaks), breaks forth in indignant protest as follows:—

"From this you can perceive the fatality there was in this family from its
beginning to its end, to the disadvantage of the Carlovingians. And more-
over, how ignorant the Italian poet Dante was, when in his book entitled
Purgatory he says that our Hugh Capet was the son of a butcher. Which
word, once written erroneously and carelessly by him, has so crept into the
heads of some simpletons, that many who never investigated the antiquities
of our France have fallen into this same heresy. François de Villon, more
studious of taverns and ale-houses than of good books, says in some part of
his works,

> 'Si feusse les hoirs de Capet
> Qui fut extrait de boucherie.'

And since then Agrippa Alamanni, in his book on the Vanity of Science,
chapter *Of Nobility,* on this first ignorance declares impudently against the
genealogy of our Capet. If Dante thought that Hugh the Great, Capet's father,
was a butcher, he was not a clever man. But if he used this expression figu-
ratively, as I am willing to believe, those who cling to the shell of the word
are greater blockheads still. . . . .

"This passage of Dante being read and explained by Luigi Alamanni, an
Italian, before Francis the First of that name, he was indignant at the impos-
ture, and commanded it to be stricken out. He was even excited to interdict
the reading of the book in his kingdom. But for my part, in order to excul-
pate this author, I wish to say that under the name of Butcher he meant that
Capet was son of a great and valiant warrior. . . . . If Dante understood it
thus, I forgive him; if otherwise, he was a very ignorant poet."

Benvenuto says that the name of Capet comes from the fact that Hugh,
in playing with his companions in boyhood, "was in the habit of pulling off
their caps and running away with them." Ducange repeats this story from an
old chronicle, and gives also another and more probable origin of the name,
as coming from the hood or cowl which Hugh was in the habit of wearing.

The belief that the family descended from a butcher was current in Italy in Dante's time. Villani, IV. 3, says: "Most people say that the father was a great and rich burgher of Paris, of a race of butchers or dealers in cattle."

53. When the Carlovingian race were all dead but one. And who was he? The *Ottimo* says it was Rudolph, who became a monk and afterwards Archbishop of Rheims. Benvenuto gives no name, but says only "a monk in poor, coarse garments." Buti says the same. Daniello thinks it was some Friar of St. Francis, perhaps St. Louis, forgetting that these saints did not see the light till some two centuries after the time here spoken of. Others say Charles of Lorraine; and Biagioli decides that it must be either Charles the Simple, who died a prisoner in the castle of Péronne, in 922; or Louis of Outre-Mer, who was carried to England by Hugh the Great, in 936. The Man in Cloth of Grey remains as great a mystery as the Man in the Iron Mask.

59. Hugh Capet was crowned at Rheims, in 987. The expression which follows shows clearly that it is Hugh the Great who speaks, and not Hugh the founder of the Capetian dynasty.

61. Until the shame of the low origin of the family was removed by the marriage of Charles of Anjou, brother of Saint Louis, to the daughter of Raimond Berenger, who brought him Provence as her dower.

65. Making amends for one crime by committing a greater. The particular transaction here alluded to is the seizing by fraud and holding by force these provinces in the time of Philip the Fair.

67. Charles of Anjou.

68. Curradino, or Conradin, son of the Emperor Conrad IV., a beautiful youth of sixteen, who was beheaded in the square of Naples by order of Charles of Anjou, in 1268. Voltaire, in his rhymed chronology at the end of his *Annales de l'Empire,* says,

> "C'est en soixante-huit que la main d'un bourreau
> Dans Conradin son fils éteint un sang si beau."

Endeavouring to escape to Sicily after his defeat at Tagliacozzo, he was carried to Naples and imprisoned in the Castel dell' Uovo. "Christendom heard with horror," says Milman, *Lat. Christ.,* Book XI. Ch. 3, "that the royal brother of St. Louis, that the champion of the Church, after a mock trial, by the sentence of one judge, Robert di Lavena,—after an unanswerable pleading by Guido de Suzaria, a famous jurist,—had condemned the last heir of the Swabian house—a rival king who had fought gallantly for his hereditary throne—to be executed as a felon and a rebel on a public scaffold. So little did Conradin dread his fate, that, when his doom was announced, he was playing at chess with Frederick of Austria. 'Slave,' said Conradin to Robert of Bari, who read the fatal sentence, 'do you dare to condemn as a criminal the son and heir of kings? Knows not your master that he is my equal, not my judge?' He added, 'I am a mortal, and must die; yet ask the kings of the earth if a prince be criminal for seeking to win back the heritage of his ancestors. But if there be no pardon for me, spare, at least, my faithful companions; or if they must die, strike me first, that I may not behold their death.' They died devoutly, nobly. Every circumstance aggravated the abhorrence; it was said—perhaps it was the invention of that abhorrence—that Robert of Flanders, the brother of Charles, struck dead the judge who had presumed to read the iniquitous sentence. When Conradin knelt, with uplifted hands, awaiting the blow of the executioner, he uttered these last words, 'O my mother! how deep will be thy sorrow at the news of this clay!' Even the followers of Charles could hardly restrain their pity and indignation. With Conradin died his young and valiant friend, Frederick of Austria, the two Lancias, two of the noble house of Donaticcio di Pisa. The inexorable Charles would not permit them to be buried in consecrated ground."

69. Thomas Aquinas, the Angelic Doctor of the Schools, died at the convent of Fossa Nuova in the Campagna, being on his way to the Council of Lyons, in 1274. He is supposed to have been poisoned by his physician, at the instigation of Charles of Anjou.

71. Charles of Valois, who came into Italy by invitation of Boniface the Eighth, in 1301. See *Inf.* VI. 69.

74. There is in old French literature a poem entitled *Le Tournoyement de l'Antechrist,* written by Hugues de Méry, a monk of the Abbey of St. Germain-des-Prés, in the thirteenth century, in which he describes a battle between the Virtues under the banner of Christ, and the Vices under that of Antichrist.

In the *Vision of Piers Ploughman,* there is a joust between Christ and the foul fiend:—

> "Thanne was Feith in a fenestre,
> And cryde a *fili David,*
> As dooth a heraud of armes,
> Whan aventrous cometh to justes.
> Old Jewes of Jerusalem
> For joye thei songen,
> *Benedictus qui venit in nomine Domini.*
>
> "Than I frayned at Feith,
> What all that fare by-mente,
> And who sholde juste in Jerusalem.
> 'Jhesus,' he seide,
> 'And fecche that the fend claymeth,
> Piers fruyt the Plowman.'
>   . . . . . .
> "'Who shal juste with Jhesus?' quod I,
> 'Jewes or scrybes?'
> "'Nay,' quod he: 'The foule fend,
> And fals doom and deeth.'"

75. By the aid of Charles of Valois the Neri party triumphed in Florence, and the Bianchi were banished, and with them Dante.

76. There is an allusion here to the nickname of Charles of Valois, Senzaterra, or Lackland.

79. Charles the Second, son of Charles of Anjou. He went from France to recover Sicily after the Sicilian Vespers. In an engagement with the Spanish fleet under Admiral Rugieri d'Oria, he was taken prisoner. Dante says he sold his daughter, because he married her for a large sum of money to Azzo the Sixth of Este.

82. *Æneid,* III. 56. "Cursed thirst of gold, to what dost thou not drive the hearts of men."

86. The flower-de-luce is in the banner of France. Borel, *Tresor de Recherches,* cited by Roquefort, *Glossaire,* under the word *Leye,* says: "The oriflamme is so called from gold and flame; that is to say, a lily of the marshes. The lilies are the arms of France on a field of azure, which denotes water, in memory that they (the French) came from a marshy country. It is the most ancient and principal banner of France, sown with these lilies, and was borne around our kings on great occasions."

Roquefort gives his own opinion as follows: "The Franks, afterwards called French, inhabited (before entering Gaul properly so called) the environs of the Lys, a river of the Low Countries, whose banks are still covered with a kind of iris or flag of a yellow colour, which differs from the common lily and more nearly resembles the flower-de-luce of our arms. Now it seems to me very natural that the kings of the Franks, having to choose a symbol to which the name of armorial bearings has since been given, should take in its composition a beautiful and remarkable flower, which they had before their eyes, and that they should name it, from the place where it grew in abundance, *flower of the river Lys.*"

These are the lilies of which Drayton speaks in his *Ballad of Agincourt:*—

> ". . . . when our grandsire great,
>   Claiming the regal seat,
>   By many a warlike feat
>   Lopped the French lilies."

87. This passage alludes to the seizure and imprisonment of Pope Boniface the Eighth by the troops of Philip the Fair at Alagna or Anagni, in 1303. Milman, *Lat. Christ.,* Book XI. Ch. 9, thus describes the event:—

"On a sudden, on the 7th September (the 8th was the day for the publication of the Bull), the peaceful streets of Anagni were disturbed. The Pope and the Cardinals, who were all assembled around him, were startled with the trampling of armed horse, and the terrible cry, which ran like wildfire through the city, 'Death to Pope Boniface! Long live the King of France!' Sciarra Colonna, at the head of three hundred horsemen, the Barons of Cercano and Supino, and some others, the sons of Master Massio of Anagni,

were marching in furious haste, with the banner of the king of France dis-
played. The ungrateful citizens of Anagni, forgetful of their pride in their
holy compatriot, of the honour and advantage to their town from the splen-
dour and wealth of the Papal residence, received them with rebellious and
acclaiming shouts.

"The bell of the city, indeed, had tolled at the first alarm; the burghers
had assembled; they had chosen their commander; but that commander,
whom they ignorantly or treacherously chose, was Arnulf, a deadly enemy
of the Pope. The banner of the Church was unfolded against the Pope by
the captain of the people of Anagni. The first attack was on the palace of the
Pope, on that of the Marquis Gaetani, his nephew, and those of three Cardinals,
the special partisans of Boniface. The houses of the Pope and of his nephew
made some resistance. The doors of those of the Cardinals were beaten down,
the treasures ransacked and carried off; the Cardinals themselves fled from
the backs of the houses through the common sewer. Then arrived, but not
to the rescue, Arnulf, the Captain of the People; he had perhaps been suborned
by Reginald of Supino. With him were the sons of Chiton, whose father was
pining in the dungeons of Boniface. Instead of resisting, they joined the attack
on the palace of the Pope's nephew and his own. The Pope and his nephew
implored a truce; it was granted for eight hours. This time the Pope employed
in endeavouring to stir up the people to his defence; the people coldly
answered, that they were under the command of their Captain. The Pope
demanded the terms of the conspirators. 'If the Pope would save his life, let
him instantly restore the Colonna Cardinals to their dignity, and reinstate the
whole house in their honours and possessions; after this restoration the Pope
must abdicate, and leave his body at the disposal of Sciarra.' The Pope groaned
in the depths of his heart. 'The word is spoken.' Again the assailants thundered
at the gates of the palace; still there was obstinate resistance. The principal
church of Anagni, that of Santa Maria, protected the Pope's palace. Sciarra
Colonna's lawless band set fire to the gates; the church was crowded with
clergy and laity and traders who had brought their precious wares into the
sacred building. They were plundered with such rapacity that not a man
escaped with a farthing.

"The Marquis found himself compelled to surrender, on the condition
that his own life, that of his family and of his servants, should be spared. At
these sad tidings the Pope wept bitterly. The Pope was alone; from the first
the Cardinals, some from treachery, some from cowardice, had fled on all
sides, even his most familiar friends: they had crept into the most ignoble
hiding-places. The aged Pontiff alone lost not his self-command. He had
declared himself ready to perish in his glorious cause; he determined to fall
with dignity. 'If I am betrayed like Christ, I am ready to die like Christ.' He
put on the stole of St. Peter, the imperial crown was on his head, the keys
of St. Peter in one hand and the cross in the other: he took his seat on the
Papal throne, and, like the Roman senators of old, awaited the approach of
the Gaul.

"But the pride and cruelty of Boniface had raised and infixed deep in the hearts of men passions which acknowledged no awe of age, of intrepidity, or religious majesty. In William of Nogaret the blood of his Tolosan ancestors, in Colonna, the wrongs, the degradation, the beggary, the exile of all his house, had extinguished every feeling but revenge. They insulted him with contumelious reproaches; they menaced his life. The Pope answered not a word. They insisted that he should at once abdicate the Papacy. 'Behold my neck, behold my head,' was the only reply. But fiercer words passed between the Pope and William of Nogaret. Nogaret threatened to drag him before the Council of Lyons, where he should be deposed from the Papacy. 'Shall I suffer myself to be degraded and deposed by Paterins like thee, whose fathers were righteously burned as Paterins?' William turned fiery red, with shame thought the partisans of Boniface, more likely with wrath. Sciarra, it was said, would have slain him outright; he was prevented by some of his own followers, even by Nogaret. 'Wretched Pope, even at this distance the goodness of my lord the King guards thy life.'

"He was placed under close custody, not one of his own attendants permitted to approach him. Worse indignities awaited him. He was set on a vicious horse, with his face to the tail, and so led through the town to his place of imprisonment. The palaces of the Pope and of his nephew were plundered; so vast was the wealth, that the annual revenues of all the kings in the world would not have been equal to the treasures found and carried off by Sciarra's freebooting soldiers. His very private chamber was ransacked; nothing left but bare walls.

"At length the people of Anagni could no longer bear the insult and the sufferings heaped upon their illustrious and holy fellow-citizen. They rose in irresistible insurrection, drove out the soldiers by whom they had been over-awed, now gorged with plunder, and doubtless not unwilling to withdraw. The Pope was rescued, and led out into the street, where the old man addressed a few words to the people: 'Good men and women, ye see how mine enemies have come upon me, and plundered my goods, those of the Church and of the poor. Not a morsel of bread have I eaten, not a drop have I drunk, since my capture. I am almost dead with hunger. If any good woman will give me a piece of bread and a cup of wine, if she has no wine, a little water, I will absolve her, and any one who will give me their alms, from all their sins.' The compassionate rabble burst into a cry, 'Long life to the Pope!' They carried him back to his naked palace. They crowded, the women especially, with provisions, bread, meat, water, and wine. They could not find a single vessel: they poured a supply of water into a chest. The Pope proclaimed a general absolution to all, except the plunderers of his palace. He even declared that he wished to be at peace with the Colonnas and all his enemies. This perhaps was to disguise his intention of retiring, as soon as he could, to Rome.

"The Romans had heard with indignation the sacrilegious attack on the person of the Supreme Pontiff. Four hundred horse under Matteo and Gaetano Orsini were sent to conduct him to the city. He entered it almost in triumph;

the populace welcomed him with every demonstration of joy. But the awe of his greatness was gone; the spell of his dominion over the minds of men was broken. His overweening haughtiness and domination had made him many enemies in the Sacred College, the gold of France had made him more. This general revolt is his severest condemnation. Among his first enemies was the Cardinal Napoleon Orsini. Orsini had followed the triumphal entrance of the Pope. Boniface, to show that he desired to reconcile himself with all, courteously invited him to his table. The Orsini coldly answered, 'that he must receive the Colonna Cardinals into his favour; he must not now disown what had been wrung from him by compulsion.' 'I will pardon them,' said Boniface, 'but the mercy of the Pope is not to be from compulsion.' He found himself again a prisoner.

"This last mortification crushed the bodily, if not the mental strength of the Pope. Among the Ghibellines terrible stories were bruited abroad of his death. In an access of fury, either from poison or wounded pride, he sat gnawing the top of his staff, and at length either beat out his own brains against the wall, or smothered himself (a strange notion!) with his own pillows. More friendly, probably more trustworthy, accounts describe him as sadly but quietly breathing his last, surrounded by eight Cardinals, having confessed the faith and received the consoling offices of the Church. The Cardinal-Poet anticipates his mild sentence from the Divine Judge.

"The religious mind of Christendom was at once perplexed and horror-stricken by this act of sacrilegious violence on the person of the Supreme Pontiff; it shocked some even of the sternest Ghibellines. Dante, who brands the pride, the avarice, the treachery of Boniface in his most terrible words, and has consigned him to the direst doom, (though it is true that his alliance with the French, with Charles of Valois, by whom the poet had been driven into exile, was among the deepest causes of his hatred to Boniface,) nevertheless expresses the almost universal feeling. Christendom shuddered to behold the Fleur-de-lis enter into Anagni, and Christ again captive in his Vicar, the mockery, the gall and vinegar, the crucifixion between living robbers, the insolent and sacrilegious cruelty of the second Pilate."

Compare this scene with that of his inauguration as Pope, *Inf.* XIX. Note 53.

91. This "modern Pilate" is Philip the Fair, and the allusion in the following lines is to the persecution and suppression of the Order of the Knights Templars, in 1307–1312. See Milman, *Lat. Christ.,* Book XII. Ch. 2, and Villani, VIII. 92, who says the act was committed *per cupidigia di guadagnare,* for love of gain; and says also: "The king of France and his children had afterwards much shame and adversity, both on account of this sin and on account of the seizure of Pope Boniface."

97. What he was saying of the Virgin Mary, line 19.

103. The brother of Dido and murderer of her husband. *Æneid,* I., 350: "He, impious and blinded with the love of gold, having taken Sichæus by

surprise, secretly assassinates him before the altar, regardless of his sister's great affection."

106. The Phrygian king, who, for his hospitality to Silenus, was endowed by Bacchus with the fatal power of turning all he touched to gold. The most laughable thing about him was his wearing ass's ears, as a punishment for preferring the music of Pan to that of Apollo.

Ovid, XI., Croxall's Tr.:—

> "Pan tuned the pipe, and with his rural song
>   Pleased the low taste of all the vulgar throng:
>   Such songs a vulgar judgment mostly please:
>   Midas was there, and Midas judged with these."

See also Hawthorne's story of *The Golden Touch* in his *Wonder-Book*.

109. *Joshua* vii. 21: "When I saw among the spoils a goodly Babylonish garment, and two hundred shekels of silver, and a wedge of gold of fifty shekels weight, then I coveted them, and took them; and behold, they are hid in the earth in the midst of my tent, and the silver under it."

112. *Acts* v. 1, 2: "But a certain man named Ananias, with Sapphira his wife, sold a possession, and kept back part of the price, his wife also being privy to it, and brought a certain part, and laid it at the apostles' feet."

113. The hoof-beats of the miraculous horse in the Temple of Jerusalem, when Heliodorus, the treasurer of King Seleucus, went there to remove the treasure. 2 *Maccabees* iii. 25: "For there appeared unto them an horse with a terrible rider upon him, and adorned with a very fair covering, and he ran fiercely, and smote at Heliodorus with his forefeet, and it seemed that he that sat upon the horse had complete harness of gold."

115. *Æneid*, III. 49, Davidson's Tr.: "This Polydore unhappy Priam had formerly sent in secrecy, with a great weight of gold, to be brought up by the king of Thrace, when he now began to distrust the arms of Troy, and saw the city with close siege blocked up. He, [Polymnestor,] as soon as the power of the Trojans was crushed, and their fortune gone, espousing Agamemnon's interest and victorious arms, breaks every sacred bond, assassinates Polydore, and by violence possesses his gold. Cursed thirst of gold, to what dost thou not drive the hearts of men!"

116. Lucinius Crassus, surnamed the Rich. He was Consul with Pompey, and on one occasion displayed his vast wealth by giving an entertainment to the populace, at which the guests were so numerous that they occupied ten thousand tables. He was slain in a battle with the Parthians, and his head was sent to the Parthian king, Hyrodes, who had molten gold poured down its throat. Plutarch does not mention this circumstance in his Life of Crassus, but says:—

"When the head of Crassus was brought to the door, the tables were just taken away, and one Jason, a tragic actor of the town of Tralles, was singing

the scene in the Bacchæ of Euripides concerning Agave. He was receiving
much applause, when Sillaces coming to the room, and having made obeisance
to the king, threw down the head of Crassus into the midst of the company.
The Parthians receiving it with joy and acclamations, Sillaces, by the king's
command, was made to sit down, while Jason handed over the costume of
Pentheus to one of the dancers in the chorus, and taking up the head of
Crassus, and acting the part of a bacchante in her frenzy, in a rapturous,
impassioned manner, sang the lyric passages,

> 'We've hunted down a mighty chase to-day,
> And from the mountain bring the noble prey.'"

122. This is in answer to Dante's question, line 35:—

> "And why only
> Thou dost renew these praises well deserved?"

128. The occasion of this quaking of the mountain is given, Canto XXI.
58:—

> "It trembles here, whenever any soul
> Feels itself pure, so that it soars, or moves
> To mount aloft, and such a cry attends it."

130. An island in the Ægean Sea, in the centre of the Cyclades. It was
thrown up by an earthquake, in order to receive Latona, when she gave birth
to Apollo and Diana,—the Sun and the Moon.

136. *Luke* ii. 13, 14: "And suddenly there was with the angel a multitude
of the heavenly host, praising God, and saying, Glory to God in the highest,
and on earth peace, good will toward men."

140. Gower, *Conf. Amant.*, III. 5:—

> "When Goddes sone also was bore,
> He sent his aungel down therfore,
> Whom the shepherdes herden singe:
> Pees to the men of welwillinge
> In erthe be amonge us here."

Canto XXI

1. This canto is devoted to the interview with the poet Statius, whose
release from punishment was announced by the earthquake and the outcry
at the end of the last canto.

3. *John* iv. 14, 15: "Whosoever drinketh of the water that I shall give him, shall never thirst. . . . . The woman saith unto him, Sir, give me this water, that I thirst not, neither come hither to draw."

7. *Luke* xxiv. 13–15: "And, behold, two of them went that same day to a village called Emmaus, which was from Jerusalem about threescore furlongs. And they talked together of all these things which had happened. And it came to pass, that, while they communed together and reasoned, Jesus himself drew near, and went with them."

15. Among the monks of the Middle Ages there were certain salutations, which had their customary replies or countersigns. Thus one would say, "Peace be with thee!" and the answer would be, "And with thy spirit!" Or, "Praised be the Lord!" and the answer, "World without end!"

22. The letters upon Dante's forehead.

25. Lachesis. Of the three Fates, Clotho prepared and held the distaff, Lachesis spun the thread, and Atropos cut it.

"These," says Plato, *Republic,* X., "are the daughters of Necessity, the Fates, Lachesis, Clotho, and Atropos; who, clothed in white robes, with garlands on their heads, chant to the music of the Sirens; Lachesis the events of the Past, Clotho those of the Present, Atropos those of the Future."

33. See Canto XVIII. 46:——

> "What reason seeth here,
> Myself can tell thee; beyond that await
> For Beatrice, since 'tis a work of faith."

So also Cowley, in his poem on the *Use of Reason in Divine Matters:*——

> "Though Reason cannot through Faith's mysteries see,
> It sees that there and such they be;
> Leads to heaven's door, and there does humbly keep,
> And there through chinks and keyholes peep;
> Though it, like Moses, by a sad command
> Must not come into the Holy Land,
> Yet thither it infallibly does guide,
> And from afar 'tis all descried."

40. Nothing unusual ever disturbs the *religio loci,* the sacredness of the mountain.

44. This happens only when the soul, that came from heaven, is received back into heaven; not from any natural causes affecting earth or air.

48. The gate of Purgatory, which is also the gate of Heaven.

50. Iris, one of the Oceanides, the daughter of Thaumas and Electra; the rainbow.

65. The soul in Purgatory feels as great a desire to be punished for a sin, as it had to commit it.

82. The siege of Jerusalem under Titus, surnamed the "Delight of Mankind,"
took place in the year 70. Statius, who is here speaking, was born at Naples
in the reign of Claudius, and had already become famous "under the name
that most endures and honours," that is, as a poet. His works are the *Silvæ*,
or miscellaneous poems; the *Thebaid,* an epic in twelve books; and the *Achilleid,*
left unfinished. He wrote also a tragedy, *Agave,* which is lost.

Juvenal says of him, *Satire* VII., Dryden's Tr.:—

> "All Rome is pleased when Statius will rehearse,
> And longing crowds expect the promised verse;
> His lofty numbers with so great a gust
> They hear, and swallow with such eager lust;
> But while the common suffrage crowned his cause,
> And broke the benches with their loud applause,
> His Muse had starved, had not a piece unread,
> And by a player bought, supplied her bread."

Dante shows his admiration of him by placing him here.

89. Statius was not born in Toulouse, as Dante supposes, but in Naples,
as he himself states in his *Silvæ,* which work was not discovered till after
Dante's death. The passage occurs in Book III. Eclogue V., *To Claudia his
Wife,* where he describes the beauties of Parthenope, and calls her the mother
and nurse of both, *amborum genetrix altrixque.*

Landino thinks that Dante's error may be traced to Placidus Lactantius, a
commentator of the *Thebaid,* who confounded Statius the poet of Naples
with Statius the rhetorician of Toulouse.

101. Would be willing to remain another year in Purgatory.

114. Petrarca uses the same expression,—the lightning of the angelic smile,
il lampeggiar dell' angelico riso.

131. See Canto XIX. 133.

Canto XXII

1. The ascent to the Sixth Circle, where the sin of Gluttony is punished.

5. *Matthew* v. 6: "Blessed are they which do hunger and thirst after righ-
teousness; for they shall be filled."

13. The satirist Juvenal, who flourished at Rome during the last half of
the first century of the Christian era, and died at the beginning of the second,
aged eighty. He was a contemporary of Statius, and survived him some thirty
years.

40. *Æneid,* III. 56: "O cursed hunger of gold, to what dost thou not drive
the hearts of men."

42. The punishment of the Avaricious and Prodigal. *Inf.* VII. 26:—

> "With great howls
> Rolling weights forward by main force of chest."

46. Dante says of the Avaricious and Prodigal, *Inf.* VII. 56:—

> "These from the sepulchre shall rise again
> With the fist closed, and these with tresses shorn."

56. Her two sons, Eteocles and Polynices, of whom Statius sings in the *Thebaid,* and to whom Dante alludes by way of illustration, *Inf.* XXVI. 54. See also the Note.

58. Statius begins the *Thebaid* with an invocation to Clio, the Muse of History, whose office it was to record the heroic actions of brave men, I. 55:—

> "What first, O Clio, shall adorn thy page,
> The expiring prophet, or Ætolian's rage?
> Say, wilt thou sing how, grim with hostile blood,
> Hippomedon repelled the rushing flood,
> Lament the Arcadian youth's untimely fate,
> Or Jove, opposed by Capaneus, relate?"

Skelton, *Elegy on the Earl of Northumberland:*—

> "Of hevenly poems, O Clyo calde by name
> In the college of musis goddess hystoriale."

63. Saint Peter.

70. Virgil's *Bucolics,* Ecl. IV. 5, a passage supposed to foretell the birth of Christ: "The last era of Cumæan song is now arrived; the great series of ages begins anew; now the Virgin returns, returns the Saturnian reign; now a new progeny is sent down from the high heaven."

92. The Fourth Circle of Purgatory, where Sloth is punished. Canto XVII. 85:—

> "The love of good, remiss
> In what it should have done, is here restored;
> Here plied again the ill-belated oar."

97. Some editions read in this line, instead of *nostro amico,—nostro antico,* our ancient Terence; but the epithet would be more appropriate to Plautus, who was the earlier writer.

97, 98. Plautus, Cæcilius, and Terence, the three principal Latin dramatists; Varro, "the most learned of the Romans," the friend of Cicero, and author of some five hundred volumes, which made St. Augustine wonder how he who wrote so many books could find time to read so many; and how he who read so many could find time to write so many.

100. Persius, the Latin satirist.

101. Homer.

106. Mrs. Browning, *Wine of Cyprus*:—

> "Our Euripides, the human,—
>   With his droppings of warm tears;
> And his touchings of things common,
>   Till they rose to touch the spheres."

But why does Dante make no mention here of "Æschyles the thunderous" and "Sophocles the royal"?

Antiphon was a tragic and epic poet of Attica, who was put to death by Dionysius because he would not praise the tyrant's writings. Some editions read Anacreon for Antiphon.

107. Simonides, the poet of Cos, who won a poetic prize at the age of eighty, and is said to be the first poet who wrote for money.

Agatho was an Athenian dramatist, of whom nothing remains but the name and a few passages quoted in other writers.

110. Some of the people that Statius introduces into his poems. Antigone, daughter of Œdipus; Deiphile, wife of Tideus; Argia, her sister, wife of Polynices; Ismene, another daughter of Œdipus, who is here represented as still lamenting the death of Atys, her betrothed.

112. Hypsipile, who pointed out to Adrastus the fountain of Langia, when his soldiers were perishing with thirst on their march against Thebes.

113. Of the three daughters of Tiresias only Manto is mentioned by Statius in the *Thebaid*. But Dante places Manto among the Soothsayers, *Inf.* XX. 55, and not in Limbo. Had he forgotten this?

113, 114. Thetis, the mother of Achilles, and Deidamia, the daughter of Lycomedes. They are among the personages in the *Achilleid* of Statius.

118. Four hours of the day were already passed.

131. Cowley, *The Tree of Knowledge*:—

> "The sacred tree 'midst the fair orchard grew,
>   The phœnix Truth did on it rest
>   And built his perfumed nest,
> That right Porphyrian tree which did true Logic show;
>   Each leaf did learned notions give
>   And th' apples were demonstrative;
>   So clear their colour and divine
> The very shade they cast did other lights outshine."

This tree of Temptation, however, is hardly the tree of Knowledge, though sprung from it, as Dante says of the next, in Canto XXIV. 117. It is meant

only to increase the torment of the starving souls beneath it, by holding its
fresh and dewy fruit beyond their reach.

142. *John* ii. 3: "And when they wanted wine, the mother of Jesus saith
unto him, They have no wine."

146. *Daniel* i. 12: "Prove thy servants, I beseech thee, ten days; and let
them give us pulse to eat and water to drink. . . . . . And Daniel had under-
standing in all visions and dreams."

148. Compare the description of the Golden Age in Ovid, *Met.,* I.:—

> "The golden age was first; when man, yet new,
> No rule but uncorrupted reason knew,
> And, with a native bent, did good pursue.
> Unforced by punishment, unawed by fear,
> His words were simple, and his soul sincere;
> Needless was written law, where none opprest:
> The law of man was written in his breast:
> No suppliant crowds before the judge appeared,
> No court erected yet, nor cause was heard:
> But all was safe, for conscience was their guard.
> The mountain-trees in distant prospect please,
> Ere yet the pine descended to the seas;
> Ere sails were spread, new oceans to explore;
> And happy mortals, unconcerned for more,
> Confined their wishes to their native shore.
> No walls were yet: nor fence, nor mote, nor mound,
> Nor drum was heard, nor trumpet's angry sound:
> Nor swords were forged; but, void of care and crime,
> The soft creation slept away their time.
> The teeming earth, yet guiltless of the plough,
> And unprovoked, did fruitful stores allow:
> Content with food, which nature freely bred,
> On wildings and on strawberries they fed;
> Cornels and bramble-berries gave the rest,
> And falling acorns furnished out a feast.
> The flowers unsown in fields and meadows reigned;
> And western winds immortal spring maintained.
> In following years, the bearded corn ensued
> From earth unasked, nor was that earth renewed.
> From veins of valleys milk and nectar broke,
> And honey sweating through the pores of oak."

Also Boëthius, Book II. Met. 5, and the Ode in Tasso's *Aminta,* Leigh
Hunt's Tr., beginning:—

> "O lovely age of gold!
> Not that the rivers rolled

With milk, or that the woods wept honeydew;
Not that the ready ground
Produced without a wound,
Or the mild serpent had no tooth that slew;
Not that a cloudless blue
For ever was in sight,
Or that the heaven which burns,
And now is cold by turns,
Looked out in glad and everlasting light;
No, nor that even the insolent ships from far
Brought war to no new lands, nor riches worse than war:

"But solely that that vain
And breath-invented pain,
That idol of mistake, that worshipped cheat,
That Honour,—since so called
By vulgar minds appalled,—
Played not the tyrant with our nature yet.
It had not come to fret
The sweet and happy fold
Of gentle human-kind;
Nor did its hard law bind
Souls nursed in freedom; but that law of gold,
That glad and golden law, all free, all fitted,
Which Nature's own hand wrote,—What pleases, is permitted."

Also Don Quixote's address to the goatherds, *Don Quix.*, Book II. Ch. 3, Jarvis's Tr.:—

"After Don Quixote had satisfied his hunger, he took up an handful of acorns, and, looking on them attentively, gave utterance to expressions like these:—

"'Happy times, and happy ages! those to which the ancients gave the name of golden, not because gold (which, in this our iron age, is so much esteemed) was to be had, in that fortunate period, without toil and labour; but because they who then lived were ignorant of these two words Meum and Tuum. In that age of innocence, all things were in common; no one needed to take any other pains for his ordinary sustenance, than to lift up his hand and take it from the sturdy oaks, which stood inviting him liberally to taste of their sweet and relishing fruit. The limpid fountains, and running streams, offered them, in magnificent abundance, their delicious and transparent waters. In the clefts of rocks, and in the hollow of trees, did the industrious and provident bees form their commonwealths, offering to every hand, without usury, the fertile produce of their most delicious toil. The stout cork trees, without any other inducement than that of their own courtesy, divested themselves of their light and expanded bark, with which men began to cover their houses, supported by rough poles, only for a defence against the inclemency of the seasons. All then was peace, all amity, all concord. As yet the heavy coulter of the crooked plough had not dared to force open, and search into, the tender bowels of our first mother, who unconstrained offered, from every part of her fertile and spacious bosom, whatever might feed, sustain, and delight those her children, who then had her in possession. Then did the simple and beauteous young shepherdesses trip it from dale to dale, and from hill to hill, their tresses sometimes plaited, sometimes loosely flowing, with no more clothing than was necessary modestly to cover what modesty has always required to be concealed; nor were there ornaments like those now-a-days in fashion, to which the Tyrian purple and the so-many-ways martyred silk give a value; but composed of green dock-leaves and ivy interwoven; with which, perhaps, they went as splendidly and elegantly decked as our court-ladies do now, with all those rare and foreign inventions which idle curiosity hath taught them. Then were the amorous conceptions of the soul clothed in simple and sincere expressions, in the same way and manner they were conceived, without seeking artificial phrases to set them off. Nor as yet were fraud, deceit, and malice intermixed with truth and plain-dealing. Justice kept within her proper bounds; favour and interest, which now so much depreciate, confound, and persecute her, not daring then to disturb or offend her. As yet the judge did not make his own will the measure of justice; for then there was neither cause nor person to be judged.'"

Canto XXIII

1. The punishment of the sin of Gluttony.
3. Shakespeare, *As You Like It,* II. 7:—

> "Under the shade of melancholy boughs
> Lose and neglect the creeping hours of time."

11. *Psalm* li. 15: "O Lord, open thou my lips; and my mouth shall show forth thy praise."
26. Erisichthon the Thessalian, who in derision cut down an ancient oak in the sacred groves of Ceres. He was punished by perpetual hunger, till, other food failing him, at last he gnawed his own flesh. Ovid, *Met.* VIII., Vernon's Tr.:—

> "Straight he requires, impatient in demand,
> Provisions from the air, the seas, the land;
> But though the land, air, seas, provisions grant,
> Starves at full tables, and complains of want.
> What to a people might in dole be paid,

Or victual cities for a long blockade,
Could not one wolfish appetite assuage;
For glutting nourishment increased its rage.
As rivers poured from every distant shore
The sea insatiate drinks, and thirsts for more;
Or as the fire, which all materials burns,
And wasted forests into ashes turns,
Grows more voracious as the more it preys,
Recruits dilate the flame, and spread the blaze:
So impious Erisichthon's hunger raves,
Receives refreshments, and refreshments craves.
Food raises a desire for food, and meat
Is but a new provocative to eat.
He grows more empty as the more supplied,
And endless cramming but extends the void."

30. This tragic tale of the siege of Jerusalem by Titus is thus told in Josephus, *Jewish War,* Book VI. Ch. 3, Whiston's Tr.:—

"There was a certain woman that dwelt beyond Jordan; her name was Mary; her father was Eleazar, of the village Bethezub, which signifies the house of Hyssop. She was eminent for her family and her wealth, and had fled away to Jerusalem with the rest of the multitude, and was with them besieged therein at this time. The other effects of this woman had been already seized upon, such I mean as she had brought with her out of Perea, and removed to the city. What she had treasured up besides, as also what food she had contrived to save, had been also carried off by the rapacious guards, who came every day running into her house for that purpose. This put the poor woman into a very great passion, and by the frequent reproaches and imprecations she cast at these rapacious villains, she had provoked them to anger against her; but none of them, either out of the indignation she had raised against herself, or out of commiseration of her case, would take away her life. And if she found any food, she perceived her labours were for others and not for herself; and it was now become impossible for her any way to find any more food, while the famine pierced through her very bowels and marrow, when also her passion was fired to a degree beyond the famine itself. Nor did she consult with anything but with her passion and the necessity she was in. She then attempted a most unnatural thing, and, snatching up her son who was a child sucking at her breast, she said, 'O thou miserable infant! For whom shall I preserve thee in this war, this famine, and this sedition? As to the war with the Romans, if they preserve our lives, we must be slaves. This famine also will destroy us, even before that slavery comes upon us. Yet are these seditious rogues more terrible than both the other. Come on, be thou my food, and be thou a fury to these seditious varlets, and a byword to the world; which is all that is now wanting to complete the calamities of the Jews.' As soon as she had said this, she slew her son, and then roasted him, and ate the one half of him, and kept the other half by her concealed. Upon this the seditious came in presently, and, smelling the horrid scent of this food, they threatened her that they would cut her throat immediately, if she did not show them what food she had gotten ready. She replied, that she had saved a very fine portion of it for them; and withal uncovered what was left of her son. Hereupon they were seized with a horror and amazement of mind, and stood astonished at the sight, when she said to them: 'This is mine own son, and what hath been done was mine own doing. Come, eat of this food; for I have eaten of it myself. Do not you pretend to be either more tender than a woman, or more compassionate than a mother. But if you be so scrupulous, and do abominate this my sacrifice, as I have eaten the one-half, let the rest be reserved for me also.' After which those men went out trembling, being never so much affrighted at anything as they were at this, and with some difficulty they left the rest of that meat to the mother. Upon which the whole city was full of this horrid action immediately; and while everybody laid this miserable case before their own eyes, they trembled as if this unheard of action had been done by themselves. So those that were thus distressed by the famine were very desirous to die, and those already dead were esteemed happy, because they had not lived long enough either to hear or to see such miseries."

31. Shakespeare, *King Lear*, V. 3:—

>   "And in this habit
> Met I my father with his bleeding rings,
> Their precious stones new lost."

32. In this fanciful recognition of the word *omo* (*homo*, man) in the human face, so written as to place the two *o's* between the outer strokes of the *m*, the former represent the eyes, and the latter the nose and cheekbones:

Brother Berthold, a Franciscan monk of Regensburg, in the thirteenth century, makes the following allusion to it in one of his sermons. See Wackernagel, *Deutsches Lesebuch*, I. 678. The monk carries out the resemblance into still further detail:—

"Now behold, ye blessed children of God, the Almighty has created you soul and body. And he has written it under your eyes and on your faces, that you are created in his likeness. He has written it upon your very faces with ornamented letters. With great diligence are they embellished and ornamented. This your learned men will understand, but the unlearned may not understand it. The two eyes are two *o's*. The *h* is properly no letter; it only helps the others; so that *homo* with an *h* means Man. Likewise the brows arched above and the nose down between them are an *m*, beautiful with three strokes. So is the ear a *d,* beautifully rounded and ornamented. So are the nostrils beautifully formed like a Greek ε, beautifully rounded and ornamented. So is the mouth an *i,* beautifully adorned and ornamented. Now behold, ye good Christian people, how skilfully he has adorned you with these six letters, to show that ye are his own, and that he has created you! Now read me an *o* and an *m* and another *o* together; that spells *homo.* Then read me a *d* and an *e* and an *i* together; that spells *dei. Homo dei,* man of God, man of God!"

48. Forese Donati, the brother-in-law and intimate friend of Dante. "This Forese," says Buti, "was a citizen of Florence, and was brother of Messer Corso Donati, and was very gluttonous; and therefore the author feigns that he found him here, where the Gluttons are punished."

Certain vituperative sonnets, addressed to Dante, have been attributed to Forese. If authentic, they prove that the friendship between the two poets was not uninterrupted. See Rossetti, *Early Italian Poets,* Appendix to Part II.

74. The same desire that sacrifice and atonement may be complete.

75. *Matthew* xxvii. 46: "Eli, Eli, lama sabachthani? that is to say, My God, my God, why hast thou forsaken me?"

83. Outside the gate of Purgatory, where those who had postponed repentance till the last hour were forced to wait as many years and days as they had lived impenitent on earth, unless aided by the devout prayers of those on earth. See Canto IV.

87. Nella, contraction of Giovannella, widow of Forese. Nothing is known of this good woman but the name, and what Forese here says in her praise.

94. Covino, *Descriz. Geograf. dell' Italia,* p. 52, says: "In the district of Arborea, on the slopes of the Gennargentu, the most vast and lofty mountain range of Sardinia, spreads an alpine country which in Dante's time, being almost barbarous, was called the *Barbagia."*

102. Sacchetti, the Italian novelist of the fourteenth century, severely criticises the fashions of the Florentines, and their sudden changes, which he says it would take a whole volume of his stories to enumerate. In Nov. 1378, he speaks of their wearing their dresses "far below their arm-pits," and then "up to their ears;" and continues, in Napier's version, *Flor. Hist.,* II. 539:—

"The young Florentine girls, who used to dress so modestly, have now changed the fashion of their hoods to resemble courtesans, and thus attired they move about laced up to the throat, with all sorts of animals hanging as ornaments about their necks. Their sleeves, or rather their sacks, as they should be called,—was there ever so useless and pernicious a fashion! Can any of them reach a glass or take a morsel from the table without dirtying herself or the cloth by the things she knocks down? And thus do the young men, and worse; and such sleeves are made even for sucking babes. The women go about in hoods and cloaks; most of the young men without cloaks, in long, flowing hair, and if they throw off their breeches, which from their smallness may easily be done, all is off, for they literally stick their posteriors into a pair of socks and expend a yard of cloth on their wristbands, while more stuff is put into a glove than a cloak-hood. However, I am comforted by one thing, and that is, that all now have begun to put their feet in chains, perhaps as a penance for the many vain things they are guilty of; for we are but a day in this world, and in that day the fashion is changed a thousand times: all seek liberty, yet all deprive themselves of it: God has made our feet free, and many with long pointed toes to their shoes can scarcely walk: he has supplied the legs with hinges, and many have so bound them up with close lacing that they can scarcely sit: the bust is tightly bandaged up; the arms trail their drapery along; the throat is rolled in a capuchin; the head so loaded and bound round with caps over the hair that it appears as though it were sawed off. And thus I might go on for ever discoursing of female absurdities, commencing with the immeasurable trains at their feet, and proceeding regularly upwards to the head, with which they may always be seen occupied in their chambers; some curling, some smoothing, and some whitening it, so that they often kill themselves with colds caught in these vain occupations."

132. Statius.

Canto XXIV

1. Continuation of the punishment of Gluttony.

7. Continuing the words with which the preceding canto closes, and referring to Statius.

10. Picarda, sister of Forese and Corso Donati. She was a nun of Santa Clara, and is placed by Dante in the first heaven of Paradise, which Forese calls "high Olympus." See *Par.* III. 48, where her story is told more in detail.

19. Buonagiunta Urbisani of Lucca is one of the early minor poets of Italy, a contemporary of Dante. Rossetti, *Early Italian Poets,* 77, gives some specimens of his sonnets and canzoni. All that is known of him is contained in Benvenuto's brief notice: "Buonagiunta of Urbisani, an honourable man of the city of Lucca, a brilliant orator in his mother tongue, a facile producer of rhymes, and still more facile consumer of wines; who knew our author in his lifetime, and sometimes corresponded with him."

Tiraboschi also mentions him, *Storia della Lett.,* IV. 397: "He was seen by Dante in Purgatory punished among the Gluttons, from which vice, it is proper to say, poetry did not render him exempt."

22. Pope Martin the Fourth, whose fondness for the eels of Bolsena brought his life to a sudden close, and his soul to this circle of Purgatory, has been ridiculed in the well-known epigram,—

> "Gaudent anguillæ, quod mortuus hic jacet ille
> Qui quasi morte reas excoriabat eas."

"Martin the Fourth," says Milman, *Hist. Lat. Christ.,* VI. 143, "was born at Mont. Pencè in Brie; he had been Canon of Tours. He put on at first the

show of maintaining the lofty character of the Churchman. He excommu-
nicated the Viterbans for their sacrilegious maltreatment of the Cardinals;
Rinaldo Annibaldeschi, the Lord of Viterbo, was compelled to ask pardon
on his knees of the Cardinal Rosso, and forgiven only at the intervention of
the Pope. Martin the Fourth retired to Orvieto.

"But the Frenchman soon began to predominate over the Pontiff; he
sunk into the vassal of Charles of Anjou. The great policy of his predecessor,
to assuage the feuds of Guelph and Ghibelline, was an Italian policy; it was
altogether abandoned. The Ghibellines in every city were menaced or smit-
ten with excommunication; the Lambertazzi were driven from Bologna.
Forlì was placed under interdict for harbouring the exiles; the goods of the
citizens were confiscated for the benefit of the Pope. Bertoldo Orsini was
deposed from the Countship of Romagna; the office was bestowed on John
of Appia, with instructions everywhere to coerce or to chastise the refractory
Ghibellines."

Villani, Book VI. Ch. 106, says: "He was a good man, and very favourable
to Holy Church and to those of the house of France, because he was from
Tours."

He is said to have died of a surfeit. The eels and sturgeon of Bolsena, and
the wines of Orvieto and Montefiascone, in the neighbourhood of whose
vineyards he lived, were too much for him. But he died in Perugia, not in
Orvieto.

24. The Lake of Bolsena is in the Papal States, a few miles northwest of
Viterbo, on the road from Rome to Siena. It is thus described in Murray's
Handbook of Central Italy, p. 199:—

"Its circular form, and being in the centre of a volcanic district, has led to
its being regarded as an extinct crater; but that hypothesis can scarcely be
admitted when the great extent of the lake is considered. The treacherous
beauty of the lake conceals *malaria* in its most fatal forms; and its shores,
although there are no traces of a marsh, are deserted, excepting where a few
sickly hamlets are scattered on their western slopes. The ground is cultivated
in many parts down to the water's edge, but the labourers dare not sleep for
a single night during the summer or autumn on the plains where they work
by day; and a large tract of beautiful and productive country is reduced to a
perfect solitude by this invisible calamity. Nothing can be more striking than
the appearance of the lake, without a single sail upon its waters, and with
scarcely a human habitation within sight of Bolsena; and nothing perhaps can
give the traveller who visits Italy for the first time a more impressive idea of
the effects of malaria."

Of the Vernaccia or Vernage, in which Pope Martin cooked his eels,
Henderson says, *Hist. Anc. and Mod. Wines,* p. 296: "The Vernage . . . . was
a red wine, of a bright colour, and a sweetish and somewhat rough flavour,
which was grown in Tuscany and other parts of Italy, and derived its name
from the thick-skinned grape, *vernaccia* (corresponding with the *vinaciola* of
the ancients), that was used in the preparation of it."

Chaucer mentions it in the *Merchant's Tale:*—

> "He drinketh ipocras, clarre, and vernage
> Of spices hot, to encreasen his corege."

And Redi, *Bacchus in Tuscany,* Leigh Hunt's Tr., p. 30, sings of it thus:—

> "If anybody doesn't like Vernaccia,
>   I mean that sort that's made in Pietrafitta,
>   Let him fly
>   My violent eye;
>   I curse him, clean, through all the Alpha-beta."

28. Ovid, *Met.* VII., says of Erisichthon, that he

> "Deludes his throat with visionary fare,
>   Feasts on the wind and banquets on the air."

29. Ubaldin dalla Pila was a brother of the Cardinal Ottaviano degli Ubaldini, mentioned *Inf.* X. 120, and father of the Archbishop Ruggieri, *Inf.* XXXIII. 14. According to Sacchetti, Nov. 205, he passed most of his time at his castle, and turned his gardener into a priest; "and Messer Ubaldino," continues the novelist, "put him into his church; of which one may say he made a pigsty; for he did not put in a priest, but a pig in the way of eating and drinking, who had neither grammar nor any good thing in him."

Some writers say that this Boniface, Archbishop of Ravenna, was a son of Ubaldino; but this is confounding him with Ruggieri, Archbishop of Pisa. He was of the Fieschi of Genoa. His pasturing many people alludes to his keeping a great retinue and court, and the free life they led in matters of the table.

31. Messer Marchese da Forlì, who answered the accusation made against him, that "he was always drinking," by saying, that "he was always thirsty."

37. A lady of Lucca with whom Dante is supposed to have been enamoured. "Let us pass over in silence," says Balbo, *Life and Times of Dante,* II. 177, "the consolations and errors of the poor exile." But Buti says: "He formed an attachment to a gentle lady, called Madonna Gentucca, of the family of Rossimpelo, on account of her great virtue and modesty, and not with any other love."

Benvenuto and the *Ottimo* interpret the passage differently, making *gentucca* a common noun,—*gente bassa,* low people. But the passage which immediately follows, in which a maiden is mentioned who should make Lucca pleasant to him, seems to confirm the former interpretation.

38. In the throat of the speaker, where he felt the hunger and thirst of his punishment.

50. Chaucer, *Complaint of the Blacke Knight,* 194:—

> "But even like as doth a skrivenere,
>   That can no more tell what that he shal write,
>   But as his maister beside dothe indite."

51. A canzone of the *Vita Nuova*, beginning, in Rossetti's version, *Early Italian Poets,* p. 255:—

> "Ladies that have intelligence in love,
>   Of mine own lady I would speak with you;
>   Not that I hope to count her praises through,
>   But, telling what I may, to ease my mind."

56. Jacopo da Lentino, or "the Notary," was a Sicilian poet who flourished about 1250, in the later days of the Emperor Frederick the Second. Crescimbeni, *Hist. Volg. Poesia,* III. 43, says that Dante "esteemed him so highly, that he even mentions him in his Comedy, doing him the favour to put him into Purgatory." Tassoni, and others after him, make the careless statement that he addressed a sonnet to Petrarca. He died before Petrarca was born. Rossetti gives several specimens of his sonnets and canzonette in his *Early Italian Poets,* of which the following is one:—

> "OF HIS LADY IN HEAVEN.
> "I have it in my heart to serve God so
>   That into Paradise I shall repair,—
>   The holy place through the which everywhere
> I have heard say that joy and solace flow.
> Without my lady I were loath to go,—
>   She who has the bright face and the bright hair;
>   Because if she were absent, I being there,
> My pleasure would be less than nought, I know.
> Look you, I say not this to such intent
>   As that I there would deal in any sin:
>   only would behold her gracious mien,
>   And beautiful soft eyes, and lovely face,
> That so it should be my complete content
>   To see my lady joyful in her place."

Fra Guittone d'Arezzo, a contemporary of the Notary, was one of the Frati Gaudenti, or Jovial Friars, mentioned in *Inf.* XXIII. Note 103. He first brought the Italian Sonnet to the perfect form it has since preserved, and left behind the earliest specimens of Italian letter-writing. These letters are written in a very florid style, and are perhaps more poetical than his verses, which certainly fall very far short of the "sweet new style." Of all his letters the best is that *To the Florentines,* from which a brief extract is given Canto VI. Note 76.

82. Corso Donati, the brother of Forese who is here speaking, and into whose mouth nothing but Ghibelline wrath could have put these words. Corso was the leader of the Neri in Florence, and a partisan of Charles de Valois. His death is recorded by Villani, VIII. 96, and is thus described by Napier, *Flor. Hist.,* I. 407:—

"The popularity of Corso was now thoroughly undermined, and the priors, after sounding the Campana for a general assembly of the armed citizens, laid a formal accusation before the Podestà Piero Branca d'Agobbio against him for conspiring to overthrow the liberties of his country, and endeavouring to make himself Tyrant of Florence: he was immediately cited to appear, and, not complying, from a reasonable distrust of his judges, was within one hour, against all legal forms, condemned to lose his head, as a rebel and traitor to the commonwealth.

"Not willing to allow the culprit more time for an armed resistance than had been given for legal vindication, the Seignory, preceded by the Gonfalonier of justice, and followed by the Podestà, the captain of the people, and the executor,—all attended by their guards and officers,—issued from the palace; and with the whole civic force marshalled in companies, with banners flying, moved forward to execute an illegal sentence against a single citizen, who nevertheless stood undaunted on his defence.

"Corso, on first hearing of the prosecution, had hastily barricaded all the approaches to his palace, but, disabled by the gout, could only direct the necessary operations from his bed; yet thus helpless, thus abandoned by all but his own immediate friends and vassals; suddenly condemned to death; encompassed by the bitterest foes, with the whole force of the republic banded against him, he never cowered for an instant, but courageously determined to resist, until succoured by Uguccione della Faggiola, to whom he had sent for aid. This attack continued during the greater part of the day, and generally with advantage to the Donati, for the people were not unanimous, and many fought unwillingly, so that, if the Rossi, Bardi, and other friends had joined, and Uguccioni's forces arrived, it would have gone hard with the citizens. The former were intimidated, the latter turned back on hearing how matters stood; and then only did Corso's adherents lose heart and slink from the barricades, while the townsmen pursued their advantage by breaking down a garden wall opposite the Stinche prisons and taking their enemy in the rear. This completed the disaster, and Corso, seeing no chance remaining, fled towards the Casentino; but, being overtaken by some Catalonian troopers in the Florentine service, he was led back a prisoner from Rovezzano. After vainly endeavouring to bribe them, unable to support the indignity of a public execution at the hands of his enemies, he let himself fall from his horse, and, receiving several stabs in the neck and flank from the Catalan lances, his body was left bleeding on the road, until the monks of San Salvi removed it to their convent, where he was interred next morning with the greatest privacy. Thus perished Corso Donati, 'the wisest and most worthy knight of his time; the best speaker, the most experienced statesman; the most renowned, the boldest, and most enterprising nobleman in Italy: he was handsome in person and of the most gracious manners, but very worldly, and caused infinite disturbance in Florence on account of his ambition.'* . . . .

---

* Villani, VIII. Ch. 96.

'People now began to repose, and his unhappy death was often and variously discussed, according to the feelings of friendship or enmity that moved the speaker; but in truth, his life was dangerous, and his death reprehensible. He was a knight of great mind and name, gentle in manners as in blood; of a fine figure even in his old age, with a beautiful countenance, delicate features, and a fair complexion; pleasing, wise; and an eloquent speaker. His attention was ever fixed on important things; he was intimate with all the great and noble, had an extensive influence, and was famous throughout Italy. He was an enemy of the middle classes and their supporters, beloved by the troops, but full of malicious thoughts, wicked, and artful. He was thus basely murdered by a foreign soldier, and his fellow-citizens well knew the man, for he was instantly conveyed away: those who ordered his death were Rosso della Tosa and Pazzino de' Pazzi, as is commonly said by all; and some bless him and some the contrary. Many believe that the two said knights killed him, and I, wishing to ascertain the truth, inquired diligently, and found what I have said to be true.'* Such is the character of Corso Donati, which has come down to us from two authors who must have been personally acquainted with this distinguished chief, but opposed to each other in the general politics of their country."

See also *Inf.* VI. Note 52.

99. Virgil and Statius.

105. Dante had only so far gone round the circle, as to come in sight of the second of these trees, which from distance to distance encircle the mountain.

116. In the Terrestrial Paradise on the top of the mountain.

121. The Centaurs, born of Ixion and the Cloud, and having the "double breasts" of man and horse, became drunk with wine at the marriage of Hippodamia and Pirithous, and strove to carry off the bride and the other women by violence. Theseus and the rest of the Lapithæ opposed them, and drove them from the feast. This famous battle is described at great length by Ovid, *Met.* XII., Dryden's Tr.:—

> "For one, most brutal of the brutal brood,
> Or whether wine or beauty fired his blood,
> Or both at once, beheld with lustful eyes
> The bride; at once resolved to make his prize.
> Down went the board; and fastening on her hair,
> He seized with sudden force the frighted fair.
> 'Twas Eurytus began: his bestial kind
> His crime pursued; and each, as pleased his mind,
> Or her whom chance presented, took: the feast
> An image of a taken town expressed.
>   "The cave resounds with female shrieks; we rise

---

* Dino Compagni, III. 76.

Mad with revenge, to make a swift reprise:
And Theseus first, 'What frenzy has possessed,
O Eurytus,' he cried, 'thy brutal breast,
To wrong Pirithous, and not him alone,
But, while I live, two friends conjoined in one?'"

125. *Judges* vii. 5, 6: "So he brought down the people unto the water: and the Lord said unto Gideon, Every one that lappeth of the water with his tongue, as a dog lappeth, him shalt thou set by himself; likewise every one that boweth down upon his knees to drink. And the number of them that lapped, putting their hand to their mouth, were three hundred men; but all the rest of the people bowed down upon their knees to drink water."

139. The Angel of the Seventh Circle.

Canto XXV

1. The ascent to the Seventh Circle of Purgatory, where the sin of Lust is punished.

3. When the sign of Taurus reached the meridian, the sun, being in Aries, would be two hours beyond it. It is now two o'clock of the afternoon. The Scorpion is the sign opposite Taurus.

15. Shakespeare, *Hamlet*, I. 2:—

"And did address
Itself to motion, like as it would speak."

22. Meleager was the son of Œneus and Althæa, of Calydon. At his birth the Fates were present and predicted his future greatness. Clotho said that he would be brave; Lachesis, that he would be strong; and Atropos, that he would live as long as the brand upon the fire remained unconsumed.

Ovid, *Met.* VIII.:—

"There lay a log unlighted on the hearth,
When she was labouring in the throes of birth
For th' unborn chief; the fatal sisters came,
And raised it up, and tossed it on the flame.
Then on the rock a scanty measure place
Of vital flax, and turned the wheel apace;
And turning sung, 'To this red brand and thee,
O new-born babe, we give an equal destiny;'
So vanished out of view. The frighted dame
Sprung hasty from her bed, and quenched the flame.
The log, in secret locked, she kept with care,
And that, while thus preserved, preserved her heir."

Meleager distinguished himself in the Argonautic expedition, and afterwards in the hunt of Calydon, where he killed the famous boar, and gave the boar's head to Atalanta; and when his uncles tried to take possession of it, he killed them also. On hearing this, and seeing the dead bodies, his mother in a rage threw the brand upon the fire again, and, as it was consumed, Meleager perished.

Mr. Swinburne, *Atalanta in Calydon*:

CHORUS.

"When thou dravest the men
Of the chosen of Thrace,
None turned him again
Nor endured he thy face
Clothed round with the blush of the battle, with light from a terrible place.

ŒNEUS.

"Thou shouldst die as he dies
For whom none sheddeth tears;
Filling thine eyes
And fulfilling thine ears
With the brilliance of battle, the bloom and the beauty, the splendour of spears.

CHORUS.

"In the ears of the world
It is sung, it is told,
And the light thereof hurled
And the noise thereof rolled
From the Acroceraunian snow to the ford of the fleece of gold.

MELEAGER.

"Would God ye could carry me
Forth of all these;
Heap sand and bury me
By the Chersonese
Where the thundering Bosphorus answers the thunder of Pontic seas.

ŒNEUS.

"Dost thou mock at our praise
And the singing begun
And the men of strange days
Praising my son
In the folds of the hills of home, high places of Calydon?

MELEAGER.

"For the dead man no home is;
  Ah, better to be
What the flower of the foam is
  In fields of the sea,
That the sea-waves might be as my raiment, the gulf-stream a garment for me.

. . . . .

"Mother, I dying with unforgetful tongue
Hail thee as holy and worship thee as just
Who art unjust and unholy; and with my knees
Would worship, but thy fire and subtlety,
Dissundering them, devour me; for these limbs
Are as light dust and crumblings from mine urn
Before the fire has touched them; and my face
As a dead leaf or dead foot's mark on snow,
And all this body a broken barren tree
That was so strong, and all this flower of life
Disbranched and desecrated miserably,
And minished all that god-like muscle and might
And lesser than a man's: for all my veins
Fail me, and all mine ashen life burns down."

37. The dissertation which Dante here puts into the mouth of Statius may be found also in a briefer prose form in the *Convito,* IV. 21. It so much excites the enthusiasm of Varchi, that he declares it alone sufficient to prove Dante to have been a physician, philosopher, and theologian of the highest order; and goes on to say: "I not only confess, but I swear, that as many times as I have read it, which day and night are more than a thousand, my wonder and astonishment have always increased, seeming every time to find therein new beauties and new instruction, and consequently new difficulties."

This subject is also discussed in part by Thomas Aquinas, *Sum. Theol.,* I. Quæst. cxix., *De propagatione hominis quantum ad corpus.*

Milton, in his Latin poem, *De Idea Platonica,* has touched upon a theme somewhat akin to this, but in a manner to make it seem very remote. Perhaps no two passages could better show the difference between Dante and Milton, than this canto and *Plato's Archetypal Man,* which in Leigh Hunt's translation runs as follows:—

"Say, guardian goddesses of woods,
  Aspects, felt in solitudes;
And Memory, at whose blessed knee
  The Nine, which thy dear daughters be,
  Learnt of the majestic past;
And thou, that in some antre vast

Leaning afar off dost lie,
Otiose Eternity,
Keeping the tablets and decrees
Of Jove, and the ephemerides
Of the gods, and calendars,
Of the ever festal stars;
Say, who was he, the sunless shade,
After whose pattern man was made;
He first, the full of ages, born
With the old pale polar morn,
Sole, yet all; first visible thought,
After which the Deity wrought?
Twin-birth with Pallas, not remain
Doth he in Jove's o'ershadowed brain;
But though of wide communion,
Dwells apart, like one alone;
And fills the wondering embrace,
(Doubt it not) of size and place.
Whether, companion of the stars,
With their tenfold round he errs;
Or inhabits with his lone
Nature in the neighbouring moon;
Or sits with body-waiting souls,
Dozing by the Lethæan pools:—
Or whether, haply, placed afar
In some blank region of our star,
He stalks, an unsubstantial heap,
Humanity's giant archetype;
Where a loftier bulk he rears
Than Atlas, grappler of the stars,
And through their shadow-touched abodes
Brings a terror to the gods.
Not the seer of him had sight,
Who found in darkness depths of light;*
His travelled eyeballs saw him not
In all his mighty gulfs of thought:—
Him the farthest-footed good,
Pleiad Mercury, never showed
To any poet's wisest sight
In the silence of the night:—
News of him the Assyrian priest†
Found not in his sacred list,

---

* Tiresias, who was blind.
† Sanchoniathon.

Though he traced back old king Nine,
And Belus, elder name divine,
And Osiris, endless famed.
Not the glory, triple-named,
Thrice great Hermes, though his eyes
Read the shapes of all the skies,
Left him in his sacred verse
Revealed to Nature's worshippers.
 "O Plato! and was this a dream
Of thine in bowery Academe?
Wert thou the golden tongue to tell
First of this high miracle,
And charm him to thy schools below?
O call thy poets back, if so,*
Back to the state thine exiles call,
Thou greatest fabler of them all;
Or follow through the self-same gate,
Thou, the founder of the state."

48. The heart, where the blood takes the "virtue informative," as stated in line 40.

52. The vegetative soul, which in man differs from that in plants, as being in a state of development, while that of plants is complete already.

55. The vegetative becomes a sensitive soul.

65. "This was the opinion of Averroes," says the *Ottimo,* "which is false, and contrary to the Catholic faith."

In the language of the Schools, the Possible Intellect, *intellectus possibilis,* is the faculty which receives impressions through the senses, and forms from them pictures or *phantasmata* in the mind. The Active Intellect, *intellectus agens,* draws from these pictures various ideas, notions, and conclusions. They represent the Understanding and the Reason.

70. God.

75. Redi, *Bacchus in Tuscany:*—

"Such bright blood is a ray enkindled
 Of that sun, in heaven that shines,
 And has been left behind entangled
 And caught in the net of the many vines."

79. When Lachesis has spun out the thread of life.

81. Thomas Aquinas, *Sum. Theol.,* I. Quæst. cxviii. Art. 3: "*Anima intellectiva remanet destructo corpore.*"

86. Either upon the shores of Acheron or of the Tiber.

* Whom Plato banished from his imaginary republic.

103. *Æneid*, VI. 723, Davidson's Tr.:—

"In the first place, the spirit within nourishes the heavens, the earth, and watery plains, the moon's enlightened orb, and the Titanian stars; and the mind, diffused through all the members, actuates the whole frame, and mingles with the vast body of the universe. Thence the race of men and beasts, the vital principles of the flying kind, and the monsters which the ocean breeds under its smooth plain. These principles have the active force of fire, and are of a heavenly original, so far as they are not clogged by noxious bodies, blunted by earth-born limbs and dying members. Hence they fear and desire, grieve and rejoice; and, shut up in darkness and a gloomy prison, lose sight of their native skies. Even when with the last beams of light their life is gone, yet not every ill, nor all corporeal stains, are quite removed from the unhappy beings; and it is absolutely necessary that many imperfections which have long been joined to the soul should be in marvellous ways increased and riveted therein. Therefore are they afflicted with punishments, and pay the penalties of their former ills. Some, hung on high, are spread out to the empty winds; in others, the guilt not done away is washed out in a vast watery abyss, or burned away in fire. We each endure his own manes, thence are we conveyed along the spacious Elysium, and we, the happy few, possess the fields of bliss; till length of time, after the fixed period is elapsed, hath done away the inherent stain, and hath left the pure celestial reason, and the fiery energy of the simple spirit."

121. "God of clemency supreme;" the church hymn, sung at matins on Saturday morning, and containing a prayer for purity.

128. Luke i. 34: "Then said Mary unto the angel, How shall this be, seeing I know not a man?"

131. Helice, or Callisto, was a daughter of Lycaon king of Arcadia. She was one of the attendant nymphs of Diana, who discarded her on account of an amour with Jupiter, for which Juno turned her into a bear. Arcas was the offspring of this amour. Jupiter changed them to the constellations of the Great and Little Bear.

Ovid, *Met*. II., Addison's Tr.:—

"But now her son had fifteen summers told,
Fierce at the chase, and in the forest bold;
When, as he beat the woods in quest of prey,
He chanced to rouse his mother where she lay.
She knew her son, and kept him in her sight,
And fondly gazed: the boy was in a fright,
And aimed a pointed arrow at her breast,
And would have slain his mother in the breast;
But Jove forbad, and snatched them through the air
In whirlwinds up to heaven, and fixed them there;
Where the new constellations nightly rise,
And add a lustre to the Northern skies.

"When Juno saw the rival in her height,
Spangled with stars, and circled round with light,
She sought old Ocean in his deep abodes,
And Tethys, both revered among the gods.
They ask what brings her there: 'Ne'er ask,' says she,
'What brings me here; heaven is no place for me.
You'll see, when Night has covered all things o'er,
Jove's starry bastard and triumphant whore
Usurp the heavens; you'll see them proudly roll
In their new orbs, and brighten all the pole.'"

Canto XXVI

1. The punishment of the sin of Lust.

5. It is near sunset, and the western sky is white, as the sky always is in the neighbourhood of the sun.

12. A ghostly or spiritual body.

41. Pasiphae, wife of Minos, king of Crete, and mother of the Minotaur. Virgil, *Eclogue* VI. 45, Davidson's Tr.:—

"And he soothes Pasiphae in her passion for the snow-white bull: happy woman if herds had never been! Ah, ill-fated maid, what madness seized thee? The daughters of Prœtus with imaginary lowings filled the fields; yet none of them pursued such vile embraces of a beast, however they might dread the plough about their necks, and often feel for horns on their smooth foreheads. Ah, ill-fated maid, thou now art roaming on the mountains! He, resting his snowy side on the soft hyacinth, ruminates the blanched herbs under some gloomy oak, or courts some female in the numerous herd."

43. The Riphæan mountains are in the north of Russia. The sands are the sands of the deserts.

59. Beatrice.

62. The highest heaven. *Par.* XXVII.

78. In one of Cæsar's triumphs the Roman soldiery around his chariot called him "Queen;" thus reviling him for his youthful debaucheries with Nicomedes, king of Bithynia.

87. The cow made by Dædalus.

92. Guido Guinicelli, the best of the Italian poets before Dante, flourished in the first half of the thirteenth century. He was a native of Bologna, but of his life nothing is known. His most celebrated poem is a Canzone on the Nature of Love, which goes far to justify the warmth and tenderness of Dante's praise. Rossetti, *Early Italian Poets,* p. 24, gives the following version of it, under the title of *The Gentle Heart:*—

"Within the gentle heart Love shelters him,
     As birds within the green shade of the grove.
Before the gentle heart, in Nature's scheme,

Love was not, nor the gentle heart ere Love.
    For with the sun, at once,
So sprang the light immediately; nor was
    Its birth before the sun's.
And Love hath his effect in gentleness
    Of very self: even as
Within the middle fire the heat's excess.

"The fire of Love comes to the gentle heart
    Like as its virtue to a precious stone;
To which no star its influence can impart
    Till it is made a pure thing by the sun:
    For when the sun hath smit
From out its essence that which there was vile,
    The star endoweth it.
And so the heart created by God's breath
    Pure, true, and clean from guile,
A woman, like a star, enamoureth.

"In gentle heart Love for like reason is
    For which the lamp's high flame is fanned and bowed:
Clear, piercing bright, it shines for its own bliss;
    Nor would it burn there else, it is so proud.
    For evil natures meet
With Love as it were water met with fire,
    As cold abhorring heat.
Through gentle heart Love doth a track divine,—
    Like knowing like; the same
As diamond runs through iron in the mine.

"The sun strikes full upon the mud all day;
    It remains vile, nor the sun's worth is less.
'By race I am gentle,' the proud man doth say:
    He is the mud, the sun is gentleness.
    Let no man predicate
That aught the name of gentleness should have,
    Even in a king's estate,
Except the heart there be a gentle man's.
    The star-beam lights the wave,—
Heaven holds the star and the star's radiance.

"God, in the understanding of high Heaven,
    Burns more than in our sight the living sun:
There to behold His Face unveiled is given;
    And Heaven, whose will is homage paid to One,

Fulfils the things which live
In God, from the beginning excellent.
        So should my lady give
That truth which in her eyes is glorified,
        On which her heart is bent,
To me whose service waiteth at her side.

"My lady, God shall ask, 'What daredst thou?'
        (When my soul stands with all her acts reviewed;)
'Thou passedst Heaven, into My sight, as now,
        To make Me of vain love similitude.
        To Me doth praise belong,
And to the Queen of all the realm of grace
        Who endeth fraud and wrong.'
Then may I plead: 'As though from Thee he came,
        Love wore an angel's face:
Lord, if I loved her, count it not my shame.'"

94. Hypsipyle was discovered and rescued by her sons Eumenius and
Thoas, (whose father was the "bland Jason," as Statius calls him,) just as King
Lycurgus in his great grief was about to put her to death for neglecting the
care of his child, who through her neglect had been stung by a serpent.

Statius, *Thebaid,* V. 949, says it was Tydeus who saved Hypsipyle:—

> "But interposing Tydeus rushed between,
>   And with his shield protects the Lemnian queen."

118. In the old Romance languages the name of *prosa* was applied
generally to all narrative poems, and particularly to the monorhythmic
romances. Thus Gonzalo de Berceo, a Spanish poet of the thirteenth
century, begins a poem on the *Vida del Glorioso Confessor Santo Domingo
de Silos:*—

> "De un confessor Sancto quiero fer una prosa,
>   Quiero fer una prosa en roman paladino,
>   En qual suele el pueblo fablar á su vecino,
>   Ca non so tan letrado per fer otro Latino."

120. Gerault de Berneil of Limoges, born of poor parents, but a man of
talent and learning, was one of the most famous Troubadours of the thirteenth
century. The old Provençal biographer, quoted by Raynouard, *Choix de
Poésies,* V. 166, says: "He was a better poet than any who preceded or fol-
lowed him, and was therefore called the Master of the Troubadours. . . . . .
He passed his winters in study, and his summers in wandering from court to
court with two minstrels who sang his songs."

The following specimen of his poems is from [Taylor's] *Lays of the Minnesingers and Troubadours,* p. 247. It is an *Aubade,* or song of the morning:—

"Companion dear! or sleeping or awaking,
    Sleep not again! for lo! the morn is nigh,
And in the east that early star is breaking,
    The day's forerunner, known unto mine eye;
        The morn, the morn is near.

"Companion dear! with carols sweet I call thee;
    Sleep not again! I hear the birds' blithe song
Loud in the woodlands; evil may befall thee,
    And jealous eyes awaken, tarrying long,
        Now that the morn is near.

"Companion dear! forth from the window looking,
    Attentive mark the signs of yonder heaven;
Judge if aright I read what they betoken:
    Thine all the loss, if vain the warning given;
        The morn, the morn is near.

"Companion dear! since thou from hence wert straying,
    Nor sleep nor rest these eyes have visited;
My prayers unceasing to the Virgin paying,
    That thou in peace thy backward way might tread.
        The morn, the morn is near.

"Companion dear! hence to the fields with me!
    Me thou forbad'st to slumber through the night,
And I have watched that livelong night for thee;
    But thou in song or me hast no delight,
        And now the morn is near.

ANSWER.
"Companion dear! so happily sojourning,
    So blest am I, I care not forth to speed:
Here brightest beauty reigns, her smiles adorning
    Her dwelling-place,—then wherefore should I heed
        The morn or jealous eyes?"

According to Nostrodamus he died in 1278. Notwithstanding his great repute, Dante gives the palm of excellence to Arnaud Daniel, his rival and contemporary. But this is not the general verdict of literary history.

124. Fra Guittone d'Arezzo. See Canto XXIV. Note 56.

137. Venturi has the indiscretion to say: "This is a disgusting compliment after the manner of the French; in the Italian fashion we should say, 'You

will do me a favour, if you will tell me your name.'" Whereupon Biagioli thunders at him in this wise: "Infamous dirty dog that you are, how can you call this a compliment after the manner of the French? How can you set off against it what any cobbler might say? Away! and a murrain on you!"

142. Arnaud Daniel, the Troubadour of the thirteenth century, whom Dante lauds so highly, and whom Petrarca calls "the Grand Master of Love," was born of a noble family at the castle of Ribeyrac in Périgord. Millot, *Hist. des Troub.*, II. 479, says of him: "In all ages there have been false reputations, founded on some individual judgment, whose authority has prevailed without examination, until at last criticism discusses, the truth penetrates, and the phantom of prejudice vanishes. Such has been the reputation of Arnaud Daniel."

Raynouard confirms this judgment, and says that, "in reading the works of this Troubadour, it is difficult to conceive the cause of the great celebrity he enjoyed during his life."

Arnaud Daniel was the inventor of the *Sestina,* a song of six stanzas of six lines each, with the same rhymes repeated in all, though arranged in different and intricate order, which must be seen to be understood. He was also author of the metrical romance of *Lancillotto,* or Launcelot of the Lake, to which Dante doubtless refers in his expression *prose di romanzi,* or proses of romance. The following anecdote is from the old Provençal authority, quoted both by Millot and Raynouard, and is thus translated by Miss Costello, *Early Poetry of France,* p. 37:—

"Arnaud visited the court of Richard Cœur de Lion in England, and encountered there a jongleur, who defied him to a trial of skill, and boasted of being able to make more difficult rhymes than Arnaud, a proficiency on which he chiefly prided himself. He accepted the challenge, and the two poets separated, and retired to their respective chambers to prepare for the contest. The Muse of Arnaud was not propitious, and he vainly endeavoured to string two rhymes together. His rival, on the other hand, quickly caught the inspiration. The king had allowed ten days as the term of preparation, five for composition, and the remainder for learning it by heart to sing before the court. On the third day the jongleur declared that he had finished his poem, and was ready to recite it, but Arnaud replied that he had not yet thought of his. It was the jongleur's custom to repeat his verses out loud every day, in order to learn them better, and Arnaud, who was in vain endeavouring to devise some means to save himself from the mockery of the court at being outdone in this contest, happened to overhear the jongleur singing. He went to his door and listened, and succeeded in retaining the words and the air. On the day appointed they both appeared before the king. Arnaud desired to be allowed to sing first, and immediately gave the song which the jongleur had composed. The latter, stupified with astonishment, could only exclaim: 'It is my song, it is my song.' 'Impossible!' cried the king; but the jongleur, persisting, requested Richard to interrogate Arnaud, who would not dare, he said, to deny it. Daniel confessed the fact, and related the manner in which the affair had been conducted, which amused Richard far more than the song itself. The stakes of the wager were restored to each, and the king loaded them both with presents."

According to Nostrodamus, Arnaud died about 1189. There is no other reason for making him speak in Provençal than the evident delight which Dante took in the sound of the words, and the peculiar flavour they give to the close of the canto. Raynouard says that the writings of none of the Troubadours have been so disfigured by copyists as those of Arnaud. This would seem to be true of the very lines which Dante writes for him; as there are at least seven different readings of them.

Here Venturi has again the indiscretion to say that Arnaud answers Dante in "a kind of *lingua-franca,* part Provençal and part Catalan, joining together the perfidious French with the vile Spanish, perhaps to show that Arnaud was a clever speaker of the two." And again Biagioli suppresses him with "that unbridled beast of a Venturi," and this "most potent argument of his presumptuous ignorance and impertinence."

Canto XXVII

1. The description of the Seventh and last Circle continued.
Cowley, *Hymn to Light:*—

> "Say from what golden quivers of the sky
>   Do all thy winged arrows fly?"

2. When the sun is rising at Jerusalem, it is setting on the Mountain of Purgatory; it is midnight in Spain, with Libra in the meridian, and noon in India.

"A great labyrinth of words and things," says Venturi, "meaning only that the sun was setting!" and this time the "*dolce pedagogo*" Biagioli lets him escape without the usual reprimand.

8. *Matthew* v. 8: "Blessed are the pure in heart, for they shall see God."

16. With the hands clasped and turned palm downwards, and the body straightened backward in attitude of resistance.

23. *Inf.* XVII.

33. Knowing that he ought to confide in Virgil and go forward.

37. The story of the Babylonian lovers, whose trysting-place was under the white mulberry-tree near the tomb of Ninus, and whose blood changed the fruit from white to purple, is too well known to need comment. Ovid, *Met.* IV., Eusden's Tr.:—

> "At Thisbe's name awaked, he opened wide
>   His dying eyes; with dying eyes he tried
>   On her to dwell, but closed them slow and died."

48. Statius had for a long while been between Virgil and Dante.

58. *Matthew* xxv. 34: "Then shall the king say unto them on his right hand, Come, ye blessed of my Father, inherit the kingdom prepared for you from the foundation of the world."

70. Dr. Furness's *Hymn*:—

> "Slowly by God's hand unfurled,
> Down around the weary world
> Falls the darkness."

90. Evening of the Third Day of Purgatory. Milton, *Parad. Lost,* IV. 598:—

> "Now came still Evening on, and Twilight gray
> Had in her sober livery all things clad:
> Silence accompanied; for beast and bird,
> They to their grassy couch, these to their nests
> Were slunk, all but the wakeful nightingale;
> She all night long her amorous descant sung;
> Silence was pleased: now glowed the firmament
> With living sapphires: Hesperus, that led
> The starry host, rode brightest, till the moon,
> Rising in clouded majesty, at length,
> Apparent queen, unveiled her peerless light,
> And o'er the dark her silver mantle threw."

93. The vision which Dante sees is a foreshadowing of Matilda and Beatrice in the Terrestrial Paradise. In the Old Testament Leah is a symbol of the Active Life, and Rachel of the Contemplative; as Martha and Mary are in the New Testament, and Matilda and Beatrice in the Divine Comedy. "Happy is that house," says Saint Bernard, "and blessed is that congregation, where Martha still complaineth of Mary."

Dante says in the *Convito,* IV. 17: "Truly it should be known that we can have in this life two felicities, by following two different and excellent roads, which lead thereto; namely, the Active life and the Contemplative."

And Owen Feltham in his *Resolves*:—

"The mind can walk beyond the sight of the eye, and, though in a cloud, can lift us into heaven while we live. Meditation is the soul's perspective glass, whereby, in her long remove, she discerneth God as if he were nearer hand. I persuade no man to make it his whole life's business. We have bodies as well as souls. And even this world, while we are in it, ought somewhat to be cared for. As those states are likely to flourish, where execution follows sound advisements, so is man, when contemplation is seconded by action. Contemplation generates; action propagates. Without the first, the latter is defective. Without the last, the first is but abortive and embryous. Saint

Bernard compares contemplation to Rachel, which was the more fair; but action to Leah, which was the more fruitful. I will neither always be busy and doing, nor ever shut up in nothing but thoughts. Yet that which some would call idleness, I will call the sweetest part of my life, and that is, my thinking."

95. Venus, the morning star, rising with the constellation Pisces, two hours before the sun.

100. Ruskin, *Mod. Painters,* III. 221: "This vision of Rachel and Leah has been always, and with unquestionable truth, received as a type of the Active and Contemplative life, and as an introduction to the two divisions of the Paradise which Dante is about to enter. Therefore the unwearied spirit of the Countess Matilda is understood to represent the Active life, which forms the felicity of Earth; and the spirit of Beatrice the Contemplative life, which forms the felicity of Heaven. This interpretation appears at first straightforward and certain; but it has missed count of exactly the most important fact in the two passages which we have to explain. Observe: Leah gathers the flowers to decorate *herself,* and delights in *her own* Labour. Rachel sits silent, contemplating herself, and delights in *her own* Image. These are the types of the Unglorified Active and Contemplative powers of Man. But Beatrice and Matilda are the same powers, glorified. And how are they glorified? Leah took delight in her own labour; but Matilda, *in operibus manuum Tuarum,*—in *God's labour*; Rachel, in the sight of her own face; Beatrice, in the sight of *God's face.*"

112. The morning of the Fourth Day of Purgatory.

115. Happiness.

Canto XXVIII

1. The Terrestrial Paradise. Compare Milton, *Parad. Lost,* IV. 214:—

> "In this pleasant soil
> His far more pleasant garden God ordained:
> Out of the fertile ground he caused to grow
> All trees of noblest kind for sight, smell, taste;
> And all amid them stood the Tree of Life,
> High eminent, blooming ambrosial fruit
> Of vegetable gold; and next to Life,
> Our death, the Tree of Knowledge, grew fast by,
> Knowledge of good bought dear by knowing ill.
> Southward through Eden went a river large,
> Nor changed his course, but through the shaggy hill
> Passed underneath ingulfed; for God had thrown
> That mountain as his garden mould, high raised
> Upon the rapid current, which through veins
> Of porous earth with kindly thirst up drawn,

Rose a fresh fountain, and with many a rill
Watered the garden; thence united fell
Down the steep glade, and met the nether flood,
Which from his darksome passage now appears;
And now, divided into four main streams,
Runs diverse, wandering many a famous realm
And country, whereof here needs no account;
But rather to tell how, if art could tell,
How from that sapphire fount the crisped brooks,
Rolling on orient pearl and sands of gold,
With mazy error under pendent shades
Ran nectar, visiting each plant, and fed
Flowers worthy of Paradise; which not nice art
In beds and curious knots, but nature boon
Poured forth profuse on hill, and dale, and plain;
Both where the morning sun first warmly smote
The open field, and where the unpierced shade
Imbrowned the noontide bowers. Thus was this place
A happy rural seat of various view:
Groves whose rich trees wept odorous gums and balm;
Others, whose fruit, burnished with golden rind,
Hung amiable, Hesperian fables true,
If true, here only, and of delicious taste.
Betwixt them lawns, or level downs, and flocks
Grazing the tender herb, were interposed;
Or palmy hillock, or the flowery lap
Of some irriguous valley spread her store;
Flowers of all hue, and without thorn the rose.
Another side, umbrageous grots and caves
Of cool recess, o'er which the mantling vine
Lays forth her purple grape, and gently creeps
Luxuriant: meanwhile murmuring waters fall
Down the slope hills, dispersed, or in a lake,
That to the fringed bank with myrtle crowned
Her crystal mirror holds, unite their streams.
The birds their quire apply; airs, vernal airs,
Breathing the smell of field and grove, attune
The trembling leaves; while universal Pan,
Knit with the Graces and the Hours in dance,
Led on the eternal spring."

2. Ruskin, *Mod. Painters*, III. 219: "As Homer gave us an ideal landscape, which even a god might have been pleased to behold, so Dante gives us, fortunately, an ideal landscape, which is specially intended for the terrestrial paradise. And it will doubtless be with some surprise, after our reflections

above on the general tone of Dante's feelings, that we find ourselves here first entering a *forest,* and that even a *thick* forest. . . . .

"This forest, then, is very like that of Colonos in several respects,—in its peace and sweetness, and number of birds; it differs from it only in letting a light breeze through it, being therefore somewhat thinner than the Greek wood; the tender lines which tell of the voices of the birds mingling with the wind, and of the leaves all turning one way before it, have been more or less copied by every poet since Dante's time. They are, so far as I know, the sweetest passage of wood description which exists in literature."

Homer's ideal landscape, here referred to, is in *Odyssey* V., where he describes the visit of Mercury to the Island of Calypso. It is thus translated by Buckley:—

"Immediately then he bound his beautiful sandals beneath his feet, ambrosial, golden; which carried him both over the moist wave, and over the boundless earth, with the breath of the wind. . . . . Then he rushed over the wave like a bird, a sea-gull, which, hunting for fish in the terrible bays of the barren sea, dips frequently its wings in the brine; like unto this Mercury rode over many waves. But when he came to the distant island, then, going from the blue sea, he went to the continent; until he came to the great cave in which the fair-haired Nymph dwelt; and he found her within. A large fire was burning on the hearth, and at a distance the smell of well-cleft cedar, and of frankincense, that were burning, shed odour through the island: but she within was singing with a beautiful voice, and, going over the web, wove with a golden shuttle. But a flourishing wood sprung up around her grot, alder and poplar, and sweet-smelling cypress. There also birds with spreading wings slept, owls and hawks, and wide-tongued crows of the ocean, to which maritime employments are a care. There a vine in its prime was spread about the hollow grot, and it flourished with clusters. But four fountains flowed in succession with white water, turned near one another, each in different ways; but around there flourished soft meadows of violets and of parsley. There indeed even an immortal coming would admire it when he beheld, and would be delighted in his mind; there the messenger, the slayer of Argus, standing, admired."

And again, at the close of the same book, where Ulysses reaches the shore at Phæacia:—

"Then he hastened to the wood; and found it near the water in a conspicuous place, and he came under two shrubs, which sprang from the same place; one of wild olive, the other of olive. Neither the strength of the moistly blowing winds breathes through them, nor has the shining sun ever struck them with its beams, nor has the shower penetrated entirely through them: so thick were they grown entangled with one another; under which Ulysses came."

The wood of Colonos is thus described in one of the Choruses of the *Œdipus Coloneus* of Sophocles, Oxford Tr., Anon.:—

"Thou hast come, O stranger, to the seats of this land, renowned for the steed; to seats the fairest on earth, the chalky Colonus; where the vocal knightingale, chief abounding, trills her plaintive note in the green vales, tenanting the dark-hued ivy and the leafy grove of the god, untrodden [by mortal foot], teeming with fruits, impervious to the sun, and unshaken by the winds of every storm; where Bacchus ever roams in revelry companioning his divine nurses. And ever day by day the narcissus, with its beauteous clusters, burst into bloom by heaven's dew, the ancient coronet of the mighty goddesses, and the saffron with golden ray; nor do the sleepless founts that feed the channels of Cephissus fail, but ever, each day, it rushes o'er the plains with its stainless wave, fertilizing the bosom of the earth; nor have the choirs of the Muses spurned this clime; nor Venus, too, of the golden rein. And there is a tree, such as I hear not to have ever sprung in the land of Asia, nor in the mighty Doric island of Pelops, a tree unplanted by hand, of spontaneous growth, terror of the hostile spear, which flourishes chiefly in this region, the leaf of the azure olive that nourishes our young. This shall neither any one in youth nor in old age, marking for destruction, and having laid it waste with his hand, set its divinity at naught; for the eye that never closes of Morian Jove regards it, and the blue-eyed Minerva."

We have also Homer's description of the Garden of Alcinoüs, *Odyssey,* VII., Buckley's Tr.:—

"But without the hall there is a large garden, near the gates, of four acres; but around it a hedge was extended on both sides. And there tall, flourishing trees grew, pears, and pomegranates, and apple-trees producing beautiful fruit, and sweet figs, and flourishing olives. Of these the fruit never perishes, nor does it fail in winter or summer, lasting throughout the whole year; but the west wind ever blowing makes some bud forth, and ripens others. Pear grows old after pear, apple after apple, grape also after grape, and fig after fig. There a fruitful vineyard was planted: one part of this ground, exposed to the sun in a wide place, is dried by the sun; and some [grapes] they are gathering, and others they are treading, and further on are unripe grapes, having thrown off the flower, and others are slightly changing colour. And there are all kinds of beds laid out in order, to the furthest part of the ground, flourishing throughout the whole year: and in it are two fountains, one is spread through the whole garden, but the other on the other side goes under the threshold of the hall to the lofty house, from whence the citizens are wont to draw water."

Dante's description of the Terrestrial Paradise will hardly fail to recall that of Mount Acidale in Spenser's *Faerie Queene,* VI. x. 6:—

> "It was an Hill plaste in an open plaine,
> That round about was bordered with a wood
> Of matchlesse hight, that seemed th' earth to disdaine;
> In which all trees of honour stately stood,
> And did all winter as in sommer bud,
> Spredding pavilions for the birds to bowre,
> Which in their lower braunches sung aloud;
> And in their tops the soring hauke did towre,
> Sitting like king of fowles in maiesty and powre.

> "And at the foote thereof a gentle flud
>   His silver waves did softly tumble downe,
>   Unmard with ragged mosse or filthy mud;
>   Ne mote wylde beastes, ne mote the ruder clowne,
>   Thereto approch; ne filth mote therein drowne:
>   But Nymphes and Faeries by the bancks did sit
>   In the woods shade which did the waters crowne,
>   Keeping all noysome things away from it,
> And to the waters fall tuning their accents fit.

> "And on the top thereof a spacious plaine
>   Did spred itselfe, to serve to all delight,
>   Either to daunce, when they to daunce would faine,
>   Or else to course-about their bases light;
>   Ne ought there wanted, which for pleasure might
>   Desired be, or thence to banish bale:
>   So pleasauntly the Hill with equall hight
>   Did seeme to overlooke the lowly vale;
> Therefore it rightly cleeped was Mount Acidale."

See also Tasso's Garden of Armida, in the *Gerusalemme,* XVI.

20. Chiassi is on the sea-shore near Ravenna. "Here grows a spacious pine forest," says Covino, *Descr. Geog.,* p. 39, "which stretches along the sea between Ravenna and Cervia."

25. The river Lethe.

40. This lady, who represents the Active life to Dante's waking eyes, as Leah had done in his vision, and whom Dante afterwards, Canto XXXIII. 119, calls Matilda, is generally supposed by the commentators to be the celebrated Countess Matilda, daughter of Boniface, Count of Tuscany, and wife of Guelf, of the house of Suabia. Of this marriage Villani, IV. 21, gives a very strange account, which, if true, is a singular picture of the times. Napier, *Flor. Hist.,* I. Ch. 4 and 6, gives these glimpses of the Countess:—

"This heroine died in 1115, after a reign of active exertion for herself and the Church against the Emperors, which generated the infant and as yet nameless factions of Guelf and Ghibelline. Matilda endured this contest with all the enthusiasm and constancy of a woman, combined with a manly courage that must ever render her name respectable, whether proceeding from the bigotry of the age, or to oppose imperial ambition in defence of her own defective title. According to the laws of that time, she could not as a female inherit her father's states, for even male heirs required a royal confirmation. Matilda therefore, having no legal right, feared the Emperor and clung to the Popes, who already claimed, among other prerogatives, the supreme disposal of kingdoms. . . . .

"The Church had ever come forward as the friend of her house, and from childhood she had breathed an atmosphere of blind and devoted submission to its authority; even when only fifteen she had appeared in arms against its enemies, and made two successful expeditions to assist Pope Alexander the Second during her mother's lifetime.

"No wonder, then, that in a superstitious age, when monarchs trembled at an angry voice from the Lateran, the habits of early youth should have mingled with every action of Matilda's life, and spread an agreeable *mirage* over the prospect of her eternal salvation: the power that tamed a Henry's pride, a Barbarossa's fierceness, and afterwards withstood the vast ability of a Frederic, might without shame have been reverenced by a girl whose feelings so harmonized with the sacred strains of ancient tradition and priestly dignity. But from whatever motive, the result was a continual aggrandizement of ecclesiastics; in prosperity and adversity; during life and after death; from the lowliest priest to the proudest pontiff.

"The fearless assertion of her own independence by successful struggles with the Emperor was an example not overlooked by the young Italian communities under Matilda's rule, who were already accused by imperial legitimacy of political innovation and visionary notions of government. . . . .

"Being then at a place called Monte Baroncione, and in her sixty-ninth year, this celebrated woman breathed her last, after a long and glorious reign of incessant activity, during which she displayed a wisdom, vigour, and determination of character rarely seen even in men. She bequeathed to the Church all those patrimonial estates of which she had previously disposed by an act of gift to Gregory the Seventh, without, however, any immediate royal power over the cities and other possessions thus given, as her will expresses it, 'for the good of her soul, and the souls of her parents.'

"Whatever may now be thought of her chivalrous support, her bold defence, and her deep devotion to the Church, it was in perfect harmony with the spirit of that age, and has formed one of her chief merits with many even in the present. Her unflinching adherence to the cause she had so conscientiously embraced was far more noble than the Emperor Henry's conduct. Swinging between the extremes of unmeasured insolence and abject humiliation, he died a victim to Papal influence over superstitious minds; an influence which, amongst other debasing lessons, then taught the world that a breach of the most sacred ties and dearest affections of human nature was one means of gaining the approbation of a Being who is all truth and beneficence.

"Matilda's object was to strengthen the chief spiritual against the chief temporal power, but reserving her own independence; a policy subsequently pursued, at least in spirit, by the Guelphic states of Italy. She therefore protected subordinate members of the Church against feudal chieftains, and its head against the feudal Emperor. True to her religious and warlike character, she died between the sword and the crucifix, and two of her last acts, even when the hand of death was already cold on her brow, were the chastisement of revolted Mantua, and the midnight celebration of Christ's nativity in the depth of a freezing and unusually inclement winter."

50. Ovid, *Met.* V., Maynwaring's Tr.:—

"Here, while young Proserpine, among the maids,
Diverts herself in these delicious shades;
While like a child with busy speed and care
She gathers lilies here, and violets there;
While first to fill her little lap she strives,
Hell's grizzly monarch at the shade arrives;
Sees her thus sporting on the flowery green,
And loves the blooming maid, as soon as seen.
His urgent flame impatient of delay,
Swift as his thought he seized the beauteous prey,
And bore her in his sooty car away.
The frighted goddess to her mother cries,
But all in vain, for now far off she flies.
Far she behind her leaves her virgin train;
To them too cries, and cries to them in vain.
And while with passion she repeats her call,
The violets from her lap, and lilies fall:
She misses them, poor heart! and makes new moan;
Her lilies, ah! are lost, her violets gone."

65. Ovid, *Met.* X., Eusden's Tr.:—

"For Cytherëa's lips while Cupid prest,
He with a heedless arrow razed her breast.
The goddess felt it, and, with fury stung,
The wanton mischief from her bosom flung:
Yet thought at first the danger slight, but found
The dart too faithful, and too deep the wound.
Fired with a mortal beauty, she disdains
To haunt th' Idalian mount, or Phrygian plains.
She seeks not Cnidos, nor her Paphian shrines,
Nor Amathus, that teems with brazen mines:
Even Heaven itself with all its sweets unsought,
Adonis far a sweeter Heaven is thought."

72. When Xerxes invaded Greece he crossed the Hellespont on a bridge of boats with an army of five million. So say the historians. On his return he crossed it in a fishing-boat almost alone,—"a warning to all human arrogance."

Leander naturally hated the Hellespont, having to swim it so many times. The last time, according to Thomas Hood, he met with a sea nymph, who, enamoured of his beauty, carried him to the bottom of the sea. See *Hero and Leander,* stanza 45:—

"His eyes are blinded with the sleety brine,
His ears are deafened with the wildering noise;

He asks the purpose of her fell design,
But foamy waves choke up his struggling voice,
Under the ponderous sea his body dips,
And Hero's name dies bubbling on his lips.

"Look how a man is lowered to his grave,
A yearning hollow in the green earth's lap;
So he is sunk into the yawning wave,
The plunging sea fills up the watery gap;
Anon he is all gone, and nothing seen,
But likeness of green turf and hillocks green.

"And where he swam, the constant sun lies sleeping,
Over the verdant plain that makes his bed;
And all the noisy waves go freshly leaping,
Like gamesome boys over the churchyard dead;
The light in vain keeps looking for his face,
Now screaming sea-fowl settle in his place."

80. *Psalm* xcii. 4: "For thou, Lord, hast made me glad through thy work: I will triumph in the works of thy hands."
87. Canto XXI. 46:—

"Because that neither rain, nor hail, nor snow,
Nor dew, nor hoar-frost any higher falls
Than the short, little stairway of three steps."

94. Only six hours, according to Adam's own account in *Par.,* XXI. 139:—

"Upon the mount which highest o'er the wave
Rises was I, with life or pure or sinful,
From the first hour to that which is the second,
As the sun changes quadrant, to the sixth."

102. Above the gate described in Canto IX.
146. Virgil and Statius smile at this allusion to the dreams of poets.

Canto XXIX

1. The Terrestrial Paradise and the Apocalyptic Procession of the Church Triumphant.
3. *Psalm* xxxii. 1: "Blessed is he whose transgression is forgiven, whose sin is covered."

10. Counted together, their steps were not a hundred in all.

41. The Muse of Astronomy, or things celestial, represented as crowned with stars and robed in azure. Milton, *Parad. Lost,* VII. 1, makes the same invocation:—

> "Descend from heaven, Urania, by that name
> If rightly thou art called, whose voice divine
> Following, above the Olympian hill I soar,
> Above the flight of Pegasean wing.
> The meaning, not the name, I call: for thou
> Nor of the Muses nine, nor on the top
> Of old Olympus dwell'st; but, heavenly-born,
> Before the hills appeared, or fountain flowed,
> Thou with Eternal Wisdom didst converse,
> Wisdom thy sister, and with her didst play
> In presence of the Almighty Father, pleased
> With thy celestial song."

47. The general form which objects may have in common, and by which they resemble each other.

49. The faculty which lends discourse to reason is apprehension, or the faculty by which things are first conceived. See Canto XVIII. 22:—

> "Your apprehension from some real thing
>   An image draws, and in yourselves displays it,
>   So that it makes the soul turn unto it."

50. *Revelation* i. 12, 20: "And I turned to see the voice that spake with me. And, being turned, I saw seven golden candlesticks. . . . . And the seven candlesticks. . . . . are the seven churches."

Some commentators interpret them as the seven Sacraments of the Church; others, as the seven gifts of the Holy Ghost.

78. Delia or Diana, the moon; and her girdle, the halo, sometimes seen around it.

83. *Revelation* iv. 4: "And round about the throne were four and twenty seats: and upon the seats I saw four and twenty elders sitting, clothed in white raiment; and they had on their heads crowns of gold."

These four and twenty elders are supposed to symbolize here the four and twenty books of the Old Testament. The crown of lilies indicates the purity of faith and doctrine.

85. The salutation of the angel to the Virgin Mary. *Luke* i. 28: "Blessed art thou among women." Here the words are made to refer to Beatrice.

92. The four Evangelists, of whom the four mysterious animals in Ezekiel are regarded as symbols. Mrs. Jameson, *Sacred and Legendary Art,* I. 99:—

"The general application of the Four Creatures to the Four Evangelists is of much earlier date than the separate and individual application of each symbol, which has varied at different times; that propounded by St. Jerome, in his commentary on Ezekiel, has since his time prevailed universally. Thus, then,—1. To St. Matthew was given the CHERUB, or human semblance, because he begins his Gospel with the human generation of Christ; or, according to others, because in his Gospel the human nature of the Saviour is more insisted on than the divine. In the most ancient mosaics, the type is human, not angelic, for the head is that of a man with a beard. 2. St. Mark has the LION, because he has set forth the royal dignity of Christ; or, according to others, because he begins with the mission of the Baptist,—'*the voice of one crying in the wilderness*,'—which is figured by the lion: or, according to a third interpretation, the lion was allotted to St. Mark because there was, in the Middle Ages, a popular belief that the young of the lion was born dead, and after three days was awakened to vitality by the breath of its sire; some authors, however, represent the lion as vivifying his young, not by his breath, but by his roar. In either case the application is the same; the revival of the young lion was considered as symbolical of the resurrection, and Mark was commonly called the 'historian of the resurrection.' Another commentator observes that Mark begins his Gospel with 'roaring,'—'the voice of one crying in the wilderness;' and ends it fearfully with a curse,— 'He that believeth not shall be damned;' and that, therefore, his appropriate attribute is the most terrible of beasts, the lion. 3. Luke has the Ox, because he has dwelt on the priesthood of Christ, the *ox* being the emblem of sacrifice. 4. John has the EAGLE, which is the symbol of the highest inspiration, because he soared upwards to the contemplation of the divine nature of the Saviour."

100. *Ezekiel* i. 4: "And I looked, and behold, a whirlwind came out of the north, a great cloud, and a fire infolding itself, and a brightness was about it, and out of the midst thereof, as the colour of amber, out of the midst of the fire. Also out of the midst thereof came the likeness of four living creatures. And this was their appearance; they had the likeness of a man. And every one had four faces, and every one had four wings. And their feet were straight feet; and the sole of their feet was like the sole of a calf's foot; and they sparkled like the colour of burnished brass."

105. In *Revelation* iv. 8, they are described as having "each of them six wings;" in Ezekiel, as having only four.

107. The triumphal chariot is the Church. The two wheels are generally interpreted as meaning the Old and New Testaments; but Dante, *Par.* XII. 106, speaks of them as St. Dominic and St. Francis.

108. The Griffin, half lion and half eagle, is explained by all the commentators as a symbol of Christ, in his divine and human nature. Didron, in his *Christian Iconography,* interprets it differently. He says, Millington's Tr., I. 458:—

"The mystical bird of two colours is understood in the manuscript of Herrade to mean the Church; in Dante, the biformed bird is the representative of the Church, the Pope. The Pope, in fact, is both priest and king; he directs the souls and governs the persons of men; he reigns over things in heaven. The Pope, then, is but one single person in two natures, and under two forms; he is both eagle and lion. In his character of Pontiff, or as an eagle, he hovers in the heavens, and ascends even to the throne of God to receive his commands; as the lion or king he walks upon the earth in strength and power."

He adds in a note: "Some commentators of Dante have supposed the griffin to be the emblem of Christ, who, in fact, is one single person with two natures; of Christ, in whom God and man are combined. But in this they are mistaken; there is, in the first place, a manifest impropriety in describing the car as drawn by God as by a beast of burden. It is very doubtful even whether Dante can be altogether freed from the imputation of a want of reverence in harnessing the Pope to the car of the Church."

110. The wings of the Griffin extend upward between the middle list or trail of splendour of the seven candles and the three outer ones on each side.

117. The chariot of the sun, which Phaeton had leave to drive for a day, is thus described by Ovid, *Met.* II., Addison's Tr.:—

> "A golden axle did the work uphold,
>   Gold was the beam, the wheels were orbed with gold.
>   The spokes in rows of silver pleased the sight,
>   The seat with party-coloured gems was bright;
>   Apollo shined amid the glare of light."

120. In smiting Phaeton with a thunderbolt. Ovid, *Met.* II.:—

> "Jove called to witness every power above,
> And even the god whose son the chariot drove,
> That what he acts he is compelled to do,
> Or universal ruin must ensue.
> Straight he ascends the high ethereal throne,
> From whence he used to dart his thunder down,
> From whence his showers and storms he used to pour,
> But now could meet with neither storm nor shower;
> Then, aiming at the youth, with lifted hand,
> Full at his head he hurled the forky brand,
> In dreadful thund'rings. Thus th' almighty sire
> Suppressed the raging of the fires with fire."

See also *Inf.* XVII. Note 107.

121. The three Theological or Evangelical Virtues, Charity, Hope, and Faith. For the symbolism of colours in Art, see Mrs. Jameson, *Sacred and Legendary Art,* quoted Canto VIII. Note 28.

130. The four Cardinal Virtues, Justice, Prudence, Fortitude, and Temperance. They are clothed in purple to mark their nobility. Prudence is represented with three eyes, as looking at the past, the present, and the future.

133. St. Luke and St. Paul.

136. St. Luke is supposed to have been a physician; a belief founded on *Colossians* iv. 14, "Luke, the beloved physician." The animal that nature holds most dear is man.

140. The sword with which St. Paul is armed is a symbol of warfare and martyrdom; "I bring not peace, but a sword." St. Luke's office was to heal; St. Paul's to destroy. Mrs. Jameson, *Sacred and Legendary Art,* I. 188, says:—

"At what period the sword was given to St. Paul as his distinctive attribute is with antiquaries a disputed point; certainly much later than the keys were given to Peter. If we could be sure that the mosaic on the tomb of Otho the Second, and another mosaic already described, had not been altered in successive restorations, these would be evidence that the sword was given to St. Paul as his attribute as early as the sixth century; but there are no monuments which can be absolutely trusted as regards the introduction of the sword before the end of the eleventh century; since the end of the fourteenth century it has been so generally adopted, that in the devotional effigies I can remember no instance in which it is omitted. When St. Paul is leaning on the sword, it expresses his martyrdom; when he holds it aloft, it expresses also his warfare in the cause of Christ: when two swords are given to him, one is the attribute, the other the emblem; but this double allusion does not occur in any of the older representations. In Italy I never met with St. Paul bearing two swords, and the only instance I can call to mind is the bronze statue by Peter Vischer, on the shrine of St. Sebald, at Nuremberg."

142. The four Apostles James, Peter, John, and Jude, writers of the Canonical Epistles. The red flowers, with which their foreheads seem all aflame, are symbols of martyrdom. Massinger, *Virgin Martyr,* V. 1:—

> "What flowers are these?
> In Dioclesian's gardens, the most beauteous
> Compared with these are weeds."

143. St. John, writer of the Apocalypse; here represented as asleep; as if he were "in the spirit on the Lord's day, and heard behind him a great voice as of a trumpet." Or perhaps the allusion may be to the belief of the early Christians that John did not die, but was sleeping till the second coming of Christ. This subject has been represented in mediæval Art as follows. Mrs. Jameson, *Sacred and Legendary Art,* I. 139:—

"St. John, habited in priest's garments, descends the steps of an altar into an open grave, in which he lays himself down, not in death, but in sleep, until the coming of Christ; 'being reserved alive with Enoch and Elijah (who also knew not death), to preach against the Antichrist in the last days.' This fanciful legend is founded on the following text: 'Peter, seeing the disciple whom Jesus loved following, saith unto Jesus, Lord, and what shall this man do? Jesus saith unto him, If I will that he tarry till I come, what is that to thee? Then went this saying abroad among the brethren that that disciple should not die.' (John xxi. 21, 22.)"

154. Of this canto and those that follow, Dr. Barlow, *Study of the Div. Com.*, p. 270, says:—

"Dante's sublime pageant of the Church Militant is one of the most marvellous processions ever marshalled on paper. In the invention, arrangement, grouping, and colouring the poet has shown himself a great master in art, familiar with all the stately requirements of solemn shows, festivals, and triumphs. Whatever he may have gathered from the sacred records, and from classic writers, or seen in early mosaics, or witnessed in the streets of Florence with her joyous population, her May-day dancers, and the military pomp of her magnificent Carroccio, like the ark of the covenant going forth with the host, has here been surpassed in invention and erudition, and a picture produced at once as original as it is impressive, as significant as it is grand. Petrarca was, probably, indebted to it for his 'Trionfi,' so frequently in favour with Italian artists.

"This canto with the four that follow form a poem which, though an essential portion of the Divina Commedia, may be separately considered as the continuation of the poetic vision mentioned in the Vita Nuova, and the fulfilment of the intention there expressed.

"It represents the symbolical passage of the Christian Church, preceded by the Hebrew dispensation, and followed by the disastrous effects of schism, and the corruptions induced by the unholy conduct of political Pontiffs. The soul of this solemn exhibition, the living and glorified principle of the beatitude which Religion pure and holy confers upon those who embrace it, is personified in the 'Donna,' to whom Dante from his earliest youth had been more or less devoted, the Beatrice of the Vita Nuova, 'Loda di Dio vera,' who concentrates in herself the divine wisdom with which the Church is inspired, whom angels delight to honour, and whose advent on earth had been prepared from all eternity by the moral virtues.

"Beatrice is here presented as the principle of divine beatitude, or that which confers it, and bears a resemblance to the figure of the New Jerusalem seen by St. John descending from heaven 'as a bride adorned for her husband' (Rev. xxi. 2); a representation of which, in the manner of Raphael, occurs in one of the tapestries of the Vatican, and, though not arrayed in the colours of the Christian virtues, Faith, Hope, and Charity, white and green and red, as was Beatrice, may yet be regarded as a Roman version of her."

Didron, describing the painting of the Triumph of Christ in the Church of Notre Dame de Brou, *Christian Iconography*, Millington's Tr., I. 315, says:—

"In the centre of all rises the Hero of the Triumph, Jesus Christ, who is seated in an open car with four wheels. He alone is adorned with a nimbus formed of rays, departing from each point of the head, and which illumines everything around. With one glance he embraces the past which precedes, and the future which is to succeed him. His face resembles that drawn by Raphael and the masters of the period of Renaissance, agreeing with the description given by Lentulus and Damascenus; it is serious and gentle. In the centre of the chariot is placed a starry globe traversed by the ecliptic, on which the twelve signs of the zodiac are brilliantly figured. This globe is symbolic of the world, and forms a throne for Christ: the Son of God is seated on its summit. The car is placed upon four wheels, and drawn by the four attributes or symbols of the Evangelists. The angel of St. Matthew, and the eagle of St. John, are of celestial whiteness; the lion of St. Mark, and the ox of St. Luke, are of a reddish yellow, symbolizing the earth on which they dwell. The eagle and angel do, in fact, fly; while the lion and the ox walk. Yet upon the painted window all the four have wings. A rein of silver, passing round the neck of each of the four symbols, is attached to the pole of the chariot. The Church, represented by the four most elevated religious potentates, by the Pope, the Cardinal, the Archbishop, and Bishop, or by the four chief Fathers, St. Gregory, St. Jerome, St. Ambrose, and St. Augustine, drives the four-wheeled car, and, in conjunction with the Evangelists, urges it onward. Jesus guides his triumph, not holding reins, but shedding blessings from his right hand wherever he passes.

"The entire assemblage of persons represented on the window are seen marching onwards, singing with joy. Within the spaces formed by the mullions which trellis the upper part of the window, forty-six angels are represented with long golden hair, white transparent robes, and wings of yellow, red, violet, and green; they are all painted on a background of azure, like the sky, and celebrate with blended voices, or with musical instruments, the glory of Christ. Some have in their hands instruments of different forms, others books of music. The four animals of the Evangelists seem with sonorous voice to swell the acclamations of the hosts of saints; the ox with his bellowing, the lion with his roar, the eagle with his cry, and the angel with his song, accompany the songs of the forty-six angels who fill the upper part of the window. At the head of the procession is an angel who leads the entire company, and, with a little cross which he holds in his hand, points out to all the Paradise they are to enter. Finally, twelve other angels, blue as the heaven into which they melt, join in adoration before the triumph of Christ. . . . .

"Dante has given a description of a similar triumph, but marked by some interesting differences. The Florentine poet formed his cortége of figures taken from the Apocalypse and Christian symbolism. At Brou, with the exception of the attributes of the Evangelists, everything is historical. In the sixteenth century, in fact, history began to predominate over symbolism, which in the thirteenth and fourteenth centuries had reigned supreme. Dante, who was a politic poet, drew the triumph, not of Christ, but of the Church; the triumph of Catholicism rather than of Christianity. The chariot by which he represents the Church is widowed of Christ, whose figure is so important on the window of Brou; the chariot is empty, and Dante neither discovered this deficiency, nor was concerned to rectify it; for he was less anxious to

celebrate Christ and his doctrine, for their own sake, than as connected with
the organization and administration of the Church. He described the car as
drawn by a griffin, thereby representing the Pope, for the griffin unites in
itself the characteristics of both eagle and lion. Now the Pope is also twofold
in character; as priest he is the eagle floating in the air; as king, he is a lion,
walking upon the earth. The Ultramontane poet regarded the Church, that
is the Papacy, in the light of an absolute monarchy; not a limited monarchy
as with us, and still less a republic, as amongst the schismatics of Greece and
of the East. Consequently, while, at Brou, the Cardinal, the Archbishop, and
Bishop assist the Pope in guiding the car of the Church, in the 'Divina
Commedia,' the Pope is alone, and accepts of no assistance from the other
great ecclesiastical dignitaries. At Brou the car is guided by the Evangelists,
or by their attributes; ecclesiastical power is content merely to lend its aid.
According to the Italian poet, the Evangelists, although present at the Triumph,
do not conduct it; the Pope is himself the sole guide of the Church, and
permits neither the Evangelists to direct nor ecclesiastics to assist him. The
Pope seems to require no assistance; his eye and arm alone are sufficient
for him."

Canto XXX

1. In this canto Beatrice appears.

The Seven Stars, or Septentrion of the highest heaven, are the seven lights
that lead the procession, the seven gifts of the Holy Ghost, by which all men
are guided safely in things spiritual, as the mariner is by the Septentrion, or
Seven Stars of the Ursa Minor, two of which are called the "Wardens of the
Pole," and one of which is the Cynosure, or Pole Star. These lights precede
the triumphal chariot, as in our heaven the Ursa Minor precedes, or is nearer
the centre of rest, than the Ursa Major or Charles's Wain.

In the Northern Mythology the God Thor is represented as holding these
constellations in his hand. The old Swedish *Rhyme Chronicle,* describing the
statues in the church of Upsala, says:—

> "The God Thor was the highest of them;
>   He sat naked as a child,
>   Seven stars in his hand and Charles's Wain."

Spenser, *Faerie Queene,* I. ii. 1:—

> "By this the northern wagoner had set
>   His sevenfold teme behind the steadfast starre
>   That was in ocean waves yet never wet,
>   But firme is fixt, and sendeth light from farre
>   To all that in the wide deep wandering arre."

11. *Song of Solomon* iv. 8: "Come with me from Lebanon, my spouse, with me from Lebanon."

17. At the voice of so venerable an old man.

19. The cry of the multitude at Christ's entry into Jerusalem. Matthew xxi. 9: "Blessed is he that cometh in the name of the Lord."

21. *Æneid*, VI. 833: "Give me lilies in handfuls; let me scatter purple flowers."

25. Milton, *Parad. Lost*, I. 194:—

> "As when the sun new-risen
> Shines through the horizontal misty air
> Shorn of his beams."

32. It will be observed that Dante makes Beatrice appear clothed in the colours of the three Theological Virtues described in Canto XXIX. 121. The white veil is the symbol of Faith; the green mantle, of Hope; the red tunic, of Charity. The crown of olive denotes wisdom. This attire somewhat resembles that given by artists to the Virgin. "The proper dress of the Virgin," says Mrs. Jameson, *Legends of the Madonna,* Introd., liii., "is a close, red tunic, with long sleeves, and over this a blue robe or mantle. . . . Her head ought to be veiled."

35. Beatrice had been dead ten years at the date of the poem, 1300.

36. Fully to understand and feel what is expressed in this line, the reader must call to mind all that Dante says in the *Vita Nuova* of his meetings with Beatrice, and particularly the first, which is thus rendered by Mr. Norton in his *New Life of Dante,* p. 20:—

"Nine times now, since my birth, the heaven of light had turned almost to the same point in its gyration, when first appeared before my eyes the glorious lady of my mind, who was called Beatrice by many who did not know why they thus called her. She had now been in this life so long, that in its course the starry heaven had moved toward the east one of the twelfth parts of a degree; so that about the beginning of her ninth year she appeared to me, and I near the end of my ninth year saw her. She appeared to me clothed in a most noble colour, a becoming and modest crimson, and she was girt and adorned in the style that became her extreme youth. At that instant, I say truly, the spirit of life, which dwells in the most secret chamber of the heart, began to tremble with such violence, that it appeared fearfully in the least pulses, and, trembling, said these words: *Ecce deus fortior me, qui veniens dominabitur mihi!* 'Behold a god, stronger than I, who, coming, shall rule me!'

"At that instant, the spirit of the soul, which dwells in the high chamber to which all the spirits of the senses bring their perceptions, began to marvel greatly, and, addressing the spirits of the sight, said these words: *Apparuit jam beatitudo vestra,*—'Now hath appeared your bliss.' At that instant the natural spirit, which dwells in that part where the nourishment is supplied, began to weep, and, weeping, said these words: *Heu miser! quia frequenter impeditus ero deinceps,*—'Woe is me wretched! because frequently henceforth shall I be hindered.'

"From this time forward I say that Love lorded it over my soul, which had been thus quickly put at his disposal; and he began to exercise over me such control and such lordship, through the power which my imagination gave to him, that it behoved me to perform completely all his pleasure. He commanded me many times that I should seek to see this youthful angel, so that I in my boyhood often went seeking her, and saw her of such noble and praiseworthy deportment, that truly of her might be said that saying of the poet Homer: 'She does not seem the daughter of mortal man, but of God.' And though her image, which stayed constantly with me, inspired confidence in Love to hold lordship over me, yet it was of such noble virtue, that it never suffered that Love should rule without the faithful counsel of Reason in those matters in which such counsel could be useful."

48. Dante here translates Virgil's own words, as he has done so many times before. *Æneid,* IV. 23: *Agnosco veteris vestigia flammæ.*

52. The Terrestrial Paradise lost by Eve.

83. *Psalm* xxxi. 1, 8: "In thee, O Lord, have I put my trust. . . . . Thou hast set my feet in a large room."

85. *Æneid,* VI. 180: "Down drop the firs; crashes, by axes felled, the ilex; and the ashen rafters and the yielding oaks are cleft by wedges."

And IX. 87: "A wood . . . . dark with gloomy firs, and rafters of the maple."

Denistoun, *Mem. of the Duke of Urbino,* I. 4, says: "On the summit grew those magnificent pines, which gave to the district of Massa the epithet of *Trabaria,* from the beams which were carried thence for the palaces of Rome, and which are noticed by Dante as

> 'The living rafters
> Upon the back of Italy.'"

87. Shakespeare, *Winter's Tale,* IV. 3:—

> "The fanned snow
> That's bolted by the northern blast twice o'er."

And *Midsummer Night's Dream:*—

> "High Taurus' snow
> Fanned with the eastern wind."

113. Which are formed in such lofty regions, that they are beyond human conception.

125. Beatrice died in 1290, at the age of twenty-five.

136. How far these self-accusations of Dante were justified by facts, and how far they may be regarded as expressions of a sensitive and excited

conscience, we have no means of determining. It is doubtless but simple justice to apply to him the words which he applies to Virgil, Canto III. 8:—

> "O noble conscience, and without a stain,
> How sharp a sting is trivial fault to thee!"

This should be borne in mind when we read what Dante says of his own shortcomings; as, for instance, in his conversation with his brother-in-law Forese, Canto XXIII. 115:—

> "If thou bring back to mind
> What thou with me hast been and I with thee,
> The present memory will be grievous still."

But what shall we say of this sonnet addressed to Dante by his intimate friend, Guido Cavalcanti? Rossetti, *Early Italian Poets*, p. 358:—

> "I come to thee by daytime constantly,
>   But in thy thoughts too much of baseness find:
>   Greatly it grieves me for thy gentle mind,
>   And for thy many virtues gone from thee.
> It was thy wont to shun much company,
>   Unto all sorry concourse ill inclined:
>   And still thy speech of me, heartfelt and kind,
>   Had made me treasure up thy poetry.
> But now I dare not, for thine abject life,
>   Make manifest that I approve thy rhymes;
>   Nor come I in such sort that thou may'st know.
> Ah! prythee read this sonnet many times:
>   So shall that evil one who bred this strife
>   Be thrust from thy dishonoured soul, and go."

Canto XXXI

1. In this canto Dante, having made confession of his sins, is drawn by Matilda through the river Lethe.

2. Hitherto Beatrice has directed her discourse to her attendant hand-maidens around the chariot. Now she speaks directly to Dante.

25. As in a castle or fortress.

30. As one fascinated and enamoured with them.

42. The sword of justice is dulled by the wheel being turned against its edge. This is the usual interpretation; but a friend suggests that the allusion may be to the wheel of St. Catherine, which is studded with sword-blades.

46. The grief which is the cause of your weeping.

59. There is a good deal of gossiping among the commentators about this little girl or *Pargoletta*. Some suppose it to be the same as the Gentucca of Canto XXIV. 37, and the Pargoletta of one of the poems in the *Canzoniere,* which in Mr. Lyell's translation runs as follows:—

> "Ladies, behold a maiden fair, and young;
>   To you I come heaven's beauty to display,
>   And manifest the place from whence I am.
>   In heaven I dwelt, and thither shall return,
>   Joy to impart to angels with my light.
>   He who shall me behold nor be enamoured,
>   Of Love shall never comprehend the charm;
>   For every pleasing gift was freely given,
>   When Nature sought the grant of me from him
>   Who willed that your companion I should be.
> Each star upon my eyes its influence sheds,
>   And with its light and virtue I am blest:
>   Beauties are mine the world hath never seen,
>   For I obtained them in the realms above;
>   And ever must their essence rest unknown,
>   Unless through consciousness of him in whom
>   Love shall abide through pleasure of another.
> These words a youthful angel bore inscribed
>   Upon her brow, whose vision we beheld;
>   And I, who to find safety gazed on her,
>   A risk incur that it may cost my life;
>   For I received a wound so deep and wide
>   From one I saw entrenched within her eyes,
>   That still I weep, nor peace I since have known."

Others think the allusion is general. The *Ottimo* says: "Neither that young woman, whom in his *Rime* he called Pargoletta, nor that Lisetta, nor that other mountain maiden, nor this one, nor that other." He might have added the lady of Bologna, of whom Dante sings in one of his sonnets:—

> "And I may say
> That in an evil hour I saw Bologna,
> And that fair lady whom I looked upon."

Buti gives a different interpretation of the word *pargoletta,* making it the same as *pargultà* or *pargolezza,* "childishness or indiscretion of youth."

In all this unnecessary confusion one thing is quite evident. As Beatrice is speaking of the past, she could not possibly allude to Gentucca, who is spoken of as one who would make Lucca pleasant to Dante at some future time:—

> " 'A maid is born, and wears not yet the veil,'
>   Began he, 'who to thee shall pleasant make
>   My city, howsoever men may blame it.' "

Upon the whole, the interpretation of the *Ottimo* is the most satisfactory, or at all events the least open to objection.

63. *Proverbs* i. 17: "Surely in vain the net is spread in the sight of any bird."

72. Iarbas, king of Gætulia, from whom Dido bought the land for building Carthage.

77. The angels described in Canto XXX. 20, as

> "Scattering flowers above and round about."

92. Matilda, described in Canto XXVIII. 40:—

> "A lady all alone, who went along
>   Singing and culling floweret after floweret,
>   With which her pathway was all painted over."

95. Bunyan, *Pilgrim's Progress,* the river without a bridge:—

"Now I further saw that betwixt them and the gate was a river; but there was no bridge to go over: the river was very deep. At the sight therefore of this river, the pilgrims were much stunned; but the men that went with them said, 'You must go through, or you cannot come at the gate.' . . . .

"They then addressed themselves to the water, and, entering, Christian began to sink, and crying out to his good friend Hopeful, he said, 'I sink in deep waters; the billows go over my head, all his waves go over me. Selah.' . . . .

"Now upon the bank of the river, on the other side, they saw the two shining men again, who there waited for them. Wherefore being come out of the river, they saluted them, saying, 'We are ministering spirits, sent forth to minister for those that shall be heirs of salvation.' "

98. *Psalm* li. 7: "Purge me with hyssop, and I shall be clean: wash me and I shall be whiter than snow."

104. The four attendant Nymphs on the left of the triumphal chariot. See Canto XXIX. 130:—

> "Upon the left hand four made holiday
>   Vested in purple."

106. See Canto I. Note 23.

111. These four Cardinal Virtues lead to Divine Wisdom, but the three Evangelical Virtues quicken the sight to penetrate more deeply into it.

114. Standing upon the chariot still; she does not alight till line 36 of the next canto.

116. The colour of Beatrice's eyes has not been passed over in silence by the commentators. Lani, in his *Annotazioni,* says: "They were of a greenish blue, like the colour of the sea." Mechior Messirini, who thought he had discovered a portrait of Beatrice as old as the fourteenth century, affirms that she had "splendid brown eyes." Dante here calls them emeralds; upon which the *Ottimo* comments thus: "Dante very happily introduces this precious stone, considering its properties, and considering that griffins watch over emeralds. The emerald is the prince of all green stones; no gem nor herb has greater greenness; it reflects an image like a mirror; increases wealth; is useful in litigation and to orators; is good for convulsions and epilepsy; preserves and strengthens the sight; restrains lust; restores memory; is powerful against phantoms and demons; calms tempests; stanches blood, and is useful to soothsayers."

The beauty of green eyes, *ojuelos verdes,* is extolled by Spanish poets; and is not left unsung by poets of other countries. Lycophron in his "tenebrous poem" of *Cassandra,* says of Achilles:—

> "Lo! the warlike eagle come,
> Green of eye, and black of plume."

And in one of the old French Mysteries, *Hist. Théat. Franç.,* I. 176, Joseph describes the child Jesus as having

> "Les yeulx vers, la chair blanche et tendre
> Les cheveulx blonds."

122. Monster is here used in the sense of marvel or prodigy.

123. Now as an eagle, now as a lion. The two natures, divine and human, of Christ are reflected in Theology, or Divine Wisdom. Didron, who thinks the Griffin a symbol of the Pope, applies this to his spiritual and temporal power: "As priest he is the eagle floating in the air; as king he is a lion walking on the earth."

132. The Italian *Caribo,* like the English Carol or Roundelay, is both song and dance. Some editions read in this line "singing," instead of "dancing."

Canto XXXII

1. A mystical canto, in which is described the tree of the forbidden fruit, and other wonderful and mysterious things.

2. Beatrice had been dead ten years.

10. Goethe, *Hermann and Dorothea,* Cochrane's Tr., p. 103:—

> "Ev'n as the wanderer, who, ere the sun dips his orb in the ocean,
> One last look still takes of the day-god, fast disappearing;

> Then, amid rocks rude-piled, umbrageous forests, and copsewoods,
> Sees his similitude float, wherever he fixes his vision;
> Finding it glancing before him, and dancing in magical colours."

35. A *disfrenata saetta,* an uncurbed arrow, like that which Pandarus shot at Menelaus, *Iliad,* IV. 124: "The sharp-pointed arrow sprang forth, eager to rush among the crowd."

38. *Genesis* ii. 16: "Of every tree of the garden thou mayest freely eat. But of the tree of the knowledge of good and evil, thou shalt not eat of it: for in the day that thou eatest thereof, thou shalt surely die."

Some commentators suppose that Dante's mystic tree is not only the tree of knowledge of good and evil, but also a symbol of the Roman Empire.

41. Virgil, *Georgics,* II. 123: "The groves which India, nearer the ocean, the utmost skirts of the globe, produces, where no arrows by their flight have been able to surmount the airy summit of the tree; and yet that nation is not slow at archery."

43. Christ's renunciation of temporal power.

51. The pole of the chariot, which was made of this tree, he left bound to the tree.

Buti says: "This chariot represents the Holy Church, which is the congregation of the faithful, and the pole of this chariot is the cross of Christ, which he bore upon his shoulders, so that the author well represents him as dragging the pole with his neck." The statement that the cross was made of the tree of knowledge, is founded on an old legend. When Adam was dying, he sent his son Seth to the Garden of Paradise to bring him some drops of the oil of the mercy of God. The angel at the gate refused him entrance, but gave him a branch from the tree of knowledge, and told him to plant it upon Adam's grave; and that, when it should bear fruit, then should Adam receive the oil of God's mercy. The branch grew into a tree, but never bore fruit till the passion of Christ; but "of a branch of this tree and of other wood," says Buti, "the cross was made, and from that branch was suspended such sweet fruit as the body of our Lord Jesus Christ, and then Adam and other saints had the oil of mercy, inasmuch as they were taken from Limbo and led by Christ into eternal life."

54. In the month of February, when the sun is in the constellation of the Fishes. Dante here gives it the title of the Lasca, the Roach or Mullet.

58. The red and white of the apple-blossoms is symbolical of the blood and water which flowed from the wound in Christ's side. At least so thinks Vellutelli.

Ruskin, *Mod. Painters,* III, 226, says: "Some three arrow-flights farther up into the wood we come to a tall tree, which is at first barren, but, after some little time, visibly opens into flowers, of a colour 'less than that of roses, but more than that of violets.' It certainly would not be possible, in words, to come nearer to the *definition* of the exact hue which Dante meant,—that of the apple-blossom. Had he employed any simple colour-phrase, as a 'pale

pink,' or 'violet pink,' or any other such combined expression, he still could
not have completely got at the delicacy of the hue; he might perhaps have
indicated its kind, but not its tenderness; but by taking the rose-leaf as the
type of the delicate red, and then enfeebling this with the violet gray, he gets,
as closely as language can carry him, to the complete rendering of the vision,
though it is evidently felt by him to be in its perfect beauty ineffable; and
rightly so felt, for of all lovely things which grace the spring-time in our fair
temperate zone, I am not sure but this blossoming of the apple-tree is the
fairest."

65. The eyes of Argus, whom Mercury lulled asleep by telling him the
story of Syrinx, and then put to death.

Ovid, *Met.*, I., Dryden's Tr.:—

> "While Hermes piped, and sung, and told his tale,
> The keeper's winking eyes began to fail,
> And drowsy slumber on the lids to creep;
> Till all the watchman was at length asleep.
> Then soon the god his voice and song supprest,
> And with his powerful rod confirmed his rest;
> Without delay his crooked falchion drew,
> And at one fatal stroke the keeper slew."

73. The Transfiguration. The passage in the *Song of Solomon,* ii. 3, "As the
apple-tree among the trees of the wood, so is my beloved among the sons,"
is interpreted as referring to Christ; and Dante here calls the Transfiguration
the blossoming of that tree.

77. *Matthew* xvii. 5: "While he yet spake, behold, a bright cloud over-
shadowed them: and, behold, a voice out of the cloud, which said, This is
my beloved Son, in whom I am well pleased; hear ye him. And when the
disciples heard it, they fell on their face, and were sore afraid. And Jesus came
and touched them, and said, Arise, and be not afraid. And when they had
lifted up their eyes, they saw no man, save Jesus only."

82. Matilda.

98. The seven Virtues holding the seven golden candlesticks, or the seven
gifts of the Holy Spirit.

112. The descent of the eagle upon the tree is interpreted by Buti as the
persecution of the Christians by the Emperors. The rending of the bark of
the tree is the "breaking down of the constancy and fortitude of holy men";
the blossoms are "virtuous examples or prayers," and the new leaves, "the
virtuous deeds that holy men had begun to do, and which were interrupted
by these persecutions."

115. Buti says: "This descent of the eagle upon the chariot, and the smit-
ing it, mean the persecution of the Holy Church and of the Christians by
the Emperors, as appears in the chronicles down to the time of Constantine."

119. The fox is Heresy.

126. The gift of Constantine to the Church. *Inf.* XIX. 125:—

> "Ah, Constantine! of how much woe was mother,
> Not thy conversion, but that marriage-dower
> Which the first wealthy Father took from thee!"

131. Mahomet. *Revelation* xii. 3: "And there appeared another wonder in heaven; and, behold, a great red dragon, having seven heads and ten horns, and seven crowns upon his heads. And his tail drew the third part of the stars of heaven, and did cast them to the earth."

144. These seven heads, say the *Ottimo* and others, "denote the seven deadly sins." But Biagioli, following Buti, says: "There is no doubt that these heads and the horns represent the same that we have said in Canto XIX. of the *Inferno;* namely, the ten horns, the Ten Commandments of God; and the seven heads, the Seven Sacraments of the Church." Never was there a wider difference of interpretation. The context certainly favours the first.

150. Pope Boniface the Eighth.

152. Philip the Fourth of France. For his character see Canto XX. Note 43.

156. This alludes to the maltreatment of Boniface by the troops of Philip at Alagna. See Canto XX. Note 87.

159. The removal of the Papal See from Rome to Avignon.

The principal points of the allegory of this canto may be summed up as follows. The triumphal chariot, the Church; the seven Nymphs, the Virtues Cardinal and Evangelical; the seven candlesticks, the seven gifts of the Holy Spirit; the tree of knowledge, Rome; the Eagle, the Imperial power; the Fox, heresy; the Dragon, Mahomet; the shameless whore, Pope Boniface the Eighth; and the giant, Philip the Fair of France.

Canto XXXIII

1. In this canto Dante is made to drink of the river Eunoë, the memory of things good.

Psalm lxxix., beginning: "O God, the heathen are come into thine inheritance; thy holy temple have they defiled." The three Evangelical and four Cardinal Virtues chant this psalm, alternately responding to each other. The Latin words must be chanted, in order to make the lines rhythmical, with an equal emphasis on each syllable.

7. When their singing was ended.

10. *John* xvi. 16: "A little while, and ye shall not see me: and again, a little while, and ye shall see me; because I go to the Father."

15. Dante, Matilda, and Statius.

27. As in Canto XXXI. 7:—

> "My faculties were in so great confusion,
>   That the voice moved, but sooner was extinct,
>   Than by its organs it was set at large."

34. Is no longer what it was. *Revelation* xvii. 8: "The beast that thou sawest was, and is not."

36. In the olden time in Florence, if an assassin could contrive to eat a sop of bread and wine at the grave of the murdered man, within nine days after the murder, he was free from the vengeance of the family; and to prevent this they kept watch at the tomb. There is no evading the vengeance of God in this way. Such is the interpretation of this passage by all the old commentators.

37. The Roman Empire shall not always be without an Emperor, as it was then in the eyes of Dante, who counted the "German Albert," *Alberto tedesco,* as no Emperor, because he never came into Italy. See the appeal to him, Canto VI. 96, and the malediction, because he suffered

> "The garden of the empire to be waste."

43. The Roman numerals making DVX, or Leader. The allusion is to Henry of Luxemburgh, in whom Dante placed his hopes of the restoration of the Imperial power. He was the successor of the German Albert of the preceding note, after an interregnum of one year. He died in 1312, shortly after his coronation in Rome. See Canto VI. Note 97.

Villani, though a Guelf, pays this tribute of respect to his memory, Book IX. Ch. 1: "He was wise and just and gracious, valiant in arms, dignified, and catholic; and although of low estate in lineage, he was of a magnanimous heart, feared and redoubted, and if he had lived longer, he would have done great things."

When Henry entered Italy in September, 1310, Dante hastened to meet him, full of faith and hope. Whether this interview took place at Susa, Turin, or Milan, is uncertain; nor is there any record of it, except the allusion in the following extract from a letter of Dante, "written in Tuscany, at the sources of the Arno, on the 14th of May, 1311, in the first year of the happy journey of the divine Henry into Italy." Dante was disappointed that his hero should linger so long in the Lombard towns, and wished him to march at once against Florence, the monster "that drinketh neither of the headlong Po, nor of thy Tyber." In this letter, Mr. Greene's Tr., he says:—

"The inheritance of peace, as the immense love of God witnesseth, was left us, that in the marvellous sweetness thereof our hard warfare might be softened, and by the use thereof we might deserve the joys of our triumphant country. But the hatred of the ancient and implacable enemy, who ever and secretly layeth snares for human prosperity,—disinheriting some of those who were willing,—impiously, in the absence of our protector, despoiled us also, who were unwilling. Wherefore we wept long by the rivers of confusion, and incessantly implored the protection of the just king, to scatter the satellites of the cruel tyrant, and restore us to our just rights. And when thou, successor of Cæsar and of Augustus, crossing the chain of the Apennines, brought back the venerable Tarpeian ensigns, our long sighings straightway ceased, the fountains of our tears were stayed, and a new hope of a better age, like a sun suddenly risen, shed its beams over Latium. Then many, breaking forth into jubilant vows, sang with Mars the Saturnian reign, and the return of the Virgin.

"But since our sun (whether the fervour of desire suggests it, or the aspect of truth) is already believed to have delayed, or is supposed to be going back in his course, as if a new Joshua or the son of Amos had commanded, we are compelled in our uncertainty to doubt, and to break forth in the words of the Forerunner: 'Art thou he that should come, or look we for another?' And although the fury of long thirst turns into doubt, as is its wont, the things which are certain because they are near, nevertheless we believe and hope in thee, asserting thee to be the minister of God, and the son of the Church, and the promoter of the Roman glory. And I, who write as well for myself as for others, when my hands touched thy feet and my lips performed their office, saw thee most benignant, as becometh the Imperial majesty, and heard thee most clement. Then my spirit exulted within me, and I silently said to myself, 'Behold the lamb of God, who taketh away the sins of the world.'"

Dante, *Par.* XXX. 133, sees the crown and throne that await the "noble Henry" in the highest heaven:—

> "On that great throne on which thine eyes are fixed
>   For the crown's sake already placed upon it,
>   Before thou suppest at this wedding feast,
> Shall sit the soul (that is to be Augustus
>   On earth) of noble Henry, who shall come
>   To reform Italy ere she be prepared."

47. Themis, the daughter of Cœlus and Terra, whose oracle was famous in Attica, and who puzzled Deucalion and Pyrrha by telling them that, in order to repeople the earth after the deluge, they must throw "their mother's bones behind them."

The Sphinx, the famous monster born of Chimæra, and having the head of a woman, the wings of a bird, the body of a dog, and the paws of a lion; and whose riddle "What animal walks on four legs in the morning, on two at noon, and on three at night?" so puzzled the Thebans, that King Creon offered his crown and his daughter Jocasta to any one who should solve it, and so free the land of the uncomfortable monster; a feat accomplished by Œdipus apparently without much difficulty.

49. The Naiades having undertaken to solve the enigmas of oracles, Themis, offended, sent forth a wild beast to ravage the flocks and fields of the Thebans; though why they should have been held accountable for the doings of the

Naiades is not very obvious. The tradition is founded on a passage in Ovid, *Met.*, VII. 757:—

> "Carmina Naïades non intellecta priorum
>   Solvunt."

Heinsius and other critics say that the lines should read,—

> "Carmina Laïades non intellecta priorum
>   Solverat;"

referring to Œdipus, son of Laius. But Rosa Moranda maintains the old reading, and says there is authority in Pausanias for making the Naiades interpreters of oracles.

54. *Coplas de Manrique:*—

> "Our cradle is the starting place,
>   Life is the running of the race."

57. First by the Eagle, who rent its bark and leaves; then by the giant, who bore away the chariot which had been bound to it.

61. The sin of Adam, and the death of Christ.

66. Widening at the top, instead of diminishing upward like other trees.

68. The Elsa is a river in Tuscany, rising in the mountains near Colle, and flowing northward into the Arno, between Florence and Pisa. Its waters have the power of incrusting or petrifying anything left in them. "This power of incrustation," says Covino, *Descriz. Geog. dell' Italia,* "is especially manifest a little above Colle, where a great pool rushes impetuously from the ground."

69. If the vain thoughts thou hast been immersed in had not petrified thee, and the pleasure of them stained thee; if thou hadst not been

> "Converted into stone and stained with sin."

78. The staff wreathed with palm, the cockle-shell in the hat, and the sandal-shoon were all marks of the pilgrim, showing he had been beyond sea and in the Holy Land. Thus in the old ballad of *The Friar of Orders Gray:*—

> "And how should I your true love know
>   From many another one?
>   O by his cockle-hat and staff,
>   And by his sandal-shoone."

In the *Vita Nuova,* Mr. Norton's Tr., p. 71, is this passage: "Moreover, it is to be known that the people who travel in the service of the Most High are called by three distinct terms. Those who go beyond the sea, whence often they bring back the palm, are called *palmers*. Those who go to the house of Galicia are called *pilgrims,* because the burial-place of St. James was more distant from his country than that of any other of the Apostles. And those are called *romei* who go to Rome."

85. How far Philosophy differs from Religion. Isaiah lv. 8: "For my thoughts are not your thoughts, neither are your ways my ways, saith the Lord. For as the heavens are higher than the earth, so are my ways higher than your ways, and my thoughts than your thoughts."

104. Noon of the Fourth Day of Purgatory.

112. Two of the four rivers that watered Paradise. Here they are the same as Lethe and Eunoë, the oblivion of evil, and the memory of good.

127. Bunyan, *Pilgrim's Progress:*—

"I saw then, that they went on their way to a pleasant river, which David the king called 'the river of God;' but John, 'the river of the water of life.' Now their way lay just upon the bank of the river: here therefore Christian and his companion walked with great delight: they drank also of the water of the river, which was pleasant, and enlivening to their weary spirits. Besides, on the banks of this river, on either side, were green trees for all manner of fruit; and the leaves they ate to prevent surfeits and other diseases that are incident to those that heat their blood by travels. On either side of the river was also a meadow, curiously beautified with lilies; and it was green all the year long. In this meadow they lay down and slept; for here they might lie down safely. When they awoke, they gathered again of the fruits of the trees, and drank again of the water of the river, and then lay down again to sleep."

129. Sir John Denham says:—

> "The sweetest cordial we receive at last
> Is conscience of our virtuous actions past."

145. The last word in this division of the poem, as in the other two, is the suggestive word "Stars."

FICTION

FLATLAND: A ROMANCE OF MANY DIMENSIONS, Edwin A. Abbott. (0-486-27263-X)

PRIDE AND PREJUDICE, Jane Austen. (0-486-28473-5)

CIVIL WAR SHORT STORIES AND POEMS, Edited by Bob Blaisdell. (0-486-48226-X)

THE DECAMERON: Selected Tales, Giovanni Boccaccio. Edited by Bob Blaisdell. (0-486-41113-3)

JANE EYRE, Charlotte Brontë. (0-486-42449-9)

WUTHERING HEIGHTS, Emily Brontë. (0-486-29256-8)

THE THIRTY-NINE STEPS, John Buchan. (0-486-28201-5)

ALICE'S ADVENTURES IN WONDERLAND, Lewis Carroll. (0-486-27543-4)

MY ÁNTONIA, Willa Cather. (0-486-28240-6)

THE AWAKENING, Kate Chopin. (0-486-27786-0)

HEART OF DARKNESS, Joseph Conrad. (0-486-26464-5)

LORD JIM, Joseph Conrad. (0-486-40650-4)

THE RED BADGE OF COURAGE, Stephen Crane. (0-486-26465-3)

THE WORLD'S GREATEST SHORT STORIES, Edited by James Daley. (0-486-44716-2)

A CHRISTMAS CAROL, Charles Dickens. (0-486-26865-9)

GREAT EXPECTATIONS, Charles Dickens. (0-486-41586-4)

A TALE OF TWO CITIES, Charles Dickens. (0-486-40651-2)

CRIME AND PUNISHMENT, Fyodor Dostoyevsky. Translated by Constance Garnett. (0-486-41587-2)

THE ADVENTURES OF SHERLOCK HOLMES, Sir Arthur Conan Doyle. (0-486-47491-7)

THE HOUND OF THE BASKERVILLES, Sir Arthur Conan Doyle. (0-486-28214-7)

BLAKE: PROPHET AGAINST EMPIRE, David V. Erdman. (0-486-26719-9)

WHERE ANGELS FEAR TO TREAD, E. M. Forster. (0-486-27791-7)

BEOWULF, Translated by R. K. Gordon. (0-486-27264-8)

THE RETURN OF THE NATIVE, Thomas Hardy. (0-486-43165-7)

THE SCARLET LETTER, Nathaniel Hawthorne. (0-486-28048-9)

SIDDHARTHA, Hermann Hesse. (0-486-40653-9)

THE ODYSSEY, Homer. (0-486-40654-7)

THE TURN OF THE SCREW, Henry James. (0-486-26684-2)

DUBLINERS, James Joyce. (0-486-26870-5)

NONFICTION

POETICS, Aristotle. (0-486-29577-X)

MEDITATIONS, Marcus Aurelius. (0-486-29823-X)

THE WAY OF PERFECTION, St. Teresa of Avila. Edited and Translated by
E. Allison Peers. (0-486-48451-3)

THE DEVIL'S DICTIONARY, Ambrose Bierce. (0-486-27542-6)

GREAT SPEECHES OF THE 20TH CENTURY, Edited by Bob Blaisdell.
(0-486-47467-4)

THE COMMUNIST MANIFESTO AND OTHER REVOLUTIONARY WRITINGS:
Marx, Marat, Paine, Mao Tse-Tung, Gandhi and Others, Edited by Bob Blaisdell.
(0-486-42465-0)

INFAMOUS SPEECHES: From Robespierre to Osama bin Laden, Edited by Bob
Blaisdell. (0-486-47849-1)

GREAT ENGLISH ESSAYS: From Bacon to Chesterton, Edited by Bob Blaisdell.
(0-486-44082-6)

GREEK AND ROMAN ORATORY, Edited by Bob Blaisdell. (0-486-49622-8)

THE UNITED STATES CONSTITUTION: The Full Text with Supplementary
Materials, Edited and with supplementary materials by Bob Blaisdell.
(0-486-47166-7)

GREAT SPEECHES BY NATIVE AMERICANS, Edited by Bob Blaisdell.
(0-486-41122-2)

GREAT SPEECHES BY AFRICAN AMERICANS: Frederick Douglass, Sojourner
Truth, Dr. Martin Luther King, Jr., Barack Obama, and Others, Edited by
James Daley. (0-486-44761-8)

GREAT SPEECHES BY AMERICAN WOMEN, Edited by James Daley.
(0-486-46141-6)

HISTORY'S GREATEST SPEECHES, Edited by James Daley. (0-486-49739-9)

GREAT INAUGURAL ADDRESSES, Edited by James Daley. (0-486-44577-1)

GREAT SPEECHES ON GAY RIGHTS, Edited by James Daley. (0-486-47512-3)

ON THE ORIGIN OF SPECIES: By Means of Natural Selection, Charles Darwin.
(0-486-45006-6)

NARRATIVE OF THE LIFE OF FREDERICK DOUGLASS, Frederick Douglass.
(0-486-28499-9)

THE SOULS OF BLACK FOLK, W. E. B. Du Bois. (0-486-28041-1)

NATURE AND OTHER ESSAYS, Ralph Waldo Emerson. (0-486-46947-6)

SELF-RELIANCE AND OTHER ESSAYS, Ralph Waldo Emerson. (0-486-27790-9)

THE LIFE OF OLAUDAH EQUIANO, Olaudah Equiano. (0-486-40661-X)

WIT AND WISDOM FROM POOR RICHARD'S ALMANACK, Benjamin Franklin.
(0-486-40891-4)

THE AUTOBIOGRAPHY OF BENJAMIN FRANKLIN, Benjamin Franklin.
(0-486-29073-5)